GENDER AND POWER IN PREHISPANIC MESOAMERICA

T0355734

ROSEMARY A. JOYCE

Gender and Power in

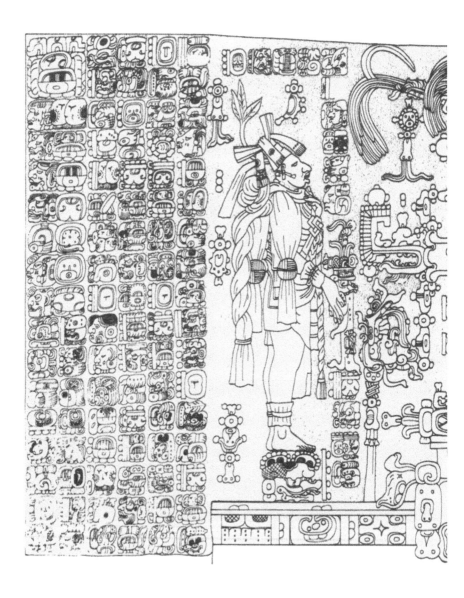

Prehispanic Mesoamerica

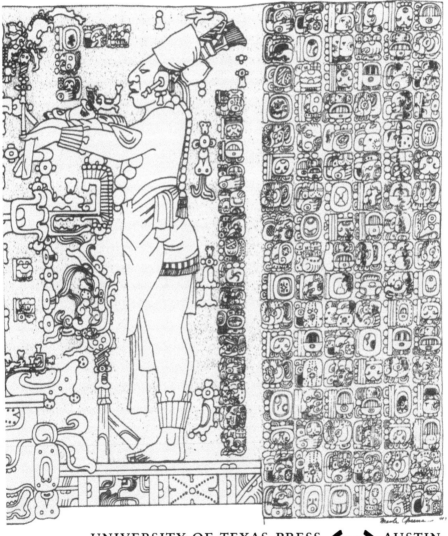

UNIVERSITY OF TEXAS PRESS AUSTIN

Library of Congress Cataloging-in-Publication Data
Joyce, Rosemary A., 1956–
Gender and power in Prehispanic Mesoamerica / Rosemary A. Joyce.— 1st ed.
   p.   cm.
Includes bibliographical references and index.
ISBN 0-292-74065-4 (pbk. : alk. paper)

   1. Indians of Central America—Social life and customs.
   2. Indians of Mexico—Social life and customs.   3. Sex role—Central America   4. Sex role—Mexico.   5. Maya women.   6. Aztec women.
   I. Title
F1434.2.S63   J69   2000
305.3′0972—dc21
00-008033

For Rus, always

Contents

Figures

Tables

Acknowledgments

There are a number of debts that I incurred in the writing of this book. Parts of the arguments included in Chapters 1 and 3 appeared in different form in "Performing the Body in Prehispanic Central America," in *Res: Anthropology and Aesthetics* 33 (spring 1998):147–165; in "Women's Work: Images of Production and Reproduction in Prehispanic Southern Central America," *Current Anthropology* 34, no. 3 (1993):255–274; and in *Embodying Personhood in Prehispanic Costa Rica*, Davis Museum and Cultural Center, Wellesley, Massachusetts (1993). Other material in Chapters 1 and 2 was previously incorporated in "Social Dynamics of Exchange: Changing Patterns in the Honduran Archaeological Record," in *Chieftains, Power, and Trade: Regional Interaction in the Intermediate Area of the Americas,* edited by Carl Henrik Langebaek and Felipe Cárdenas-Arroyo, pp. 31–46, published by the Departamento de Antropología, Universidad de los Andes, Bogotá, Colombia (1996). Parts of the analyses incorporated in Chapter 2 were presented in much different form in "Social Dimensions of Pre-Classic Burials," in *Social Patterns in Pre-Classic Mesoamerica,* edited by David C. Grove and Rosemary A. Joyce, published by Dumbarton Oaks, Washington, D.C. (1999); and in "Innovation, Communication, and the Archaeological Record: A Reassessment of Middle Formative Honduras," *Journal of the Steward Anthropological Society* 20, nos. 1–2 (1992):235–256. The arguments presented in Chapters 3 and 4 were refined through previous presentation in "Classic Maya Images of Gender and Labor," in *Exploring Gender through Archaeology: Selected Papers from the 1991 Boone Conference,* edited by Cheryl Claassen, Monographs in World Archaeology, No. 11, Prehistory Press, Madison, Wisconsin (1992); in "Dimensiones simbólicas del traje en monumentos clásicos mayas: La construcción del género a través del vestido," in *La indumentaria y el tejido mayas a través del tiempo,* edited by Linda Asturias and Dina Fernández, Monograph 8 of the Museo Ixchel del Traje Indígena, Guatemala, pp. 29–38 (1992); in a Comment on "Engendering Tomb 7 at Monte Alban: Respinning an Old Yarn," by Geoffrey and Sharisse McCafferty, *Current Anthropology* (1995); and in "The Construction of Gender in Classic Maya Monuments," in *Gender in Archaeology,* edited by Rita Wright, pp. 167–195, University of Pennsylvania Press (1996).

I gratefully acknowledge the support of a fellowship at the Bunting Institute at Radcliffe College, where several of these preliminary works were drafted in 1993 when I began work on this project. Florence Ladd, then director of the Bunting Institute, provided particularly urgent moral support beyond the requirements of her position. The Getty Grant Program supported my research leave as a Fellow at the University of California Humanities Research Institute in spring 1999, when I completed final revisions on the manuscript.

The work in progress benefited from invitations to present material in a variety of venues, which I also gratefully acknowledge. Foremost among these opportunities was the invitation extended by Veronica Kann and Geoffrey McCafferty to participate in a session they organized at the 1990 meeting of the American Anthropological Association. The idea that a book like this might be of interest first occurred to me after this stimulating session. Cheryl Claassen ensured that this thought would become a reality through her invitation to the First Boone Conference, where I found an audience prepared to encourage me to improve my analysis without discouraging me from doing so. Cheryl deserves the primary credit for any persistence I have shown in trying to disentangle what I mean when I say sex and gender, although the end result is that I no longer can answer those questions. My participation at the Second and Third Boone Conferences, which she organized, provided me with a great sense of community and continuing encouragement. Mary Weismantel and Stephen Eisenman reinforced the good work Cheryl, Ronnie, and Geoff began through a series of invitations to speak at Occidental College. These good friends all pushed me to read and deal with the work of Judith Butler; I hope they find the results of that effort in this book a worthwhile credit to their guidance.

While I have been particularly gifted in having friends of many years who generously invited me to present material in safe spaces where I could learn and develop my arguments, I have a similar debt to a number of then-strangers (now also friends) who took the risk of providing opportunities to talk through these ideas, and who have opened my eyes to dimensions of my own work that I might otherwise have failed to consider as seriously. Rita Wright's decision to put together a series of talks at New York University in 1991 in which she included me, followed by her invitation to participate in a session on women in states at the American Anthropological Association meetings in 1993, were particularly important opportunities to work through the political and economic aspects of the Maya material, especially the transition to the Postclassic. Liz Chilton and Mary Ann Levine made me realize that age was as important a variable in my analyses as sex by including me in a panel discussion at the University of Massachusetts, Amherst, in 1993, and subsequently in a session on childhood at the Society for American Archaeology's (SAA) annual meeting in 1994.

Michelle Marcus provided similar impetus for the development of my understanding of the importance of body modification through her invitation to act as the discussant for a 1994 College Art Association session, "The Decorated Body," and to contribute to a session on gender and the body at the annual meeting of the Archaeological Institute of America in 1995. The first versions of this work were developed for an exhibit at Wellesley College in 1993, and for a paper for the 1994 Conference on Gender and Material Culture at the University of Exeter. I would like to thank Judy Hoos Fox and Joe Giuffre of the Wellesley College museum for their advocacy for the exhibit, and Meredith Chesson and John Gerry for seeing that my paper was delivered at Exeter while I was in the field. Jeffrey Quilter, director of Pre-Columbian Studies at Dumbarton Oaks, provided a significant stimulus to the development of these arguments with his invitation to participate in a roundtable discussion, "Pre-Columbian States of Being," in 1996. Cecelia Klein's kind invitation to present my research in the Dumbarton Oaks conference "Recovering Gender in Pre-Columbian America" gave me a further opportunity to refine this material. I pursued some of the points raised by the paper I presented at the latter conference in the 1998 SAA session "Archaeologies of Sexuality," organized by Barb Voss and Rob Schmidt, and am particularly grateful to them for their vision in creating this session. Other aspects of this material were the subject of the paper I presented at the 1998 Lampeter Workshop, "Thinking through the Body." I am grateful to the conference organizers, Yannis Hamilakis, Sarah Tarlow, and Mark Pluciennek, for including me in the program, and to Lynn

Meskell and Roberta Gilchrist for exchanges about the issues included in this book, both on the occasion of that conference and subsequently.

The danger of attempting this kind of recognition of significant aid received is that much of the help developing a long-simmering set of arguments cannot be attributed to specific events, but rather to ongoing interchange of ideas. At Harvard I was privileged to work with Bob Preucel, who provided a hearing for many of the first kernels of ideas developed more fully here. He may even, against all odds, have improved some of them. Since coming to Berkeley I have been able to count on the constant support and stimulation of my colleagues in archaeology, particularly those from whom I have learned through shared teaching, Meg Conkey, Christine Hastorf, and Ruth Tringham. The Berkeley anthropology faculty as a whole was kind enough to allow me to present aspects of these ideas in a department colloquium and at a faculty research dinner, and I gratefully thank Marianne Ferme, Nelson Graburn, Donald Moore, and Laura Nader for specific comments on these presentations. I may not have incorporated all of their suggestions, but each was deeply appreciated.

The most continuous ongoing dialogues reflected in the existence of this book are with my colleagues Susan Gillespie and Julia Hendon. Each has been in her own way a model of scholarship for me, and the many debts I owe them are only partly indicated by citations of their work in the text. Each has her own unique perspective on most, if not all, of the issues raised here, and I look forward eagerly to continuing to read their writing on these issues.

Finally, as always, I would like to thank the first audience for all of this work, the most patient of all men, and the reliable provider of an environment where I can think and write, my husband, Rus.

GENDER AND POWER IN PREHISPANIC MESOAMERICA

CHAPTER ONE

Gender, Performance, Power, and Representation

When European observers came face to face with the pristine societies of Central America in the late fifteenth and early sixteenth centuries, they began a process of reinterpretation of the exotic and unintelligible features of those societies into more comfortable concepts with which they could govern their new colonies. Native peoples acted as collaborators in this radical reformulation, first of the concepts of their own societies, and then of the institutions and ways of life that shaped those societies. Anyone trying, from the vantage point of the late twentieth century, to recover some of the quality of precolumbian society faces a formidable task. If we take as our goal the aim of making precolumbian Mesoamerica more intelligible, as did the earliest Europeans to enter into a dialogue with its people, then we ensure that we will come to understand these societies as different versions of the same thing, lesser or distorted mirror images of Europe.

Our alternative could rather be to make precolumbian Mesoamerica more distinct, to push at the limits of its strangeness from the Europe that absorbed and reformulated it over half a millennium. I try to do just that in this study, which began as a consideration of the ways that sexual difference affected the formation of political power in prehispanic Mesoamerica (Figure 1). In it I attempt to reexamine materials that have served to characterize Mesoamerican attitudes toward gender and status, guided not by the goal of increasing their

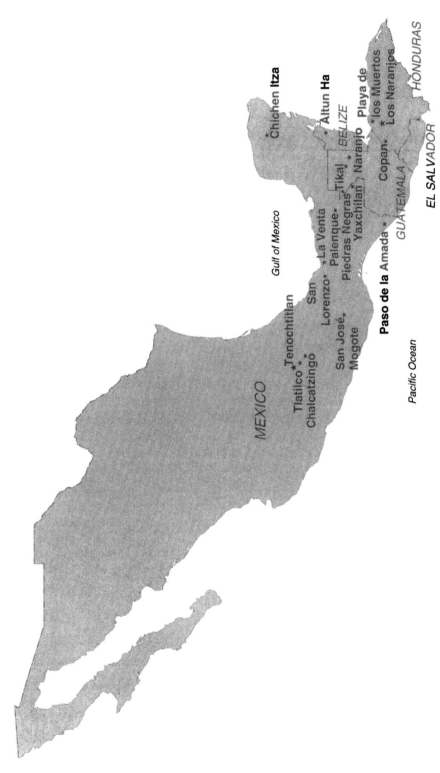

Figure 1. Map of prehispanic Mesoamerica, showing sites discussed in text.

Table 1. CHRONOLOGICAL CHART OF MAJOR MESOAMERICAN
TIME PERIODS

Period	Beginning	Ending	Beginning Marked by
Archaic	9000 B.C.	2300 B.C.	
Formative	2300 B.C.	250 A.D.	Use of pottery in
Early	2300 B.C.	900 B.C.	sedentary villages
Middle	900 B.C.	400 B.C.	
Late	400 B.C.	250 A.D.	
Classic	250 A.D.	1000 A.D.	Formation of Teotihuacan,
Early	250 A.D.	400 A.D.	Monte Albán, and
Middle	400 A.D.	550 A.D.	Classic Maya states
Late	550 A.D.	850 A.D.	
Terminal	850 A.D.	1000 A.D.	
Postclassic	1000 A.D.	1521 A.D.	Collapse of Classic
Early	1000 A.D.	1200 A.D.	Period states
Late	1200 A.D.	1521 A.D.	

transparency but by that of capturing hints they provide of the development of distinctive practices and ideas over more than three millennia (Table 1).

The difficulties encountered in approaching Mesoamerica illuminate several issues that have emerged as central in recent cross-cultural analyses of gender and power. Among these, the most critical are the paradoxical nature of gender, as presumptively concerned with biological difference but at the same time not determined by such differences; and the erosion of genders as central categories of identity that follows from attention to the unlinking of gender from its "natural" grounding. While other themes— including the relationship between gender, status, and the value of work, and the ways that changing contexts and scales of interaction can affect relationships proposed between gender and status—are considered in the chapters that follow, these two concepts provide the fundamental grounding for the trail I pick through the rich evidence for men's and women's lives and actions in those later sections. It is with an analysis of these concepts that we must begin.

Gender, Nature, and Culture

When a consideration of women's existence and status became an explicit topic of anthropological research, with the publication of works like *Woman, Culture, and Society* in the early 1970s, the reality of "woman" as a unitary category was taken as a necessary starting point.[1] Women were seen to be, as a category, universally disadvantaged with respect to men, a proposition stated as axiomatic in at least one influential introduction to kinship studies.[2] Some of the most important early anthropological analysis of gender was devoted to explaining this presumed reality, and such explanation quickly focused on the symbolic dimension of femininity, as determined by women's biological role.[3] Woman was to man as nature was to culture; and unlike man, who could remake himself socially, woman was irrevocably marked as of nature through the biological processes of menstruation and childbirth. In the most self-empowering versions of this logic, being the embodiment of the forces of nature was presented as a source of power for women; a power that—threatening as it was to men, who lacked this resource—was denied by men as a means to assert control over women. In its most blunt form, this thread led directly to the development of a mythology of an earlier stage of human society when women, representing a generalized Goddess, exercised the power rightfully theirs as the unique vessels of reproduction.[4]

Although anthropological analyses of gender have long since abandoned this original schematic, and historical research has demonstrated its roots in conventional historical speculation of the nineteenth century, a residue of the original formulation of gender as a problem has remained and continually arises within even the most sophisticated analyses. While the historical narrative of women's natural power and fall from grace may have been thoroughly debunked, the naturalness of woman as a category of study, or even as the primary category of social analysis, has proven more tenacious. The major spurs to recognizing problems with the initial conceptualization of women's status in anthropological analysis have undoubtedly been analyses that introduce crosscutting dimensions of seniority, race, class, and sexuality into the presumed unity of the category woman. These studies, which by no means speak with one coherent voice, nonetheless share a beginning commitment to the ideas that gender cannot be taken as the original and natural ground for identity, that sharing specific biological features does not imply a unity of purpose or viewpoint, and that perhaps the presumption that the question to be studied is how given biological features are valued in a society is not, in fact, a particularly productive question.[5]

Under the assumptions of a biologically based analysis of women's status, the goal of this book would be to trace the ways that women's association with fertility served as fodder for discourses that associated women's bodies and their potential with different social values. My pro-

cedure would be first to look for women in precolumbian societies—
identifying them ideally by their biological characteristics in burials, by the
depiction of such characteristics in representational media, and by the sex-
specific behaviors that might be documented by the distributions of tools,
ornaments, or vocabulary in written documents. Once having ascertained
the presence of women, we could summarize the ways their experience dif-
fered from that of men, where they were and were not allowed to act, what
they were allowed or required to do, whether and how they could claim
credit for their actions. I could ultimately construct a history of the gradual tightening of opportunities for women as Mesoamerican states became
increasingly centralized through time, and control of women's production
and reproductive potential became more critical to the men in power. In
fact, I have engaged in a series of studies that could easily be characterized in this fashion, producing in the end a narrative strangely similar to
the accounts of European Goddess literature, indulging in what Margaret
Conkey and Sarah Williams call a "narrative of closure" typical of the slide
of archaeology into "origins research." [6]

     But in the process, in order to sustain this vision, I (or those summa-
rizing my work) would have to ignore a number of uncomfortable points
of severe ambiguity. The easily detectable points of discomfort—in the face
of a procedure that should be guaranteed not to see ambiguity—include
female-sexed skeletons whose associations are more like those of male-
sexed skeletons than of other females in their own community; images in
which identifiable primary or secondary sexual characteristics are absent,
even when the body is nude; distributions of "women's" tools in settings
where men are the expected participants (and the reverse); and texts in
which gender is unmarked linguistically or apparent gender appears to be
violated. These difficulties are perhaps epitomized by the ambiguity of a
group of Classic Maya figures who wear a well-defined costume, and have
serially been identified as women, male priests, women again, royal men
dressed as women, royal men or women dressed as a bigendered deity, and
royal women dressed as men dressed as a deity.[7] How can the gender status
of the individuals depicted be so fluid? How, analytically, can we even begin
to talk about the relationships between gender and power if we cannot even
identify the gender identity of our subjects?

Gender Identity and Gendered Performance

One way out of the dilemma may be to admit that because we must rely
on secondary evidence when addressing precolumbian societies, we cannot

ever really know the gender identity of our subjects. Perhaps we should be satisfied with analyses at a scale coarser than the individual, taking as our unit of study the household (or houseful), the site, the polity, the society, the culture.

Such a strategy suffers from two flawed assumptions. The first is the notion that a concern with the way gender works is ultimately a question about individuals. As numerous examples from Mesoamerica demonstrate, realistic models at any of these scales require assumptions about the way gender works, leaving us not with ungendered models, but with models that simply project certain gender arrangements, often with no self-consciousness, into these societies. While gender is certainly a vital issue for real individuals in society, it also permeates models about society that rest on categorization and generalization about the behavior of people in groups.

The second problematic assumption embodied in the illusion of escape from the ambiguity of gender is the idea that gender is clearly an identity. This is the idea that underwrites the legacy of the original formulation of gendered research questions in anthropology, the concept that woman is a category with a privileged unitary status deriving from the common experience within society of persons with particular sexual organs. Here, confronting again the natural grounding of gender in biology, I find my thread out of this maze, the thread I will follow in the succeeding pages. What if gender is *not* simply the particularly contextualized socially valued construal of the body one is born with?

This alternative formulation of the issue has engaged a number of contemporary theorists in diverse fields. In biology itself, Ruth Hubbard has pointed out how the assumption that people are supposed to be either male or female guides action surrounding birth in North American culture, including the treatment of babies whose sexual characteristics do not conform to this expectation. Thomas Laqueur has shown how European concepts of gender difference structured the way sexual organs were represented and ideas about the development of the body were fostered, from the Classical Greek tradition through the twentieth century. His analysis demonstrates that what was seen depended on the prior existence of a theory about what there was to be seen. He specifically identifies the idea of immutable biological gender identity stemming from extreme difference (to the most basic biochemical level) as a relatively late idea in European history, replacing an ideology that saw sexual difference as a matter of degree of development of shared potential.[8] As these scholars and others have demonstrated, the assumption of fixed dichotomous genders grounded in absolute distinctions in biology is a commonplace of the modern western European intellectual tradition. There is no reason to assume that this was a feature of other societies and other times, any more than it serves for the earlier history of European society. With its presumed grounding in the body gone, an analysis of gender must go beyond the characterization of the presence, recognition, and value of biological categories, and engage a theory of gender itself.

Judith Butler has argued strongly for the decoupling of gender from the "natural" body, and indeed, from any fixity that might allow characterization of gender as an aspect of "identity," something one is. Butler offers instead a vision of gender as activity, something one does, a kind of performance. In Butler's view, people perform gender, and their performances are the fluid medium through which gender is reflexively shaped within specific social settings. As performance, gender is a way of being in the world, a way of dressing, of using the body, of revealing, concealing, modifying, and presenting the physical self. Gendered performances are learned and practiced, and they gain their intelligibility through social acts of interpretation, that is, when others understand a performing body's gender. Gendered performance, in Butler's analysis, is particularly centered on sexuality, and the readings of bodies that are interpretations of gender are always concerned with sexual possibility.[9]

Throughout the following chapters, I will pursue the argument that certain archaeological materials and settings were the media and stages for gendered performances. With Butler's insight as a guide, the confusion surrounding apparent cross-dressing in the debate about a particular Classic Maya costume becomes evidence for a gendered performance in which ambiguity of a particular kind is displayed and the lack of clarity becomes a deliberate aspect of the political manipulation that is implicit in all these images. If gender is not a fixed and biologically grounded identity, then in fact the fixing of specific gendered performance in everyday life and in representation takes on a slightly different significance and raises other questions. What were the reasons for the creation of the images, settings, and objects that appear in relation to sexual status in precolumbian Mesoamerica?

Gender, Power, and Material Culture

Material evidence is abundant for the presence of differently gendered individuals in Mesoamerican societies. Representations depicting the human form are among the earliest enduring media of Formative Period societies.

A single low-fired anthropomorphic pottery figurine from Tlapacoya, at ca. 2300 B.C., actually precedes the adoption of clay as a medium for pots in the Basin of Mexico.[10] Figurines accompany the earliest sequences of pottery known from villages on the Pacific Coast from Mexico to El Salvador, in the Mexican and Guatemalan Highlands, and along the Gulf Coast and in the Honduran lowlands, between 1500 and 800 B.C.[11] Soon after the establishment of permanent villages using pottery as a medium for representation, societies in several regions employ monumental media, especially stone, to depict anthropomorphic images. Both small-scale and large-scale media of human representation continue in use up to the epoch of Spanish contact.

The earliest Mesoamerican settlements also yield evidence of body ornaments in a variety of more or less durable materials: greenstone, shell, iron ore, and other minerals. The testimony of figurines adds an abundance of other forms of body modification, especially elaborate treatments of hair. Along with meager but suggestive evidence from Formative Period burials, discussed in the next chapter, representational images suggest that differences in costuming were already developing along lines well illustrated in later Mesoamerican societies, featuring distinctive items of male and female costume combined with other elements related to age, status, and role. Like large- and small-scale images, distinctive costume ornaments are a part of all later archaeological assemblages in Mesoamerica.

The Formative Period villages of Mesoamerica themselves provided a third material medium for the performance of difference, including gender, in the form of the spaces created through the use of architecture. The placement of residences, houses and their surrounding spaces, and, in some settlements, of larger structures, with respect to each other and in relation to natural features, created different arenas for social interaction at varied scales. It was in and among these spatial arenas that everyday performance of gender took place. It is the existence of such different settings in Maya and Mexica communities of the sixteenth century that allowed the articulation of rules of circulation dictating where women of particular ages and statuses might and might not go.[12]

The permanence of architectural settings and anthropomorphic representations contrasts with the fleeting and fluid nature of embodied gender performance. It is as if in Formative Mesoamerican villages the impermanent were being made permanent, precisely when villages were being transformed into parts of more or less stratified and centralized polities. I suggest that the flourishing of permanent media of gender during the Formative Period, including the costume ornaments cast in pottery, stone, and shell, is not an accident. I argue that rather than acting simply as reflections of a given biological identity, male or female, the media of gender — representations, costume, and action in space — were the means through which people sought to constrain and control the behavior of others in their communities. Once involved in attempts at constraint and control, these media constituted sites of discourses about what it was to enact gender within Mesoamerican societies: sites of formation of gender ideologies, but also of resistance to and transformation of those ideologies. The materiality of these media was central to their use as enduring propositions that transcended temporal limitations on the individual.

I draw here on the work of Paul Connerton about the differences that exist between what he called embodied and inscribed practices. Embodied practices — which I argue would include Butler's performances of gender — are personal, experiential, and yet inherently fleeting. While they are preserved in memory and may be the subject of social comment, accumulating reputation and surviving through oral performance, their primary power stems from their momentary sensory impact. Inscribed practices, in contrast, are social, shared among many viewers, and potentially transcend the spatial and temporal limitations of any individual. While they also have sensory impact, it is distinct from the engaged perspective of embodied practices. Connerton stresses the fact that inscribed practices are subject to conscious recognition to a degree not automatic for embodied practices, which can exist on a level of unselfconscious habit.[13]

Michael Herzfeld makes similar points in his discussion of the conversion of time into history through architectural style in a Cretan village.[14] He distinguishes between monumental time and social time, the former operating at a scale beyond the individual and the latter being measured by individual action, the embodied practice of Connerton. Herzfeld is particularly concerned with the political process through which local antiquities authorities impose on the inhabitants of particular buildings a set of requirements fixing the architectural form of the building in a particular monumental time. He illuminates how the control of the physical layout and ornamentation of space overrides the meaning with which residents imbue their house in everyday life. Herzfeld also shows that the imposition of control is not unchallenged, with the physical structure of buildings becoming the site of political conflict unavoidably publicly displayed. Houses demolished, altered, or transformed into the required form are large-scale and permanent witnesses to political gains and losses.

What Connerton and Herzfeld's analyses demonstrate is the importance of forms of material culture as media for struggles to determine what will endure within a society. Richard Parmentier discusses the way specific material features in the landscape of Belau are recognized as signs of and in history, "the permanent signs which function as present evidence of a significant past (p. 308)." [15] He argues that consideration of "the different ways history is connected to notions of time" requires attention to "the distribution within a given society of power to control the significance of events by creating or destroying historical evidence and by constructing historical discourse for specific ideological ends" (p. 5). Parmentier suggests that the selection of specific media as signs of/in history is motivated by their "sedimenting" status as "concrete embodiments" "endowed with the essentialized or reified property of historicity" as a result of their original association with the events for which they stand (pp. 11–13). Connerton, Herzfeld, and Parmentier are all explicitly concerned with the ways in which nontextual media carry extraordinary power in the creation of histories that transcend individual lives.

The media of gendered performance in precolumbian Mesoamerica served to inscribe bodily practices, to transform social time into monumental time. The efforts that were invested in creating these media throughout Mesoamerican history were substantial, including the provision of raw materials and the support of craftworkers in the exploration, mastery, and exercise of their skills. These investments of time, people, and materials become more intelligible when we take the products of this work seriously as assertions of social control. To fully explore the use of such media in dynamics related to the definition and control of sexuality and gender, however, we need to do more than recognize that they have unique kinds of power. We need to ask how they worked, in what ways they may have affected their makers and users, and in what ways they could have been creatively reworked to support alternative interpretations. These questions lead us to a consideration of the semiotics of gendered performances and representations.

Gendered Performance and Representation

Gendered performances in Mesoamerica included both everyday activities and the marked events in which concepts of gender themselves were explicitly being shaped: life-cycle rituals and ceremonies tied to the shared agricultural and divinatory calendars. While the performances themselves were fleeting, their settings and regalia could survive and provide a means to approach gendered performance archaeologically. At the same time, the inscription of bodily practices in the form of more permanent representational media provides material for examination of deliberate attempts to shape gender.

Gendered performance in everyday life left behind the residues of activities ranging from food preparation and consumption through specialized craft working. The crucial questions to ask about these performances are not the obvious ones that call for assigning tasks to fixed genders and delimiting spatial arenas for men and women from the distribution of these residues. Instead, in the pages that follow, I will examine how and why specific kinds of action came to be *representative* of certain kinds of gender, so that among the Aztecs, to weave was to be female, but not only female: young, marriageable, and perhaps primarily of the nobility. Examining those kinds of actions that were stereotyped by gender in Mesoamerica repeatedly exposes logics of everyday practice stressing interdependencies between social actors rather than hierarchies among them.[16]

Marked gendered performance in ritual or public ceremony illuminates the same logic, but here the playing out of gender is more self-conscious. In ceremonies, costume and forms of movement (athletic contests, dance, and procession) were prescribed for participants, but within the shared framework of the event, individual performances could distinguish one person from another. I suggest that Nancy Munn's concept of "beautification" as a social means to make a person more "persuasive" to others can be applied to Mesoamerican performances.

Munn describes specific social practices in Gawa, an Oceanian society, through which the sensory attraction of the body is deliberately increased by the addition of skillfully worked materials that distinguish one person from others, practices Munn labels "beautification." Beautification draws specific attention to an individual and contributes to the relative social assessment of that person, resulting in a quality of renown of great significance in this small-scale society. The identity built up through beautification and, in particular, the evaluations other people make of it become grounds for differential perceptions of effectiveness and hence of different patterns of action toward people perceived as more "persuasive" or "potent."[17] Similar statements are embedded in other ethnographies. The Amazonian Cashinahua describe feather ornamentation as promoting *dua,* a quality of health and attractiveness, by acting as "medicine" (*dau*) and by making externally visible the inherent aura of each individual. The Ama-

zonian Waiwai regard the beautification produced by wearing feather costume as "a profoundly political matter" in which individual attractiveness
provides grounds for interpersonal competition: "the efforts put into beautification are one of several means of displaying one's suitability as a good
candidate for marriage, a kind of visual persuasiveness. . . ."[18] Annette
Weiner's discussion of moments of beautified gendered performance in the
Trobriand Islands shows that some of the most important social settings
for such bodily distinction are ceremonies when newly sexually active girls
and boys perform in public dances and displays, leading to the identification of desired sexual or marital partners, as is also the case among the
Waiwai, the Papuan Gawa, and the Cashinahua.[19]

Western observers tend to see shell ornaments, feather costume, and
the like as inherently beautiful, but analysis of practices of beautification
does not require agreement between the aesthetic standards of the analyst
and the subject of study. Evidence of efforts expended to distinguish personal appearance through modification of the body can be grounds to consider beautification and its relative social evaluation. For example, while
the wearing of palm-leaf skirts in the Trobriands is described by Annette
Weiner in terms similar to Nancy Munn's discussion of beautification on
Gawa, the aesthetic dimensions of differences in these skirts are not as
immediately evident to Western sensibilities as those of shell valuables,
but they are clear to Trobriand observers. Weiner compares gender performances in the Trobriands, where male renown was created through participation in *kula* exchange and women's value was asserted through display
of the products of agricultural labor during mortuary rituals. Both performances are subject to social evaluation by others.

The recognition of shared standards for adornment and the measurement of each attempt at beautification against those standards demarcates
a community that argues about what is beautiful. The anthropological sub-
discipline of ethnoaesthetics is in fact based on this understanding.[20] Ethno-
aesthetic studies use a methodology of asking members of a production
community to rate or rank craft products, arriving through this means at an
understanding both of the general standards shared, and also of the points
of contestation, where different makers disagree. Failure of agreement is as
much a part of the establishment of a common community as is agreement.
Norman Whitten presents an ethnographic example from the Ecuadorian
Amazon in which the skillful creation of pottery and its social evaluation
are explicit bases for the formation of individual power. His ethnographic
account shows that the existence of variation in the understanding of pot-

tery decoration is intrinsic to dynamics within the community, establishing internal differences.

In performance in ancient Mesoamerica, the incorporation of common practices of body ornamentation and movement was linked with the expression of individual distinction in a tension that at times was related specifically to sexuality (see Chapter 5). The identification of marked gendered performance in precolumbian societies is possible because the regalia and settings of action were executed in permanent media, and because representational imagery further inscribed these performances. In Mesoamerica, costume was a medium for creation of specific social identity through a cumulative layering of age-, gender-, and status-appropriate ornaments and items of clothing. In images from sites such as Tikal and Calakmul, signs for individual names and titles of personages from the textual systems of the Maya were placed directly in costume, along the fringe of a robe or inserted in a feathered headdress. The incorporation of names in costume transformed dress into a literal text, an extreme version of the particularistic historical character of costume.[21]

While costume documented personal history, it also served, perhaps primarily, to beautify the body. I suggest that beautification, modification of appearance by addition of materials that enhanced the body or were themselves objects of admiration, was particularly important to newly sexually mature young adults in Mesoamerica. Because beautified persons engaged in performance were members of larger social groups, their success was both individual and social, meriting the support provided for them by the group through the creation of distinguished costumes. In Mesoamerica, as was also true in Indonesia, Oceania, and the Northwest Coast of North America,[22] costumes prepared for the use of younger members of social groups often employed heirloom objects, retained by the group and passed on through generations along with the histories they accumulated through their use in individual performances. It is no accident that such heirloom ornaments were conserved by Mesoamerican societies, including the Classic Maya, and that costume items were one of the major classes of valuables exchanged in marriage negotiations.[23] Imperishable costume ornaments survive archaeologically and provide us the permanent, inscribed evidence of fleeting performances, and testify to the social importance of performance to larger social groups.

Examples of heirloom valuables retained by Mesoamerican peoples include "Olmec" jade objects found in Postclassic settings at the Aztec Templo Mayor of Tenochtitlan and on Yucatec Maya Cozumel; jades in a

Late to Terminal Classic context in northeast Yucatan similar to Middle Formative examples from La Venta; objects deposited in Chichen Itza's Sacred Cenote during Terminal Classic to Early Postclassic times that range from Middle and Late Formative styles typical of Belize to Late Classic jades carved with inscriptions referring to Palenque and Piedras Negras; and the incised jade celt-shaped belt pendant known as the Leyden Plaque, whose inscription records Early Classic events at Tikal, but which was found near the mouth of the Motagua River in a Terminal Classic or Postclassic setting.[24]

That heirloomed costume ornaments were displayed, not simply reburied, by later peoples is supported by the image on a stela from Late Classic Yaxchilan, described by Carolyn Tate as wearing an Olmec-style figural pendant.[25] Through their re-use, heirloomed costume ornaments accrued histories. Literate societies added notations of specific events to heirloomed objects. These could be added long after the original creation of the ornament itself: a pendant from Dumbarton Oaks, stylistically Olmec, bears on the reverse a low-relief incised figure and inscription in Early Classic Maya style.[26]

The common form of the brief inscriptions on Classic Maya costume ornaments is a possessive statement: "his or her [object type], name and titles of a person."[27] More extensive texts recording political ceremonies were incised on jade and shell ornaments from sites such as Palenque, Piedras Negras, Tikal, and Altun Ha.[28] Both kinds of texts served to fix the use of the ornament at a particular point in time, and in this sense, they are equivalent: they inscribe a specific history for and on the object. This history is necessarily carried along as it is transmitted from person to person.

Many of the texts on Classic Maya inscribed heirlooms are self-referential, reinforcing the role of text in creating histories for objects. "Name-tag" texts on costume ornaments reiterate the type of object: "his ear spools," for example. The Dumbarton Oaks pendant's Early Classic Maya text and image employ the same visual form, an image of the profile view of a seated person, to inscribe the "seating" of the named noble in political office on what may be an item of regalia of that individual. The Leyden Plaque, which also records a "seating" event, depicts its standing subject wearing a belt ornamented with a set of three pendant celts like the Leyden Plaque itself, confirming the use in this ceremony of the same or similar objects.

This layering of reference reaches a peak in a pendant recovered from the Cenote at Chichen Itza that bears a text referring to events at Palenque. The bead itself was oriented horizontally when worn. Its two opposing long faces are inscribed with a text and an image, both oriented perpendicular to the orientation of the ornament when in use. The text refers to events in the heir-designation of a young Palenque lord, literally described as "taking a step into" or "entering" the succession of rulers; the image depicts a standing male figure with its heel raised in the Classic Maya stylization of movement. This figure wears on his chest a horizontally oriented long bead pendant, like the object on which the image is incised.

The self-referentiality of ornaments inscribed with texts is more obvious, but other Maya heirlooms subject to recirculation and ultimate deposition in the Cenote at Chichen Itza also historicized their own presentation on the bodies of powerful nobles. The jade pendants in what Tatiana Proskouriakoff called Nebaj style show seated rulers in elaborate costume, wearing pendants of the same general size and shape. With or without written exegesis incorporated on them, these Classic Maya ornaments (and presumably similar heirloomed costume ornaments from less literate societies) materialized the occasions of their own use and served as permanent records of specific historical events. The prior ceremonies they recorded were cited as precedents in later performances through the wearing of the same costume ornament.

Costume ornaments, the lasting media of fleeting embodied performance, are material testimony both to social investment of raw materials and craft skills in marked performances, and to the social evaluation of these performances as aesthetically realized repetitions of earlier precedents. Permanent representations of performances transformed the spatial and temporal reach of these social investments. Marked in monumental time and executed at monumental scale, they served to transform the spatial settings in which they were located. These transformations were effected through a double movement inherent in representations, the focus of much of my analysis in this study.

This analysis is what Dan Sperber called "an epidemiology of representations" that "is not about representations but about the *process* of their distribution." [29] Sperber argues that representations begin as private mental constructs. When given material form as public representations (whether performances or inscribed media) they may be transformed into new mental representations by others who witness them. Sperber's discussion views the spread of representations and the responses to them as a chain of transmission that the use of the term *epidemiology* explicitly likens to the spread of a disease: outside conscious control, moving inexorably from host to host. The beginning point of my analysis, then, is the stipulation that the anthropomorphic images and the performances that took place in the settings and using the costumes I discuss were public in this sense, inspiring new mental representations in those who viewed them.

Because these images suggest aspects of human appearance and behavior through resemblance, they are iconic, and of particular interest in the production of inequality. As Michael Herzfeld puts it, "iconic relations . . . because they either 'look natural' or can be 'naturalized,' are a good deal *more* labile [than symbols, "arbitrary" signs], and lend themselves with particular ease to totalizing cultural ideologies." [30] Because they appear to be chosen merely to establish resemblance, the ideological dimension in selection of features for iconic representations is less obvious and constitutes a subtle means to spread stereotypes of natural or essential human behavior. I assume that no detail of Mesoamerican human representations is simply natural, but rather is constrained by and constrains assumptions about what possibilities existed for living people.

Each image can then be approached as what Roland Barthes called a "pregnant moment": "In order to tell a story, the painter possesses only one moment . . . [the image] will be a hieroglyph in which can be read at a glance . . . the present, the past, and the future, i.e., the historical meaning of the represented gesture." [31] Barthes suggested that even a single still image implies its history, actions before and after the moment. But since there are many possible sequences of action that could precede or follow from a given moment, "all images are polysemous; they imply, underlying their signifiers, a 'floating chain' of signifieds, the reader able to choose some and ignore others." [32] While the patrons of Mesoamerican artists may have had in mind particular narratives, they could not completely determine how the viewers of those images would interpret and react to them.

Further, images do not exist in isolation, but in active contact with others. Contrasts between images provide one avenue to identify points of what Michael Herzfeld calls *disemia:* "At each level of social organization, the relations between insiders and outsiders are ordered according to topically distinctive principles, but they always remain predicated on the distinction between the inside and the outside of whatever social group is in question. This is disemia, a mode of organizing social knowledge *through cultural form.*" [33] Just as the evaluation of performances marks the difference between those who share standards and those who do not, so the differences that exist between images rest on differences between Herzfeld's insiders and outsiders. The profusion of detail in Mesoamerican images, often requiring extended exegesis for intelligibility, is one sign of the importance of images as sites of differentiation between groups and individuals whose narrative understandings of an image were distinct.

Barthes points to two simultaneous forms of signification that are present in any image.[34] Each feature selected excludes a range of other possibilities, and creates more-or-less arbitrary associations with other instances of the same feature. Thus Classic Maya images depicting figures dressed in a netted skirt with a shark's head at the belt recall other examples of the same costume, and suggest that there should be some uniform quality shared by these figures. But at the same time, the features selected suggest connections with earlier and later actions, giving each image a unique character: at Classic Maya Piedras Negras, images of individuals seated at the top of a ladder invoke not only the ascent up this device, but an act of human sacrifice, by the placement of a dead body at the base of the ladder and a cloth marked by dark footprints along its length.

The crowding of such elements in Mesoamerican images can be seen as a visual strategy through which an attempt is made to constrain the interpretive freedom inherent in images. The signs united in such implied narratives are bound in a relationship of "double implication: two terms presuppose one another," transforming chronological order to a logical binding "capable of integrating backwards and forwards movements" through the narrative.[35] What is shown as a sequence of action is transformed into a causal chain, where each step leads inevitably to what follows. Narrative "seems to found in nature the signs of culture."[36]

By placing politically charged images in particular spatial arrangements, Mesoamerican patrons provided a preferred body of images for this process of narrativization, and these arrangements can be used not only as guides to our understanding of preferred interpretations, but also as evidence of those topics around which the greatest tensions, and consequent desire for control, existed. The addition of text to images is yet another means adopted to further channel interpretation, a means widely used in Mesoamerica beginning in the late Formative Period. Treating texts as evidence of the desire to limit interpretation provides another indication of the sites of tension surrounding representational images, as texts selectively emphasize certain possible narratives and downplay others.

The remainder of this study, then, will trace an epidemiology of images, with particular attention to the fissures that open up in any proposed unified interpretation. I take images as a starting point because throughout prehispanic Mesoamerican history they were media for the formalization of ever more limited stereotypes of everyday and ritual performance, offering sanctioned precedents for citation. Following threads suggested by disjunctions between images, I also trace other less tractable, more diverse, less controlled media for gendered performances: the regalia and costumes through which individual members of Mesoamerican societies negotiated their own standing within social groups of varying scale. Along the way we will encounter practices and representations that I argue demonstrate that gender in precolumbian Mesoamerica was more fluid and negotiable than was suggested in the accounts left for us by the first European observers.

CHAPTER TWO

Negotiating Sex and Gender in Formative Mesoamerica

While the antiquity of the earliest people in the territory that today is Central America is still strongly debated, unequivocal evidence of populations scattered throughout the region is clear by 8000 B.C. However, it is only with the advent of larger permanent villages, marking the beginning of the Early Formative, that we have sufficient archaeological evidence to begin to address questions about the formation of individual identity, the importance of material media in fixing performance, and the relations between emerging social divisions—including gender—and the exercise of power. Once Early Formative villages appear, they immediately provide a wealth of material for such an investigation, implying that in these early sedentary settlements the negotiation of status and identity was a strong and widely shared concern.

Life in Formative Period Mesoamerica

The date of the division between the Early Formative Period and the preceding Archaic Period (Table 1) is not uniform, since it is marked in each area by the local emergence of pottery production. Evidence for the existence of pottery-using villages by 1500 B.C. has been found in virtually all areas that have been subjects of intensive investigation. From the earliest appearance of villages, interregional contact within Mesoamerica was already evident, with obsidian, the volcanic glass used for tools, being the most obvious indication of such exchange. Less durable exchange goods must have included the seeds of cultivated plants that spread throughout the region, especially maize.[1]

Early Formative villages were relatively small, and residents lived in house compounds composed of one or more wattle-and-daub buildings associated with outside work spaces and specialized below-ground storage pits. Residents of these households made and used hand-modeled figurines and produced some durable costume ornaments in pottery, shell, and stone. Debris from these villages suggests that most craft production took place in and around house compounds, a pattern that persisted to the end of the prehispanic period.[2]

In a few Early Formative sites, archaeologists have documented subtle distinctions in scale, sometimes accompanied by the use of distinctive materials, in some house compounds. Perhaps the best documented is the sequence of grand houses at a single location in the Mexican Pacific coast site of Paso de la Amada. There, a larger-than-normal house was rebuilt multiple times, raised on a platform of earlier construction debris, and made ever more visually prominent. Artifact analyses from the site do not suggest that this building served a different set of functions, but rather that it was the location of more elaborate and larger-scale versions of the same meals and craft production activities that marked most houses in the community.[3]

The general picture provided by Early Formative archaeology is one of many villages with populations low enough to sustain face-to-face social interaction. Within these villages, the occupants of individual house compounds cooperated in basic subsistence activities, and some members of some households engaged in more specialized craft work. While village plans provide no definite indications of formalized public spaces, internal distinctions might imply that the scale of activities at certain house compounds was higher, the style of material culture more elaborate, and the scope of consumption higher than was general in the community as a whole.

Most anthropological models of the workings of such small-scale, face-to-face societies are grounded in knowledge of kinship—knowledge unavailable in the case of the distant, pre-literate past. Instead, I use the concept of "house societies" defined by Claude Lévi-Strauss, further discussed by Shelly Errington and James Boon, as an alternative model of social organization that does not require assumptions about kinship systems.[4] While the concept has perhaps best been illustrated by ethnogra-

phers working in Indonesia and in Oceania,[5] Lévi-Strauss's original formulation was based on societies of the northwest United States and other
native American groups, and he also applied the model to Africa, feudal
Japan, and medieval Europe. Common to house societies is the ability to
define a physical estate through which members of a "house" conceptual-
ize themselves as a single group. The physical expression of house unity is
usually, although not always, a building, a house, the dwelling or ceremonial residence of the house elders, or sometimes that of the spirits of the ancestors.[6] Houses, it should explicitly be said, are not identical to individual
house buildings (dwellings) or groups of buildings (house compounds), nor
is coresidence a requirement for house membership. Instead, a dwelling,
ceremonial building, tomb, or the house compound of some members may
serve as the physical location on the landscape where house continuity is
anchored and made materially evident. A house, in other words, is not an
extended family.

As a social unit embodied by people, the social house endures over
time as a corporate body. The estate of the house can be "made up of both
material and immaterial wealth": in addition to such forms of property as
agricultural land, heirloom valuables, and the house building, houses often
own rights to perform particular ceremonies, to produce particular craft
goods (often regalia used in such ceremonies), and to employ particular
names and titles. It is through the transmission of house names that the
members of the house are publicly marked as part of the group, and through
the members' actions that the names of the house continue to be manifest.[7]

David Schneider's redescription of his original ethnography of kinship groups on Yap, though not explicitly framed in terms of house societies, provides an excellent example of the workings of house persistence
over time. Schneider demonstrates that what he originally identified as
facts of biological relations providing the framework for kinship are better
viewed as expressions of relative rights in landed estates physically marked
by the building platforms and fields of those estates. Rather than having
an innate right to membership in the group by blood, Yapese must perform particular kinds of service for those in authority over the estate to
which they have relative claims in order to earn their place in the estate;
in particular, they provide agricultural labor. The major sign of rights in
the estate granted to junior members are names, which are property of
the estate and are subject to revocation for poor performance of expected
duties. House names are maintained by their use by new members, and are
inalienable parts of the house property. Northwest coast Tlingit mortuary

ceremonies described by Sergei Kan exemplify the public performance of expected duties—in this case, related to deceased house members—as a means to claim names and titles, solidify their association with the house, and assert individual claims to the right to use such names.[8]

Lévi-Strauss originally developed the concept of house societies as a means to categorize groups that presented problems for his kinship analyses. Thus the house, according to Lévi-Strauss, was a combination of lineal consanguineal kin and affines. In ethnographically described house societies, a core of residents related through a combination of descent, marriage, and patron-client links cooperate in pursuit of the economic and social persistence of the house.[9] Each individual's work advances the interests of the house as a whole. At the same time, each individual is a potential member of a contending faction within the house when individual interests clash with those of the group. James Boon notes that houses "are ranked both internally and externally by birth order, by anisogamy, and by other indices of differential transmissions of estates, heirlooms, titles, prerogatives, and renown."[10] Such hierarchy is contested, constantly negotiated through alliances and exchanges, where individual and house interests may part ways.[11]

If we view Early Formative villages as house societies, then the more finely constructed house buildings that were sites of consumption of more abundant and more highly refined materials may be seen as the property of emergent noble houses. I use the term *noble* throughout this book to label an asserted social distinction. In house societies, this asserted distinction may conform to a boundary between a group of houses that formally recognize intermarriage and another group with which intermarriage is not formally recognized. As Susan McKinnon demonstrates, the boundary between noble and commoner houses is fluid and subject to different representations, as lower-ranking houses strive to formally recognize sexual alliances that noble houses choose to ignore.

The term *elite* is commonly used in Mesoamerican studies to label this distinction, but it is often conflated with other distinctions (such as variation in wealth, as measured by access to resources) that need not be correlated with asserted status. The possible correlation of distinct dimensions of social difference should itself be the subject of examination, which is not facilitated by the use of a single term for multiple aspects of social difference. For Mesoamerican societies, Joyce Marcus, based on examination of texts, has argued for a general binary distinction between nobles and commoners, while others have suggested multiple finer distinctions based on gradations of wealth, for example those evident within the Caracol site discussed by Diane and Arlen Chase.[12]

Differences between analyses based on categorical terms and distribution of resources do not simply represent adoption of emic and etic perspectives. They reflect real divergence between asserted status (nobility) and differential access to resources (wealth) at certain places and times in Mesoamerica. Where the consummation of marital alliances required economic exchanges, there will be a relationship between wealth and status, between the fluidity of the boundary demarcating noble houses and the inability of noble houses to concentrate control of wealth in their own hands. The circulation of wealth items in social exchanges related to marriage, rituals in the lives of children, and mortuary ceremonies would have been an eminently political arena for prehispanic Mesoamerican houses.[13]

Within each house compound, residents formed part of an actual or potential house whose wealth, renown, and even survival depended on the actions of individual members. House compounds formed the basic structure of all later Mesoamerican settlements, and for many of these, discussed in later chapters, there is abundant evidence for the kinds of negotiation of rank seen in ethnographic house societies. But in initial Early Formative Mesoamerica, house compounds were the *only* sites for performance, and the kinds of ceremonial performances that were enacted within them were not simply one, but the only, arena within the settlement for the enactment of aspects of social identity, including gender.

By the end of the Early Formative, new spatial settings emerged in a number of Mesoamerican villages. Although overall community size remained similar, monumental-scale features were introduced into the landscape of the village at places like San José Mogote, Chalcatzingo, Paso de la Amada, and La Venta. Taking the form of high earthen mounds, these new features were not used for residence. In some areas, they were accompanied by the deployment of monumental-scale stone carvings forming new kinds of spatial arenas, plazas, or courtyards.[14]

These new features must have intimately affected all aspects of everyday performance. As Michael Love argues, monumental architecture required new patterns of movement in space and in fact created new kinds of spatial settings in sites. I suggest that the monumentality of these new features gave them an automatic community-wide significance and omnipresence, something no previous architectural feature, however large a house it may have been, could have achieved. Monumental architecture served as the site for at least one of the kinds of marked performances that had previously taken place only in the small-scale setting of the house compound: mortuary ritual. The limitation of access to the performances taking place in such spaces, coupled with the inescapable knowledge on everyone's part that others had access to activities in these locations, was a powerful new circumstance creating different strata within late Early Formative villages.[15]

At the same time, exchange between settlements continued and the range of goods moving from one village to another was wide: greenstone, marine shell, iron ore, and more. Many of the materials were worked into intricate costume ornaments in specific areas of villages. At sites like San José Mogote, it appears that the working and use of exotic resources like these became more concentrated over time, and was particularly evident in house compounds near new zones of monumental architecture.[16] The most abundant material for understanding exchange, obsidian, clearly demonstrates that long-distance trade was changing, with fewer house compounds directly engaged in exchange and more relying on a local intermediary. Along with this linearization of trade went the development of highly skilled technologies of obsidian blade production that required constant practice, underwritten by residents of some house compounds at certain sites.[17]

The radical segregation of new spatial arenas was accompanied by a monopolization of exotic materials, worked into regalia by skilled specialists, for the use of the residents of select house compounds for their own ceremonial performances.[18] This stratification of consumption of specialized luxuries in ritual performance is the context for the spread throughout Mesoamerica of a series of representational motifs and stylistic preferences for pottery serving vessels, implied by the stylistic term "Olmec." Examination of the use across Mesoamerica of these representational motifs, stylistic preferences, and formal canons suggests more dynamic and complex histories of development than one merely spread from a single center of development by diffusion, implicit in the traditional use of the term "Olmec" both for these traits and for archaeological sites in the Gulf Coast of Mexico. David Grove has suggested limiting the term "Olmec" to the Formative Period archaeological cultures of the Gulf Coast of Mexico, represented by sites such as San Lorenzo, La Venta, and Laguna de los Cerros. For didactic purposes, he employed the term "X-complex" for those motifs that are widely distributed across Mesoamerica, including the Gulf Coast Olmec sites, in order to demonstrate that labeling them with a term implying origins has led to a lack of attention to the questions of innovation and diversity. However, to avoid reification of these motifs as an analytic cluster, Grove does not advocate the use of the term "X-complex." Arthur Demarest, while providing a sophisticated alternative to models of centers of origin and receptive peripheries that he calls a "lattice model" of interaction, nonetheless retains the term "Olmec," arguing that it need not be taken to imply origins. However, in the works of other contemporary scholars, such as John Clark, the term is used deliberately to mark interaction as beginning in the Gulf Coast and extending to other areas. I have previously employed the term "pan-Mesoamerican symbolism" for the same cluster of features. Recognizing that this terminology is more cumbersome, but that the use of the term "Olmec" does imply origins in most cases, I will use the term "Olmec" for instances of Gulf Coast origin or contact and otherwise refer to specific widespread practices of the Early or Middle Formative Period.[19]

The use of an overlapping repertoire of ceramic decoration techniques does suggest that villages in which these features were found formed a large-scale community of values, more extensive than the local, village-level arena of evaluation that was previously the highest level of integration evident archaeologically. In Michael Herzfeld's terms, use of these widespread Formative Period practices is evidence of disemia between an "us" that expands to encompass all of Mesoamerica, and a "them" that includes neighboring societies north of Guerrero, Central Mexico, and the Gulf Coast, and south of Honduras and El Salvador.

New practices of ceramic decoration widespread across Meso-america in the late Early Formative were applied to serving vessels, forms of pottery that imply the social performances associated with meals. Because these vessels are food-serving forms, they constitute metonymic or indexical signs for commensality, the enactment of a community through food sharing. Index and metonymy are special kinds of symbolic relations in which an item invokes a chain of associations by connection, not simply through arbitrary linkages. These kinds of signs have been described as "contiguity tropes." Because contiguity tropes invoke strings of associations created through living practice, they are open to analysis in ways that more arbitrary symbols are not.[20]

At least one of the entailments of serving vessels, an association that would have been always within the awareness of a viewer from these Meso-american Formative societies, was the consumption of food in social settings, or meals. And to the extent that meals united certain groups of people (and not others), meals, and the vessels that were used in them, implied an association with people with whom a viewer had certain kinds of relationships. John Clark, Michael Blake, Dennis Gosser, and Richard Lesure have presented compelling arguments for the proposition that Mesoamerica's earliest pottery was created through the replacement of perishable decorated gourd drinking vessels used in drinking rituals involving foods such as chocolate, *atole,* or corn *chicha.* These authors suggest that the ornamentation of vessels was a competitive act, conditioned by the use of pots in feasting in pursuit of prestige in these small-scale societies. John Hoopes suggests decorated vessels used in such feasting would have had a "role in impressing participants with the wealth and generosity of the feast's sponsor(s)," a quality he labels "impressiveness." Clark and Gosser add that reproducing perishable gourd drinking cups in "a new and more expensive medium (fired clay) would have enhanced their value but not tampered with meaningful social conventions."[21] Implicit in both comments is the assumption that participants in the social events in which these pots were employed would have been willing and able to judge these vessels in terms of the resource investment they represented.

William Longacre has questioned the utility of pottery vessels in such circumstances: "to be applied broadly, stylistic signals of significant social boundaries must be conspicuous and unambiguous (loud and clear). Pottery would seem to be a poor vehicle for such important information, compared with a flag, headdress, or color of dress."[22] While other media may have been better candidates than pottery to communicate "loud and clear" information about differences between bounded social groups, the use of vessels in the context of food consumption gave them a special potential not shared by Longacre's otherwise apt examples of flags, headdresses, and color of garments—which probably also played important roles in early Mesoamerican societies. Unlike these items, all of which are tied to individual actors, freestanding objects can become a focus for the creation of specifically *communal* value.[23] The characteristic contexts for the use of Early Formative bottles and bowls were meals, whether everyday or special occasion feasts, occasions of social, not merely individual, participation. As communal events on a face-to-face scale, meals, feasts, and ceremonies based on them provided a context in Early Formative Mesoamerica within which the craft work of highly decorated vessels could be appreciated as the product of individual creative action and patronage underwritten by social groups.

What distinguished vessels with decorative motifs and techniques widely employed in the later Early Formative Period was their originality, their difference from existing styles of decoration in each settlement. How they were deployed locally differs in each area that has been studied. Burials at Tlatilco in the Basin of Mexico containing vessels with widely shared motifs are among the richest, but otherwise the placement of these vessels shows little evident patterning.[24] In Oaxaca, pots with particular motifs related to the widely shared set were found in burials in specific sectors of San José Mogote and in specific sites in the Oaxaca valley hinterland. Joyce Marcus and Kent Flannery argue that the distinct motifs were used as insignia by two Oaxacan descent groups.[25]

Marcus extends the same interpretation to vessels from burials at Copan, Honduras. I argue instead that the makers of these and other pots from Formative Period Honduran sites, including the Cuyamel Caves, Los Naranjos, Playa de los Muertos, and Puerto Escondido, used motifs and techniques similar to those employed by potters in Oaxaca to differentiate their products from autochthonous traditions of decoration. The difference in our conclusions illuminates one of the ways that interpretation of ancient remains proceeds, that is, by continually questioning the adequacy of previously defined categories of analysis. Marcus assigns Copan vessels to either the category of Earth or of Lightning, defined for Oaxaca. I recognize distinct motifs that are versions of an animal based on a shark among the pots from Copan. In addition, I included in my analysis a second burial context within caves in the Copan Valley—part of a single system of burial during the Formative Period—where no separation of motifs is evident.[26]

In each area, the newly employed motifs created an appearance of difference in the local context while simultaneously connecting the users of these pots with each other both locally and at the scale of Mesoamerica as a whole. The selection of serving-vessel forms for elaboration, identified as an aspect of aggrandizing behavior in the earliest ceramic complexes of Formative Mesoamerica, implies both the existence of shared standards and differential evaluation of execution in this permanent, public medium.[27] Rather than unproblematically gaining status through their patronage of decorated ceramics, early Formative "aggrandizers" were risking rejection, inviting assessment, and framing the discourse of power, display, and wealth in the material language of the intimacy of shared meals, a social scale required to appreciate the elaboration of such hand-held vessels.

Through evaluation, particular kinds of relations were created between the makers/users of these vessels and others in their community, relations encompassing the recognition of shared standards for adornment and execution, and the measurement of each attempt at beautification against those standards. Ethnographically, such evaluation demarcates those within a group from those outside it, we who agree on what is beautiful and good from those who do not share our values.[28]

In later Early Formative Mesoamerica, the "we" formed by participation in the use of widespread motifs and practices of ceramic production is a nonlocalized network composed of only some individuals in each settlement, an emergent class claiming a different status from others in their communities. Practices of ceramic decoration appear to have spread through the same networks of exchange that provided exotic materials to be worked into distinctive costume ornaments by some houses in Early Formative villages. In burials from the very end of the Early Formative at Tlatilco, standardized iron-ore mirrors, greenstone belts, and greenstone ear ornaments were in use that are indistinguishable from ornaments employed in initial Middle Formative burials from Central Mexico to Honduras.[29]

At Tlatilco, these burials formed part of clusters placed below house compound floors, but at the slightly later sites of Chalcatzingo, La Venta, Chiapa de Corzo, and Los Naranjos, the use of such ornaments was restricted to individuals buried outside house compounds in sectors of monumental architecture. A whole suite of distinctive features that emerged late in the Early Formative Period—the construction of new spatial arenas for performance; the production of standardized costume ornaments from imperishable materials by specialists supported by the residents of select house compounds, often near the new monumental architecture; and adherence to new standards of decoration of ceremonial regalia shared across Mesoamerica—were intimately interconnected. Together, they form evidence of distinctive performances, both everyday and ceremonial, in the late Early Formative and early Middle Formative Periods, performances in which gender and power were played out and their interrelations given initial shape in the Mesoamerican tradition.

The Inscription of Gendered Performances in Figurines

Early Formative figurines from Mesoamerican sites are conventionally assigned sexual identity because they depict nude, or almost nude, bodies. Following a naturalistic model of representation, this would imply that the people of these communities were habitually nude or nearly nude as well. The identification of an item of clothing strongly identified with male sexual identity in later Mesoamerican societies, the loincloth, on a subset of figurines bolsters this naturalistic logic. But in fact the nudity of these figures is much more problematic, as the differential presence of conventional male costume and the absence of items of later conventional female costume suggests. Early Mesoamerican figurines reveal bodies, and do so differentially; it is with this aspect of the representation of gendered performance that I begin my analysis of the relationships between gender and power in emerging Mesoamerica.

The Tlatilco site in the Valley of Mexico has been the subject of extensive archaeological investigation since brickworkers mining the area found burials containing multiple pottery vessels and figurines. Over the years, more than four hundred burials have been documented. These burials were deposited in clusters, and the definition of features such as storage pits suggests the clusters were placed below the ground surfaces of house compounds. Settlements contemporary with Tlatilco in the Basin of Mexico were engaged in the production of obsidian and ground-stone tools at the household level in quantities indicating production for trade. The clustering of debris from two distinct technologies of obsidian production in burials from particular areas of the site suggests the limitation of this craft specialization to the inhabitants of these house compounds, and the importance of these crafts to house members who carried out these burial ceremonies. Concentrations of ritual regalia in certain clusters may indicate that a specific ceremonial performance was the property of other houses at the site. The wealth of some of the burials also suggests both the material success and the confidence of certain houses.[30]

More than 120 figurines were documented in these burials, providing a rich source of gendered representations from this early, prosperous community. Of these figurines, 66 were illustrated with sufficient clarity to allow determination of such features as costume and indication of sexual characteristics. More than half the figurines were provided with ear ornaments, regardless of their apparent sex. Complex, individualized hair treatments were common, and the head was the focus of most elaboration, with face painting and cranial deformation also indicated, and headdresses, ornaments on headbands, and necklaces common. The total or partial nudity of the majority of the figurines provides some basis to identify the probable sex being represented. About 30 percent of the Tlatilco figurines avoid distinctive depiction of sexual characteristics in favor of generalized features. These figurines are often classified automatically as female because they are nude and lack male genitalia. But they may better be understood as media for presenting an aspect of human identity that is independent of sharply marked dichotomous sexes, a sexually neutral human image.

Among the major indicators that have been used to identify male figurines, loincloths stand out. These garments conform in every way to the continuing depiction in later Mesoamerica of the item of male garment associated not only with maleness, but through its ornamentation and length, with specific kinds of male status as well, as when Aztec and Maya nobles wore exceptionally long loincloths.[31] By definition, figurines provided with loincloths cannot reveal male genitalia, but they have generally been identified as sexually male without any concern for possible confusion. In part an unconscious assumption of continuity and in part an adoption of the naturalistic approach to imagery, this ease of classification also reflects the presumption that female sexual status will be signaled secondarily by the presence of developed breasts on the chests exposed on these figurines, as is the case for female figures wearing loincloths in Postclassic Maya and Mexica art (Figure 2). Nothing else in the analysis of Mesoamerican imagery so obviously reveals the presumption that the subject matter of Mesoamerican art is a timeless, sexually mature adult world.

Many of the figurines from Tlatilco fit this expectation for the marking of adult female sexual status. Shown with exposed genitalia or with breasts indicated on their chests, these are the "pretty ladies" of the art world.[32] Clothing on these figurines is wholly unlike that depicted and described for adult females in images and texts from later Mesoamerican societies from which support is taken for identifying loincloths as the sign of male gender.[33] Shown nude or with very short skirts or kilts, these Formative female figurines lack the distinctive blouses and long skirts whose names in later Mesoamerican societies were metaphors for adult women. The difference in costume raises the possibility that some or all of these figurines are not meant to illustrate such fully adult women, but females of some other status. Because of their intricate hair and jewelry and costumes that reveal female bodies, I suggest that these figurines represent a record of practices of beautification linked intimately with the expression of emerging sexuality at the transition from childhood to adulthood. Burials at Tlatilco provide evidence for the everyday performance of some of the practices of beautification represented in figurines and document their strong relationship with age, not simply biological sex.

Individualization in Burials at Tlatilco

Tlatilco's female figurines, differentiated simultaneously from both sexless nude figures and depictions of properly clothed adult males, draw atten-

Figure 2. Postclassic deity wearing loincloth, marked as female by exposed breasts. Relief of Coyolxauhqui from base of the stairs of the temple of Huitzilopochtli, Templo Mayor, Tenochtitlan. From Eduardo Matos Moctezuma, *The Great Temple of the Aztecs: Treasures of Tenochtitlan.* Copyright 1988 Thames and Hudson Ltd. Reprinted by permission of the publishers.

tion to body ornamentation that is differentially distributed in burials of women, particularly young women. Out of a sample of 212 professionally excavated and completely described burials at Tlatilco, of which 86 (41%) were sexed female, 16 (8%) were buried wearing imperishable costume ornaments.[34] A disproportionate number of these (8, 50%) were female and a smaller than expected number (6, 38%) were male. The most detailed costumes were worn by young women between fifteen and twenty-five years old, who were also accompanied by the largest number of other materials, including up to 11 figurines. Small ceramic masks included in two of these burials may have been additional parts of the fancy costumes these young women wore. Ceramic stamps included in three of these burials, appropriate for ornamenting skin,[35] may document performance of a more perishable form of body modification, also indicated by painted designs preserved on 10 percent of the female figurines.

Older women, between thirty and forty-five years old, wore at most a single strand of bone or shell beads at the neck or wrist, and lacked the jade, rock crystal, and iron-ore beads and pendants found on younger women. The general simplification of costumes preserved with these slightly older women suggests a lessened emphasis on personal beautification. Unique to these older women, however, was a high frequency of ceramic rattle balls, whose form and location in burials suggests they may have been worn on the legs, and whistles that could have served as pendants. Five burials of women aged twenty-five to forty, three with no other imperishable costume ornaments, were accompanied by up to five rattles or whistles.

The age range of men buried wearing costumes was slightly older than that of women, from twenty to fifty, but again the most intricate costumes were worn by younger men, those under thirty. Among these were men who wore multiple strands of beads at neck, arm, and ankle, as well as ear spools and rings incorporating jade, bone, shell, and iron ore. As with their younger female counterparts, some males between twenty and thirty were buried with small ceramic masks and stamps that might be other media of beautification. Also like the women of Tlatilco, slightly older men, ages twenty-five to thirty-five, were buried with ceramic rattle balls. For the five youths with stamps and masks and the three older men with up to three rattles, these objects were their only form of costume ornamentation. In general, the burials of men were accompanied by less diverse and fewer objects, including much smaller numbers of figurines, suggesting differential attention to women's graves at Tlatilco. More dramatic evidence of possible asymmetry by sex in practices of beautification is presented by the modification of the shape of the skull. While 58 percent (124) of all adult burials showed evidence of such practices, a higher proportion of women (77% of female burials) had been subjected to this body modification, which began in infancy and was already evident in individuals as young as nine months.

The emphasis on the adorned bodies of youthful and young adult men and women seen in patterns of imperishable ornaments in the burials calls attention to the unrepresentative quality of figurines at the site with respect to age. Figurines at Tlatilco in general represent apparently youthful males and females. Figures identified as male have flat chests and uniformly wear loincloths and ear ornaments. Occasionally they have necklaces or helmets with chin straps. Their hair may be worn in long tresses, shaved on top, or short. Female figurines share most of these hair treatments, with the exception of shaved heads. They may wear distinctive headdresses: a band supporting one to three round disks, a beaded ornament, or a series of horns that may have been a hair treatment. Their female sexuality is signaled by small modeled breasts, sometimes accompanied by clearly delineated genitalia or, in a few cases, a swollen belly. Unlike their invariable appearance on male figurines, ear ornaments are not always present on female figurines, and in addition to necklaces, the female figurines may also wear bracelets. The most distinctive ornament of some female figurines is a real fragment of polished iron ore placed as a pendant at the neck.

Tlatilco figurines, which are more frequently of female subjects than of male or neutral sex subjects, clearly do not represent the actual patterns of differential access to ornaments and, by implication, to statuses associated with those ornaments. In burials from the site, iron-ore pendants were found in burials of both males (6) and females (2). All were among the burials with the greatest number and diversity of objects.[36] The age distribution of mirrors is consistent with the general observation that burials of youths are more complex than those of older adults, with the same shift to slightly more senior burials for males as noted for other practices of body ornamentation. Women with iron-ore ornaments ranged in age from fifteen to twenty-five, while the majority of men were between twenty-five and thirty-five years old at death (5 out of 6 examples). Three burials with these ornaments for which sex was not determined ranged between age seven and thirty. Only one exceptional burial with an iron-ore ornament was older, classified as between forty and forty-five years of age. This male was the oldest of fourteen individuals recovered from a single cluster. Four of these individuals were buried wearing costume ornaments, and five had materials suggesting involvement in obsidian craft production. The middle-aged man buried with this iron-ore ornament is a good candidate for identification as an elder of a successful house. He had one of the most lavish burial assemblages at the site, with jadeite and bone ear spools and vessels that included a unique hollow effigy of an acrobat. Patricia Ochoa suggests he could have been a ritual specialist, or shaman.[37] Despite this apparent status, none of the Tlatilco figurines represent someone of his actual age or expected experience. Instead, they overrepresent young people, especially young women, and do so in ways that emphasize their bodies.

While most often provided with no clothing, some of the female figurines wear very short flaring skirts. Intricate face and body painting is preserved on a few examples. The costumes depicted on Formative figurines revealed and accented, rather than concealed, the body. Contemporary large-scale representations (discussed below) show a knee-length skirt as the costume of women, and a similar length kilt on men, both costumes sometimes complemented by a cape. In contrast to these monuments, the body itself and its highlighting through the use of painting, hair treatment, and ornaments are the foregrounded subjects of Formative figurines, inscribing in permanent form moments of beautified, gendered performance. The inclusion of masks as part of the costume of some of the individuals buried at Tlatilco, and particularly of rattle balls, whose sound would have depended on rhythmic movement, hints that the kinds of performances in which gendered beauty was on display in this Formative society may have been ceremonies involving dancing. In the implied performances documented by the figurines and burial costumes of Tlatilco, older men and women provided the music for the display of the bodies of young, but sexually mature, women and men.

Figurines as a Discourse on Control of the Body

The burials and figurines from Tlatilco are testimony to the bodily incorporation of several kinds of differences: sex, age, seniority, and role—each a component of the emerging definition of marked young adult male and female genders. Richard Lesure, in an analysis of Formative figurines from Paso de la Amada on the Pacific coast of Mexico, has demonstrated the importance of the same axes of differentiation in a suite of very different visual representations. Two groups of human images at this site formed the assemblage created between 1250 and 1100 B.C. Standing figurines depicting armless nude figures with explicit female sexual characteristics were accompanied by seated fleshy male and female figures wearing masks and other items of ritual regalia. Lesure reports no images of youthful males and lacks burial data that would allow him to investigate differences between practice and representational imagery. Consequently, his analysis is thrown into even more stark relief than my discussion of Tlatilco. He suggests that the armless nude females reflect the objectification of young women deprived of agency as objects of marriage negotiations controlled by elders, represented by the sedentary and fleshy masked figurines.[38] Lesure's analysis suggests an undertone to the Tlatilco figurines and burial data: the possibility that the sexuality of young women—and perhaps young men—was a matter of explicit concern and control for the elders of their houses.

The differences between the two sites, however, make it evident that whatever developments are signaled by the production and manipulation of material images of the body, they are not uniform across Mesoamerica. Tlatilco female figurines do not lack arms; the strong contrast between seated and standing figurines seen at Paso de la Amada is absent from the Tlatilco assemblage; and the young male figurines of Tlatilco have no counterparts at Paso de la Amada. What both sites share with other Formative Period figurine assemblages is an astonishing emphasis on the nude body, especially sexually neutral and female bodies. At the opposite end of Mesoamerica's geography, villagers in Early to Middle Formative sites along the Ulua River in northwest Honduras produced exquisitely detailed hand-modeled figurines exhibiting the same concerns, most depicting nude or largely nude women and sexually neutral persons (Figure 3).

Honduran Formative figurines have been recovered archaeologically from burials and domestic trash at Playa de los Muertos on the Ulua River; at the Puerto Escondido and Guanchia sites, both downstream from Playa de los Muertos in the Ulua Valley; and at the sites of PACO 1 and PACO 15 in the Cuyumapa drainage east of the Ulua Valley. Doris Stone reported parts of two Playa figurines from Late Classic levels at the site of Travesía.[39] Ricardo Agurcia proposed a typology of Playa figurines divided by paste composition, based on the collection at the Middle American Research Institute (MARI) at Tulane University, which includes the examples excavated at Travesía by Stone.[40] It remains uncertain whether these paste types are products of distinct contemporary workshops or were produced at different points in time. Agurcia, Nedenia Kennedy, and Paul Healy all suggested that most of the variability in these figurines reflected social ranking.[41]

My discussion is based on my own documentation of 131 figurines from Honduras at the Peabody Museum (excavated by Gordon, Popenoe, and Strong, Kidder, and Paul) and analysis of my own excavated collections from Puerto Escondido and PACO 1 and PACO 15, and Kevin Pope's excavated examples from the Ulua Valley.[42] My concern was with the representation of different sexes, ages, and statuses within this tradition. Intersecting axes of age and sex are highlighted in these figurines to an even greater degree than at Paso de la Amada. Apparent ages depicted range from infancy to old age. Some figurines represent an adult holding a child.[43] Ricardo Agurcia suggested that some small, plump Playa de los Muertos figurines, including those that depict explicit female genitalia, represent infants. At least one such figurine, depicted with primary female sexual characteristics, lacks any indication of modeling of breasts on the

Figure 3. Formative Period figurines from Playa de los Muertos, Honduras. *Lower left:* simple medium-length hairstyle, necklace, and apron. *Upper right:* hair bound in side knot with beaded pendants hanging from headband. *Lower right:* hair bound in central knot with pendant beads, shaved stepped hairline, and necklace. Note prominent depiction of ear spools. Photograph by Steve Burger, copyright President and Fellows of Harvard College. Used by permission of the Peabody Museum, Harvard University.

chest.[44] Explicit denotation of age is evident in examples with wrinkled faces, sometimes showing mouths with a single tooth and, in exceptional cases, hunched backs.[45]

The depiction of a range of ages suggests that one of the topics of concern to the makers and users of these figurines was the transformation of personal appearance throughout the life course, a concern that may have been more strongly focused on females than on males. Of the figurines I have examined that were well-enough preserved to have presented physical sexual characteristics, 6 percent were obscured by clothing (with no examples of specifically male clothing items, such as loincloths); 35 percent are represented as immature, most lacking indications of adult sex (only 6% had body or costume suggesting specific sex, all female); and 58 percent, I argue, represent stages of adult female sexual status, primarily through costume and secondarily through the delineation of breasts.

In the Peabody collection, only 40 percent of the figurines with preserved lower bodies had identifiable clothing. Typically, this took the form of a brief skirt or apron suspended in front from a band or belt that continued around the back of the figurine. The textile in front usually extended across the front of the upper thighs only, covering the pubic region. In one example excavated at PACO 15, the frontal apron has an irregular boundary and internal patterning suggesting an animal skin. The band supporting the apron was sometimes ornamented in back with hanging strands of flexible material and beads, but does not otherwise cover any of the flesh on the back of the body. Lower-body clothing is markedly more common on standing figurines (56% of the examples in the Peabody) than in the sample as a whole.[46]

Most standardized was the treatment of hair and associated body ornaments, which provides the basis of my proposed classification of Playa figurines. The unprocessed hair of some figurines, including the infant held by an adult female, is represented by straight parallel lines and a uniform hairline. The hair on these figurines is in some sense a raw material that in other Playa de los Muertos figurines has been socially transformed. These figurines also have the lowest proportion of other ornamentation of the head. Like the actual bodies of children recovered in burials at the site, these hypothetical figural representations of children on the verge of young adulthood have a very high incidence of jewelry on their arms and legs.

A second group of figurines also has a low frequency of ear ornaments, but a distinctive hair treatment typifies them: hair drawn up into a topknot, sometimes with beading applied to locks of hair. Such figurines

suggest a concern with the moment of time when hair began to be actively transformed, by shaving and intricate dressing, into prescribed social
forms. A third group represents the peak of hair processing and of general bodily ornamentation. Beaded locks of hair are always present, shaved
patches and designs are common, and more than half have ear ornaments,
anklets, and bracelets. They include the highest proportion of standing figures and many have arms raised, hands touching the face or the back of the
head, even entwined in the hair. Their raised arms and standing postures,
combined with their detailed costuming, hint at the possibility that they
memorialize dance or similar public ceremonial movement.

Three-quarters (74%) of Playa figurines stand, regardless of the apparent age or gender they represent. The variety of their poses contrasts
vividly with the relatively static figurines from Tlatilco and encompasses
the postures that Lesure argues mark two distinct statuses at Paso de la
Amada. Like the figurines interpreted as elders from the latter site, all
Playa figurines show fleshy bodies, whether standing or sitting, regardless
of whether they depict explicitly female, sexually neutral, infantile, youthful, or aged persons. Rather than being concerned with distinctions between female and male (a category entirely unmarked in the assemblage),
the sexual characteristics depicted in Playa de los Muertos figurines may
more accurately be characterized as emphasizing transitions in age, perhaps primarily of sexually female subjects. Body form, processing of hair,
and ornamentation are combined to commemorate the gradual production of social persons, an activity concretized in the manipulation of clay
to produce the figurines themselves. It is through the selective inscription
in pottery figurines of specific gestures as typical of persons with particular sexual organs that apparently "natural" associations were made an enduring part of Ulua Valley concepts of gender. These permanent media,
through which gender was materialized, stood in dynamic tension with
actual performances within the settlement.

Bodily Performance and the Segregation of Space

The few Playa de los Muertos figurines documented archaeologically were
found within household groups, either discarded in trash or in burials under
house floors. At none of the sites where these figurines are found is there
any evidence for segregated spatial settings marked by monumental architecture or art. The figurines themselves were presumably viewed and used
in small-scale interactions in the arenas of house compounds by members

of the house and others closely connected to them. This situation stands in stark contrast to other Formative Period Honduran settlements not far from the villages where Playa de los Muertos figurines have been recovered. At Los Naranjos, on Lake Yojoa, where few figurines were identified, the site center during the contemporary Jaral phase (800–400 B.C.) boasted a ditch surrounding and setting off earthen mounds rising at least 13 meters above a plaza. At Yarumela in the Comayagua Valley, where occasional Playa de los Muertos figurines were found as trade items and were used in burials but where no local tradition of figurine manufacture has been identified, a single 20-meter-tall earthen mound was the focal point of the village. In these sites, monumental architecture created arenas for differential participation in marked performances and changed the nature of the spatial settings of everyday bodily practices.[47]

Burials within the residential group at Playa de los Muertos attest to the performance of the bodily practices that figurines suggest were important to individuals at the site.[48] In sixteen burials containing ten strings of beads, no two costumes were alike. Both juveniles and adults were buried wearing wrist and neck ornaments, with shell employed only in children's costume and greenstone used in both adult and juvenile ornaments. Ear ornaments, whether of ceramic or greenstone, were worn only by adults, but beyond this single difference, no other categorical distinctions are evident. Each set of beads is unique in arrangement, and though pendant forms are repeated within a burial, no two burials have the same pendants. Only the form of ear spools is repeated: all three pairs were of the simple napkin-ring type common throughout Honduras and El Salvador.[49] Ear spools are thus singled out as a costume element whose significance may be more standardized, perhaps as insignia of adult status. But overall, costume was individualized. The most complex costume at Playa de los Muertos was found in the burial of a child.

At contemporary Los Naranjos, in contrast, the only individual buried in costume, an adult deposited in Structure IV, wore jade ear ornaments, a jade bead necklace, and a belt of two strands of jade beads, a costume conforming to Mesoamerica-wide practices. At Chiapa de Corzo, Chalcatzingo, and La Venta, unique individuals buried within nonresidential mounds also wear highly detailed greenstone costume including double-strand belts and wide earflares (Figure 4).[50] While the inscriptions of performances through the burial of bodies wearing imperishable ornaments in house compounds manifest individuality, those associated with the spatially segregated setting of monumental architecture are distinguished by

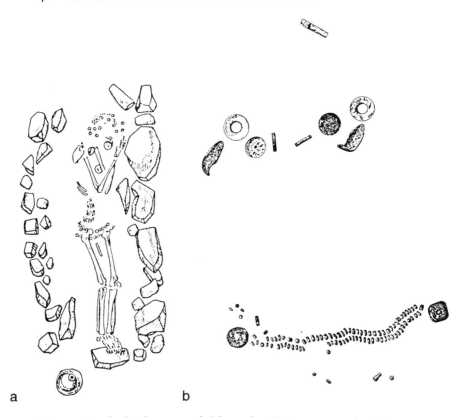

a   b

Figure 4. Standardized costume of elaborate burials in monumental architecture: (a) Chalcatzingo, Morelos; (b) La Venta. Drawing of Chalcatzingo burial courtesy of David C. Grove.

conformity to wider Mesoamerican traditions. Figurines made in settlements forming part of the Formative Mesoamerican world were shaped in response to a complex set of emerging differences and connections among people and groups.

The village sites of Tlatilco, Paso de la Amada, and Playa de los Muertos are examples both of a widespread pattern in the production of distinctive figurines in Formative Mesoamerica and of how diverse these local traditions are. No single explanation of their variety can be easily extended beyond the local community, but at the same time, they share one characteristic: an emphasis on nudity that cannot simply be treated as a naturalistic detail. It is as if bodies, and especially bodies of certain sexual status, were the center of particular tension as these early villages engaged in the face-to-face negotiation of power and status. As we would expect if the apparent subject matter of figurines was bound up in developing power relations, there are marked differences in human representation in settlements with segregated spatial arenas created through the use of monumental architecture and art.

Scale and Media in Formative Period Gendered Representations

One site with segregated spatial arenas and a well-studied figurine assemblage is Chalcatzingo, located in Morelos south of the Valley of Mexico. Already in the Early Formative the settlement contained a segregated nonresidential space formed by the conjunction of an earthen mound and an adjoining plaza. By the Middle Formative Cantera phase (ca. 700 B.C.), the formalization of this space had been enhanced by the placement of carved-stone monuments in zones of increasing exclusivity.[51]

The particularity of the body at issue in the figurines of Middle Formative Chalcatzingo, according to Ann Cyphers Guillén, is the cycle of sexual maturity, pregnancy, and parturition. Chalcatzingo figurines are entirely nude, but attention was lavished on markings that Cyphers Guillén identifies with biological features associated with reproductive stages in the female life cycle. Cyphers Guillén notes that the figurines she analyzes were distributed in household refuse, and she suggests the images of pregnant women may have served in life-cycle rituals carried out by the residents of the house compound. While Cyphers Guillén identifies the vast majority of the Chalcatzingo figurines as images of female life stages, an independent analysis of figurine heads from the site identified one type, C8, as portraits of the ruler of the site, marking the locations where they were used as participating in commemorating the ruler of the site. Susan Gillespie demonstrates that these portrait figurines were present in residential settings throughout the site, but notes some variation in their relative abundance. Significantly, they are particularly common in residences of what may be more socially distinguished houses.[52]

C8 figurines were especially common on Terrace 25, which yielded evidence of possible residential use of a distinctive stone-faced platform (16.5 m long, 4.5 m wide, 50 cm tall), as well as monumental sculpture and a sunken patio with a probable throne. They were also common at Terrace 27, the location of a second raised, rectangular, stone-faced platform (18 m long and 7.5 m wide, perhaps originally 1 m tall), rebuilt multiple times, that Prindiville and Grove characterize as like a raised house foundation.

These two locations would appear to be remarkably similar to the structure identified as a chief's house at Paso de la Amada.[53]

Other concentrations of C8 figurines were noted on Terraces 4 and 24, both sites of residential buildings of the Cantera phase. These are likely candidates for residences of houses closely involved in the assertion of status by the site's rulers. The unusually low frequency of the portrait figurines on Terrace 11 singles that location out as well. Terrace 11 was another Cantera phase house site, located at the base of the hill ornamented by monumental rock carvings. One carving was recovered at this location. It seems possible that this was the residence of a house that did not support the cult of the ruler and the assertion of status by the ruling house, itself presumably resident in buildings on Terrace 1, bordering the main Plaza.[54]

Burials at Chalcatzingo, located below house floors and within monumental architecture, are generally not accompanied by figurines. The exception is a burial containing a carved greenstone figurine of an anthropomorphic, sexually neutral nude figure.[55] Such greenstone figurines have generally been treated as unrelated to pottery figurines. The use of one in a burial at Chalcatzingo, and of others in contemporary burials at La Venta on the Gulf Coast of Mexico, places these distinctive, rare products of skilled craft production firmly within the same epidemiology of representations as pottery figurines. The contrasts between the two kinds of small-scale human representations place in perspective the individuality inherent in hand-modeled figurines. Greenstone anthropomorphic figures are substantially less varied: the majority represent standing figures, with a typical elongated head and distinctive facial features.[56] Unlike pottery figurines, the stone figures are relatively uniform throughout Mesoamerica. And while most studies report that the majority of pottery figurines that can be assigned a sex are female, the stone figures are either provided with the loincloth assumed to mark males or lack any indication of sexuality.

Consequently, the individual identity of hand-modeled pottery figurines, with their complex hair styles, carefully depicted body features, and particularistic ornaments, existed in tension with another emphasis on a generalized but inherently precious form of person. The body revealed by that form of person was as explicitly not-female as nude pottery figurines were female. The sexually neutral features of greenstone figurines echo similar traits of a minority of pottery figurines, including distinctive hollow figurines from a number of sites in the Basin of Mexico. The puffy body and face of the hollow pottery figurines have earned them the sobriquet "baby-face." Similar sexually neutral figures and their loincloth-wearing counterparts make up the exclusive subject matter not only of small-scale carved-stone figurines, but also of the monumental representations that appear in some of the same settlements at this time.

Unlike figurines, monumental anthropomorphic images do not typically depict nude figures. Thus the identification of bodily difference in monumental images is primarily through reference to differences in costume and ornament. Only one monumental image, Monument 14 from Chalcatzingo, is marked as female by the convention apparent on pottery figurines: a prominent breast exposed on a bare chest.[57] She wears a knee-length skirt and a cape suspended from her head. Contemporary low-relief and three-dimensional stone sculptures of figures wearing loincloths—for example, the figures on La Venta Altar 5 and Monument 23—may depict exposed chests with delineated pectoral muscles instead of emphasized breasts, providing a basis for their identification as sexually male. But for the most part it is costume alone that is used to create differences in appearance in monumental images.

Costume in Monumental Images and Segregated Spatial Settings

The detail in costumes of monumental images is concentrated on the head and shoulders, areas subject to the most extreme mutilation in the recycling of these monuments.[58] At Chalcatzingo most discernible ear ornaments exhibit a compound structure, with disk-shaped ear spools above pendants visible in Relief 1 and Monuments 10 and 28. The ear ornament worn by the unique woman on Monument 14 represents a disk without a pendant. Ear ornaments with pendants are also common in other late Early Formative and Middle Formative monumental images. Four colossal stone heads—La Venta Monument 2 and San Lorenzo Monuments 4, 5, and 61—each depict a hook-shaped ear ornament, most pendant from a round disk or spool. Such compound ear spools are also present on two tabletop "altars" or thrones. La Venta Altar 7 is badly battered, but the central figure emerging from a niche wears a disk-and-canine-tooth pendant ear ornament. A figure on the left side of San Lorenzo Monument 14, identified by Grove as the ruler portrayed by La Venta Monument 4, also wears the ear ornament assemblage. The disk-and-pendant ear ornament also appears on San Lorenzo Monument 30, a stone relief depicting an anthropomorphic shark. The being wears an ear ornament, shown as a disk with two long projections, like a frontal pendant and a counterweight bead.[59] The disk-and-pendant ear spool seen in these monuments corresponds to a form actually employed in a select group of highly standardized burials placed in unique locations within Middle Formative sites from Honduras to the Gulf Coast of Mexico.

Burials placed inside monumental earthen platforms at La Venta incorporate such standardized costume ornaments.[60] The ceremonial precinct dating to the Middle Formative at the site was defined by a number of earthen structures oriented with a long axis running roughly north-south. A tall, conical pyramid on the south, Complex C, forms one boundary of Complex A, a plaza outlined by two long, parallel mounds and a series of smaller platforms and courts. Mound A-2 (the northernmost structure), Mound A-3 (centrally located), and a platform on the northeast (Feature A-1-f) yielded tombs and burials or deposits of costume elements. Because of poor preservation of bones, only Tomb A, in Mound A-2, with the decayed remains of two individuals, was originally described as a human interment. Grove has previously argued, based partly on parallels to Chalcatzingo's better-preserved examples, that the bulk of the tombs and sets of costume ornaments were probably burials in which the bones have completely disintegrated.[61] The contents of the La Venta deposits were laid out in such a way as to represent stylized individual costume, whether or not all originally contained bodies.

Offerings 5, 6, and 7 from the Northeast Platform are cinnabar-coated sets of greenstone ornaments arranged to suggest costumes. Centerline earthen platforms Mound A-2 and Mound A-3 yielded a total of seven other groups of materials representing burials or burial-like caches. From north to south, these were basalt column Tomb A (1942-A, Monument 7), deposit 1942-D, basalt column Tomb E (1943-F), and Tomb B (or 1942-B), enclosed in a massive sandstone sarcophagus carved on the exterior with a saurian earth-monster depiction (Monument 6), all in Mound A-2; and stone cist Tomb C (or 1943-G) and cinnabar-stained Tomb D (1943-L) in Mound A-3. Tomb A contained two sets of objects covered in cinnabar associated with fragmentary human skeletal remains of juveniles, labeled Burial I and Burial II.

Among these ten burials, distinctions in status or function may be signaled by the presence or absence of stone enclosures (tombs, a stone sarcophagus, or a stone-outlined grave), placement on the main axis of the site (all but Offerings 5, 6, and 7), and the use of cinnabar pigment (absent in 1942-D and Tomb B). While these features vary, a small number of costume elements are repeatedly employed. Seven burials (Table 2: Pattern A) possess one or more of the following features: ear spools with pendants; a

Table 2. CONTENTS OF BURIALS AT LA VENTA

Item	1†	2	3†	4†	5†	6	7†	8†	9†	10
					Context*					
	← - - - - - - - -Pattern A- - - - - - - - →							← - -Pattern B- - →		
Ear spools with pendants		X	X	X	(X)	X	(X)			
Perforator	X	X	X							
Serrated ornament	X			X	X					
Greenstone belt			X		X	X				
Greenstone bivalve shell pendant								X	X	
Ear spools, plain									X	X
Hematite mirror							X	X		
Standing figurine	X	X	X					X		X
Greenstone maskette					X	X			X	
Greenstone bracelet							X			X
									{OR}	
Greenstone necklace							X			X

*Contexts:
  (Pattern A) 1: Tomb A, Burial II; 2: Tomb B; 3: Tomb C; 4: Tomb D;
        5: 1955 Offering 5; 6: 1955 Offering 6; 7: Tomb E;
  (Pattern B) 8: Tomb A, Burial I; 9: 1955 Offering 7; 10: 1942-D
†Contains other materials not summarized in this table.

serrated-outline greenstone ornament; a belt of greenstone beads, usually punctuated on right and left with larger beads; and perforators, including a stingray spine, a shark's tooth, greenstone "awls," and a greenstone effigy of a stingray spine. Three burials lack these elements (Table 2: Pattern B). Two of these contain greenstone bivalve shell pendants, and two have plain greenstone ear spools without pendants.

Unique in their location off the central axis of the site, Offerings 5, 6, and 7 from the Northeast Platform are the most stylized examples of these two patterns. Greenstone maskettes included in each are the same size and form as those depicted as parts of the headdress on San Martín Pajapan Monument 1, a monumental three-dimensional stone portrait sculpture.[62] Given their small size, Offerings 6 and 7 could be cached costumes incorporating such headdresses. Offering 5 also contains a small jar in a bowl and is outlined by rocks, conforming very closely to a burial practice identified at Chalcatzingo.[63] Offerings 5 and 6 exhibit Pattern A with the presence of a belt of greenstone beads and greenstone ear spools with pendants in the form of canine teeth and lobed cylinders. Offering 5 also included a diagnostic serrated outline pendant. Pattern B, as represented in Offering 7, is marked by a small effigy bivalve shell pendant and a pair of flat rings, which apparently represent the front surface (the "flare") of ear spools. The nature of these flares might suggest that they were fastened to some perishable substance, perhaps a framework for a headdress.[64]

The core costume element of Pattern A, ear spools with pendants, occurs in four other burials at La Venta. Tomb B contained a pair of greenstone ear spools with pendants in the form of canine teeth. Tomb C contained a pair of greenstone ear spools incised with the image of a supernatural bird of prey, with greenstone pendants representing deer mandibles, and a greenstone belt like those of Offerings 5 and 6. Ear spools with canine pendants also were found in Tomb D.

The perforators that form part of Pattern A were ritual tools used in bloodletting. The serrated-outline ornament included in some of these burials may also be related to bloodletting. Serrated-outline motifs incised on Early Formative ceramics were an abstract sign associated with a supernatural shark. This shark monster was directly related to bloodletting through the use of shark's teeth as actual or symbolic perforators.[65] E. Wyllys Andrews has suggested that the bivalve shell pendant of Pattern B may also be related to this ritual, as a receptacle for blood.[66] If his argument is accepted, the most distinctive features of both La Venta burial patterns are complementary actions in a single ritual. Spatial associations between burials support the idea that they are complementary in some fashion.

The elements that form Pattern A are a polythetic set, defined by the presence of one or more of four diagnostic features: ear spools with pendants, a serrated ornament, a greenstone bead belt, and perforators. The contrasting Pattern B is characterized by ear spools without pendants, a bivalve shell effigy pendant in place of the serrated ornament, and no belt or perforators. These contrasting patterns are paired in the unique occurrence of a double burial inside Tomb A. Burial II is associated with Pattern A by the presence of a serrated disk ornament and nine perforators. Burial I included the diagnostic bivalve shell effigy that marks Pattern B. The pair of burials also each included two anthropomorphic figurines: almost identical standing greenstone figures, and seated pottery figurines distinctive from each other in style and representation.

Although standing figurines are found in other La Venta burials, the seated figurines are a feature limited to this tomb. It is possible that the seated figurines are cross-references between these burials, since the figurine in Burial II wears a miniature iron-ore mirror, while the individual in Burial I was provided with a full-size iron-ore mirror. The figurine in Burial II has been identified as a female and is distinguished by a loose skirt and a combed hair treatment.[67] The figurine in Burial I appears to represent a male, since the chest is exposed and no breasts are indicated. The bare chest, high forehead, and lack of indication of hair on this figurine are features consistent with the depiction of males in monumental art — figures shown with serrated pendants and bloodletters, the objects included in Burial II.

Bivalve shell pendants, the defining feature of Pattern B, were not depicted in any monumental image of a human figure, which, with a single exception, have all been identified as male. Iron-ore mirrors, associated at La Venta in both Pattern A and Pattern B burials, are found in burials at Tlatilco with both males and females.[68] The use of this costume ornament by both men and women, documented in burials, is reflected in monumental and small-scale representations. Round, concave pectoral ornaments that have been identified as mirrors appear in monumental images of figures wearing loincloths and lacking delineated breasts: for example, on the side of La Venta Altar 5 and on La Venta Monument 23, San Lorenzo Monument 34, and Río Chiquito Monument 1.[69] Although most such sculptures were decapitated, the face of the low-relief figure on La Venta Altar 5 is intact and shows a disk ear ornament with a curved pendant, like that typical of Costume A at La Venta. John Carlson also identified the pectoral ornament on San Lorenzo Monument 34 as a mirror. This decapitated statue actually shows a serrated ornament in front of a concave pendant, perhaps symbolically combining the mirror with a motif diagnostic of Pattern A. Small-scale images, notably Tlatilco figurines with real crystalline hematite pectoral ornaments, depict females wearing mirrors. The seated figurine from La Venta Tomb A, although stylistically distinct, shares the use of a real iron-ore pendant to signify the costume ornament, perhaps reinforcing its identification as a depiction of a woman.

The virtual absence from monumental sculpture of depictions of women and of elements of La Venta Pattern B draws attention to the selectivity of these images. When contrasted with ceramic figurines, it becomes clear that even more drastic exclusion is a crucial aspect of the selection of subjects for monumental sculpture. When compared with material remains of costume and ritual tools in burials, it is evident that monumental sculpture stylizes action and appearance to a more constrained range than even the marked performances of ceremony, let alone the unmarked actions of everyday life. Monumental sculpture was the major medium through which public claims for differential status were made in early Mesoamerica. Through these images, certain members of society created restricted claims to status by excluding from representation other actors, even those who shared access to the same segregated spatial settings for burial, to products of patronized craft production, and to rare materials resulting from long-distance exchange. Preferentially representing youthful adult male actors and sexless supernatural dwarf figures, monumental images inscribed gendered, age-specific status distinctions in monumental time.

Statuo and Gender in Formative Meaoamerica

Unlike burials at most Formative Period sites, burials from Early Formative Tlatilco could be sexed. A continuum of rank was identified at Tlatilco, with both males and females among the most complex burials.[70] The presence of iron-ore mirrors, musical instruments, and masks in higher-ranked burials suggests that one source of status was ritual practice, an activity evidently open to both men and women. Human figurines at Tlatilco depicted both males and females in detailed costumes. At contemporary San José Mogote, along with the construction of the first public buildings, which are considered evidence of centralized authority, more restrictive patterns of distribution of items in burials according to gender are noted. In the succeeding Middle Formative Period, changes in burial patterns in Oaxaca, particularly an increase in male-female pairs in burials, are taken as an indication that status differences were firmly entrenched and that class affiliation was of primary importance.[71]

At contemporary Chalcatzingo, burials show evidence of a marked degree of restriction and covariation in all distinctive features, including proximity to public architecture, provision of a stone cist, and presence of greenstone items.[72] House membership, not age or sex, distinguishes the group of burials placed under the floor of a house compound located across from public architecture. Two individuals wearing complex costumes were buried in this public building, one with a greenstone belt indistinguishable from that typical of La Venta Pattern A, the other with a mirror pendant. While the sex of these individuals is uncertain, stone sculpture at the site represents a person marked as female through the delineation of an exposed breast as a focal subject. It has been suggested that this woman had a unique historical role in forming political ties between Chalcatzingo and another site through marriage alliance.[73] The selection of the breast as the physical feature marking her biological sexuality not only implies adult status but makes an implicit reference to reproduction and the nurturing of children, important aspects of noble alliance also highlighted in the treatment of the body in figurines at this site.

Both in Oaxaca and at Chalcatzingo, noble houses, made up of both men and women, are differentiated from other houses through a variety of practices: decoration and materials of the residence itself, greater consumption of exotic goods in everyday life and in mortuary ceremonies, and the support of craft specialists. Sexuality was not uniformly the primary identification of house members, becoming salient only in specific settings and circumstances, perhaps particularly when the sexual maturity of young people placed house interests under negotiation in a potential alliance through marriage.[74]

Contemporary monumental images deal not with the entire noble house, but only with selected individuals from it. Stone sculpture at Chalcatzingo and La Venta was a medium for claims of political power and status. Like all such permanent inscriptions of bodily practices, sculpture transformed certain performances into matters of monumental time transcending individual lives and memories. Grove has argued that such images include both markers of mythological significance and depictions of specific bases of human claims to power.[75] Mythological themes on monuments helped to define the character of segregated spatial arenas by associating them with cosmological forces and, presumably, shared concepts of the origin and nature of the universe. Motifs derived from mythological monuments could be incorporated schematically in narratives of human action, creating metaphoric associations with these transcendent concepts.

By presenting images of human beings embedded in depictions of the cosmological framework, and by placing the human figures in narrative sequences associated with rainfall and the growth of plants, stone sculpture presented an argument for a particular basis of power. Specific ritual actions were part of these images and consequently formed part of the new claims for political power represented by sculpture. Since the actors depicted were overwhelmingly male, the newly defined political status being formed at sites like Chalcatzingo was more limited than that gained through traditional religious practices open to both men and women.

Stone sculpture in these Formative Period settlements documents attempts to limit recognition of ritual status to males. Perforators, ear-spool pendants in the form of teeth or mandibles, and skull pendants in burials at La Venta suggest that ritual sacrifice may have been an important part of the definition of the new, or newly prominent, ritual role of men. Stone reliefs make little explicit reference to these actions, but by the selective depiction of one category of people they give more prominent place to the practitioners of these specific actions, transforming this privileged ritual status into a basis of political power. Stone reliefs fail to reflect the investment of others, notably women, in ritual and the process of sociopolitical centralization it served. The patrons of stone reliefs were presumably men with special social and ritual status who were depicted in these carvings and buried with their ceremonial regalia. Through their exclusion of women from the carved-stone record, they closed women out of the new medium in which claims to ritual status and the right to exercise power were being transacted, creating an arena of almost solely male participation.

Everyday Performance and Gendered Labor

The attempt to restrict the memory of ritual performance in Formative Period Mesoamerica, if not the actual performance itself, to one kind of person took place against a background of increasing differentiation of everyday practice through the patronage of craft specialization. The performance of gender in Mesoamerica came to encompass not only specific distinctions in dress, whose roots were already evident in the earliest villages, but also differences in action, particularly craft production. By the Postclassic Period, spinning and weaving were not only the work of women but also metaphors for womanhood. Thus the beginnings of the gendering of labor may also lie in the earliest Mesoamerican villages.

John Clark has argued that for the technology of producing long, parallel-sided blades through pressure on prepared obsidian cores to spread along the Pacific coast, patronage of full-time specialists was required, not merely to sustain the supply necessary to meet the demand, but to maintain the individual skills necessary for distinction in this craft.[76] In his model, would-be nobles invested resources to support craft elaboration as one of a suite of means to compete with others. Clark's cross-cultural survey of the patronage of craft specialization for political advantage identifies a number of cases of what he calls "hypertrophic" craft production, in which supported craft workers develop their skills to the highest point and display those skills through the making of extremely elaborate, often non-functional, items. Prominent among the cases he surveyed are examples of house societies from Polynesia.[77]

In the early development of craft production in Mesoamerica, there is no basis to presume the sexual status of the craft workers supported by noble patrons. The logic of competition through patronage would suggest that promising part-time craft workers would be singled out and encouraged individually; indeed, the most striking feature of patronized craft production is its emphasis on the individual. Support for full-time workers to hone the skills of their craft would initially have to come from the residents of the house compound in which they lived, in other words, from their house. Freed from subsistence tasks to concentrate on refining their abilities, early craft specialists would have distinguished themselves and simultaneously brought credit to their house.

Clark, Michael Blake, and Dennis Gosser suggest something like this for the production of the earliest pottery in the Pacific Coast region, the Barra complex ceramics of the initial Early Formative (ca. 1400–1550 B.C.). They argue that the highly decorated pottery vessels of this period were transformations of perishable gourd serving vessels, used in hosting feasts, into more permanent media. By adding these distinctive vessels to the common program of the feast, Barra pottery patrons distinguished themselves and their house from other houses in their community. Clark and Blake characterize the individual patrons as "aggrandizers," the literal and conceptual ancestors of later Mesoamerican nobles.[78]

Preceding the spread of core-blade technology, the production of fancy pottery vessels may be the first definable craft specialization in Mesoamerica. Later Mesoamerican pottery production was most likely work shared by diverse groups including men, women, and children, a pattern common in traditional pottery production cross-culturally.[79] Certainly pottery production never gained the gender-stereotyped status of other crafts, particularly spinning and weaving. The social character of the technology itself may have been an obstacle to associating accomplishment with an individual. In ethnographically observed situations, different people may be involved in traveling to and mining a clay source, preparing the raw clay, forming and decorating vessels, assembling them for firing, and completing the firing sequence itself. While it is common to credit the individual who formed or decorated a vessel as the potter, in reality pottery production is a social activity. But within early Mesoamerican villages, the practice of this craft may have been a site for the gradual identification of certain individuals as more deserving of credit for the success of a final product than others, a necessary move if any craft production was to be elevated as a source of personal achievement.

One possible factor in associating greater value with the contribution of one individual in the pottery production sequence may have been the opportunity for more marked personal identification provided by the use of pan-Mesoamerican motifs and standards of decoration after about 1200 B.C. While pottery decoration by specific individuals may be identifiable to experts working at the craft in even the most standardized production industries, the degree of recognition can fade among nonpotters without close links to these producers. The unique products of craft specialists working in an idiom of decoration distinct from that which is general to a community can produce a more widely recognized identity of artist with product.[80]

Without making blanket assumptions about the physical and mental capacities of persons of different sexes for certain kinds of work, or asserting preexisting ideological or symbolic associations for certain kinds of work, the only way to understand the association of specific craft activities with gender is through the individualization of craft work and the assertion of constraints on individual freedom in everyday work performance. The individualization of social credit for craft production would seem to be a prerequisite for the association of a craft role with any category of people. Whether prescriptive (entailing a rule of admission to training in a craft) or descriptive (allowing characterization of all those who practice a craft as members of a single category), assigning identity to craft workers requires a matching of individual workers with the products of their labor.

The variation in individual credit for craft work is identified as one dynamic in gendered performance in the two-spirit phenomenon of North America, in which a person performs a gender identity distinct from that of others with the same sexual characteristics. Harriet Whitehead argued that such gendered performances were defined primarily by dress and occupation and "of the two attributes, occupational preference and dress, it is the first that is most often mentioned and commented on, inclining us to believe that it was the most central of the social attributes definitive of gender." In these societies, the association of gender and occupational specialization was related to an ethic "centered largely upon individual variation in prestige-relevant occupations. The reason this ideology bore upon [two-spirit] behavior at all is that gender itself was heavily defined in terms of prestige-relevant occupations" in which a woman's production of valued goods "redounded to her own credit officially, and not simply informally."[81]

Early Mesoamerican aggrandizers supported the refinement of craft skills on the part of others in their house as a deliberate strategy to build their own personal authority and renown. The range of highly specialized crafts developed in these villages is astonishing: in addition to the production of well-made pottery and figurines and the technology of core-blade production, specializations in the manufacture of iron-ore mirrors, carving of jade and shell, and textile production (witnessed through the presence of imperishable tools) all developed within the confines of selected house compounds, located close to monumental architecture in sites with such distinctive buildings.[82] Patronized craft specialization perhaps reached its apogee in the production of monumental images in stone and other media. Reduction of roughly shaped forms near sources of the volcanic stone used by the Gulf Coast Olmec is archaeologically documented. The roughly shaped stones would have been finished in workshops at Gulf Coast centers. At San Lorenzo, a workshop for the recarving of stone monuments was not only located close to a large and specially constructed house, but was attached to that building with walls that segregated it from the rest of the site; it was further set off through specific ritual practices evident inside the workshop.[83]

Of all these everyday activities, the only ones to become associated with a specific gender in later Mesoamerica were spinning and weaving. By the Maya Classic Period, these two activities were represented as aspects of stereotypic adult female gender. The subjects of this representation were of the same age and sexual status as the gender formed through the manipulation of Formative Period figurines, that is, the young women whose sexuality may have been both a resource and a problem to their house elders, the participants in ritual whose images were not inscribed in the monumental space and time of the architectural centers of stratified Formative Period polities. How persons with this gender status were represented among the later Classic Maya exemplifies the effects of, and tensions around, political attempts by rulers and their supporters to control individual subjectivity in Mesoamerican states.

CHAPTER THREE

Narratives of Gender among the Classic Maya

The patterns of Formative Period life discussed in the preceding chapter created a distinctively Mesoamerican tradition through the formation and exercise of authority and the accrual of power within the small-scale contexts of the house compound and village and the larger-scale, nonlocalized networks of exchange and alliance that spanned Mesoamerica. The use of jade and other goods as valuables crystallized during this period. Segregated spatial settings employed a common set of architectural forms—the platform mound, the plaza, and the ballcourt—throughout Mesoamerica. These spaces were further delimited symbolically by the installation of monumental images that brought cosmological significance into these centers and inscribed in them specific valued histories of political and ritual performance. Among the variety of Mesoamerican societies, the Maya Lowlands stand out for their lack of participation in these characteristic Formative Period developments. Until the late Middle Formative and initial Late Formative, lowland Maya settlements seem to resist all these practices. Once lowland Maya settlements adopt the practices of Mesoamerican civilization, however, they engage in an unequaled record of representational documentation of their participation, employing the greatest diversity of media of representation, including writing and calendrical systems. The richness of their material record provides an abundant source for an investigation into some of the developments in relations between gender and power in maturing Classic Period Mesoamerica.

The Classic Maya World

The Maya world of the Classic Period (maximally ca. 250–1000 A.D.) encompassed dozens of individual settlements spreading from Comalcalco in the Tabasco plains of the Gulf of Mexico to the Ulua Valley of northwestern Honduras. Never politically unified, the settlements of the Maya world occupied diverse environments and were each involved in unique relations with their neighbors both within and outside that world.[1] The Maya world has been convincingly described as an anarchic states system in which independent polities are tied together by political strategies.[2] Such a system is inherently unbounded. The use of a common writing system across the area (although not in every settlement) is often assumed to indicate that the Maya Lowlands were linguistically unified. This presumed linguistic unity then forms the basis for the archaeological identity of the region. But in fact, we have no reason to assume linguistic unity. Written Classic Maya texts document two only distantly related languages from the Maya family, Yucatec and Cholan.[3] Unattested in written texts, and thus indeterminable, are the numbers of other Maya and non-Maya languages that might have been spoken in these sites. The unity of the Classic Maya has also been ascribed to the profession of a single political religion,[4] despite evidence for both variation within the region and considerable overlap with other Mesoamerican belief systems. Like linguistic unity, religion is probably not a sufficient explanation for the stylistic regularities of Classic Maya material culture that impresses all scholars.

In fact, what seems to most adequately characterize the commonalities between the settlements of the Classic Maya world is a suite of shared representational practices: the production and use of polychrome painted pottery vessels with naturalistic imagery and at times elements from the Maya writing system; small-scale reproduction in pottery of a restricted range of human images through the use of molds; and the execution at a monumental scale of carved stone, wood, modeled stucco, and polychrome painted images. Although not all of these practices are necessarily present at all times in every Maya site, some or all of them characterize the local histories of those settlements recognized as part of the Classic Maya tradition.

The Classic Maya tradition took its distinctive shape as one of the developments in a Late Formative reformulation of Mesoamerican civilization that began around 400 B.C. in successors to the Early and Middle Formative villages and states.[5] One of the most obvious developments at this

time was the incorporation of writing and calendrical notation in monumental art. In the sixteenth century, Mesoamerica's multiple polities were
participants in a single temporal system marked by the use of calendars
that combined a solar/agricultural year of 365 days with a ritual-divinatory
cycle of 260 days. These calendars, and a variety of related astronomical observational cycles, were recorded using a mathematical notation system in base 20 that employed three characters (signs for zero, one, and
five).[6] During the Late Formative Period, the shared system of mathematical and calendrical recording was combined with other varied notational
systems to create both ritual and political-historical texts.[7] This development extends the range of sponsored craft specializations to a new intellectual domain. It is quite likely that the appearance of calendrical notations
in imperishable form does not mark their first development. Nor is the implied ritual-political subject matter of the texts different from the messages
conveyed previously through imagery. What is new about these Late Formative monuments is the explicit claims they make to history, and indeed,
to a deep history, for the political actors they commemorated.

Claims to historical precedent may have aided the continuation of
earlier practices. Costume items, including mirrors and ear ornaments,
were executed in new materials but in traditional forms. Texts were added
to selected jade objects of the earlier Formative Period, inscribing them
with specific dates and the names of actors who took part in ritual and
political celebrations on those dates. Such ancient items, recycled as heirlooms, formed part of the regalia of ruling families throughout the Classic and Postclassic Periods, as the presence in the fifteenth-century Aztec
Templo Mayor of a Middle Formative mask most dramatically illustrates.

The Classic Maya tradition emerged from this Late Formative reformulation of Mesoamerican civilization. David Freidel and Linda Schele
offer a model for the abrupt emergence of Maya states in which Maya
society systematically suppressed the expression of real distinctions in social status (or more precisely, wealth) until the Late Formative.[8] They note
that across the Maya Lowlands of the Petén and Belize, over a very short
period of time, monumental architecture bearing representational imagery
referring to supernatural themes was built at a number of sites. They argue that these architectural settings provided stages for the performance
of ritual by an emergent nobility who claimed a special relationship with
the supernatural and gave it material form in ritual performances in these
settings. They note that slightly later versions of monumental platforms
inserted human portraits in places previously occupied by supernatural

beings. Finally, the medium of standing relief sculpture in the form of stelae and altars was adopted for the depiction of human actors dressed in regalia that related them to the supernatural beings previously focal in monumental images. These monuments incorporated texts that use Mesoamerican calendrical notation to specify the important dates of the nobles depicted as actors and their specific claims to legitimacy. Freidel and Schele argue that emergent Maya rulers advanced the idea that they were uniquely able to maintain the order of the cosmos through the practice of ceremonies. They identify jade items newly important in Late Formative Maya society as paraphernalia for divination.

The settlements in which these monuments were placed have been characterized as regal-ritual cities, composed of dispersed clusters of residential buildings and courtyards loosely organized around a core of monumental architecture adjacent to the residences of a small group of nobles.[9] Individual settlements varied greatly in size and length of history, from short-lived small centers like Bonampak to multicentury cities covering dozens of square kilometers, such as Tikal, Calakmul, and Caracol. The groups of houses and courtyards that make up these settlements have been described as the residences of internally ranked lineages of precisely the kinds found in house societies.[10] The outlying house compounds are integrated with the more complex compound of the reigning house by a variety of physical features, the most notable being the *sacbe*, a paved stone walkway that may mark social connections contracted through marriage or patronage between groups within these sites.[11]

The identification of noble houses in Classic Maya settlements is based on the differential consumption of luxury goods by the inhabitants of certain house compounds. Often the buildings of these compounds are more highly decorated and they may have inscriptions, testimony to access to the services of laborers and artisans. The diet of the individuals who lived in such compounds may reflect access to foods not generally available in other house compounds. Evidence of fine craft work, such as polychrome pottery painting and shell and bone ornament working, is also found in the living precincts of noble houses. In most Classic Maya archaeological sites, such characteristics are typical of a small number of house compounds, especially those located in close proximity to large-scale and specialized architecture.[12]

In addition to such direct evidence of different patterns of consumption by inhabitants of some house compounds, Maya settlements provide a secondary source of evidence of social difference in the form of now-

interpretable written texts. A language of rank is inscribed in these texts
and can be related in some aspects to representations to define different
individual and group statuses. The individuals who receive most mention in
these texts, those identified as rulers of these sites by contemporary scholars, were commonly titled with an Emblem Glyph composed of three parts:
the title *ahpo* or *ahaw;* an expression with the phonetic value *kul* or *chul,*
related to the general term for deity or sacred thing; and site-specific signs
that associate rulers with the places they are presumed to rule. The *ahaw* or
ahpo term can also appear (without *kul* or *chul*) as a title for other noble persons. At least some of these are explicitly noble women, a status indicated
by a portrait head with the phonetic value *na,* noble woman. The persons
named in texts as *ahaw* are often related to each other with terms that are
interpreted as defining kinship relations: child of father, child of mother,
mother's mother, mother's brother, father's father, mother, and spouse.
The implication that has been drawn is that *ahaw* is a status propagated
through kinship, marking off a distinct stratum of intermarrying, endoga-
mous nobles. Other titles may signify political ranks or roles, and while
they are often also attributed to individuals named as *ahaw,* there is no evidence for the inheritance of most of these statuses. Pragmatically, Classic
Maya settlements may have encompassed quite varied strata with differential economic resources, but the language of status recognizes only two
kinds of people: nobles and commoners.[13]

Texts about persons named as *ahaw* are concentrated in, if not completely restricted to, house compounds that are architecturally ornamented,
often centrally clustered, and possessed of the widest range of goods and
the highest frequencies of rare and exotic goods. Although excavation data
are much less abundant for house compounds of commoners, where they
are available, they show evidence for the same range of activities as noble
houses: the processing, cooking, and serving of corn-based foods; the consumption of diverse protein sources, although perhaps less meat or different kinds of meat; and specialized craft production of chipped stone, pottery, and other goods. Commoner houses are often occupied for shorter
periods than noble houses and are less often remodeled and architecturally ornamented. And noble houses devote greater attention to and invest
more resources in the disposal of some of the dead within the core of the
house compound itself, turning the compound into a living receptacle for
the deceased, still members of the house as ancestors.[14]

The most complex architectural groups within Classic Maya sites
are generally described as public architecture, but in form they are actually
highly decorated and differentiated, larger-scale versions of the courtyards,

tombs, and ritual facilities found in most noble house compounds, themselves more complex and differentiated versions of the house compounds of commoners. The Great Plaza of Tikal is a well-defined example that serves to illustrate the features of these compounds of reigning houses. Arrayed around the plaza are four architectural complexes.[15] To the south, with access through a multiple-doorway gallery, is the Central Acropolis, a maze of courtyards and long, multidoorwayed buildings. Rebuilt over centuries in the same location, the Central Acropolis encompassed more and more built space provided with fixed features that made it appropriate for residence: benches, sockets to suspend curtains, and roof drainage systems. A reservoir immediately to the south would have provided water for the residents of the area.

The Central Acropolis is integrated with the Great Plaza not only by its stairways and terraces but by the processional space of a miniature ballcourt located between it and the eastern Temple I. Temple I on the east, Temple II on the west, and the temples of the North Acropolis are an enlarged set of monumental shrines commemorating ancestors, many marking tombs. Only a fraction of the individuals buried under these shrines could represent the rulers recorded in inscriptions at the site. Among those buried in this area are both men and women, children and adults, a range of variation also typical of burials directly below house floors in less complex compounds. Along the edge of the North Acropolis, a series of stelae spanning most of Tikal's known history were reset by the late residents. Added to the buried dead in the temples of the Great Plaza, these royal predecessors were assimilated into the current reigning house by the control of their social memory, the histories and representations inscribed on their monuments.[16]

Within the small and large cities of the Classic Maya world, with their hereditary nobility and commoners, negotiations of social standing through the manipulation of human images have left abundant testimony of stereotypes of gender. Their context in cities with dynamic histories of development, decline, and resurgence, fueled by alliance, warfare, intermarriage, and exchange, is intensely political, and the exclusions and disjunctions in representation are formed by attempts to control the major base of power in this agricultural society: the labor of the people.

The Body and Gender in Classic Maya Representation

Unlike those of Formative Period societies, the representational traditions of the Classic Maya rarely display the naked body. Cave paintings are the major context in which nude bodies are found. There, exaggerated male genitalia are the only distinctive primary or secondary sexual characteristic displayed.[17] In some small-scale ceramic images, exposed breasts are carefully delineated, a convention that later Maya imagery (discussed in the next chapter) leads us to expect for images of adult females. But in monumental images within the space of the Classic Maya cities, neither category of bodily sign is displayed, and even the disarrangement of a woman's blouse by her breasts, modeled in three dimensions and painted in two in figurines and pottery vessels, is suppressed. The absence of overt sexual characteristics in Classic Maya monumental representations is a deliberate choice. The basic body and facial type shown is sexless, and it was only by identifying distinctive costumes or signs modifying the names of females in texts that male and female actors were identified (Figure 5).[18]

Three kinds of dress represented in monumental images have been taken to indicate female-gendered performance. Simple wrapped garments covering the breasts but leaving the arms bare are rare (although common in small-scale images). Intricately woven *huipiles* that cover the entire body appear on sculptured lintels and stelae in spatially segregated locations like the inside of buildings or the side of monuments facing away from open plazas (Figures 5 and 6). The female costume typical of monuments in more visible settings is a latticework skirt, usually interpreted as composed of interlocking jade beads (Figure 7). It may be accompanied by a cape or by a bead collar. A belt with a pendant, depicting the frontal head of a fish monster (*xoc*) with open mouth above a bivalve shell, is usually present. Tatiana Proskouriakoff initially identified this latticework beaded garment as a female costume through associated texts naming women, which seemed to act as captions. Others have challenged this conclusion, noting the use of related costumes by supernaturals: a maize god, a moon deity, and a primordial deity whose birth is recorded in texts at Palenque and who wears shell ear ornaments and has catfish barbels on his cheeks.[19]

Debate over the gender status of persons wearing these costumes has illuminated three problematic dimensions of the study of Classic Maya art with consequences for an understanding of gender. First, the attempt to determine an essential meaning of the costume (whose attribute was this originally?) by assigning it to the original mythology of the Classic Maya assumes that a stable set of characteristics formed an unchanging identity. Whether mythological or human, such fixity is unlikely to exist in a dynamic system of representations open to interpretation and transformation. The use of the costume by a maize god, by the piscine GI of creation texts

Figure 5. Paired male and female figures in Classic Maya monumental image. The male figure, shown in frontal view, holds a personified hafted axe (or manikin scepter) and wears a round shield on his wrist. The woman, in profile and to the male's left, holds a wrapped cloth bundle. Her simple cotton robe is edged with a band of astronomical symbols. Other layers of clothing are suggested by additional hems below her outer robe. Yaxchilan Lintel 1. Ian Graham and Eric von Euw, *Corpus of Maya Hieroglyphic Inscriptions, Volume 3, Part 1, Yaxchilan.* Peabody Museum of Archaeology and Ethnology. Courtesy of Ian Graham. Copyright 1977 by the President and Fellows of Harvard College.

from Palenque, and by a moon deity suggests that these three beings share characteristics or carry out similar performances, linking them with each other and to the historical characters shown wearing this garment. A more productive avenue of exploration than the search for an initial owner of this costume would be the identification of what these performances have in common.[20] I return to this point below.

Figure 6. Paired male and female figures in Classic Maya monumental image. The male figure, posed in profile, wears costume incorporating forest materials: jaguar-skin sandals and flaps of bark paper around his waist, ornamented with a motif representing a cave-mouth earth entry. Most of his skin is exposed. The woman on his left, kneeling below him but presented as focal by her frontal position, wears a robe ornamented with diagonal rows of earth-entry motifs. Her robe is edged with a version of the sky band, and drapes on the ground, enveloping her almost completely except for her head and hands. Yaxchilan Lintel 24. Ian Graham and Eric von Euw, *Corpus of Maya Hieroglyphic Inscriptions, Volume 3, Part 1, Yaxchilan.* Peabody Museum of Archaeology and Ethnology. Courtesy of Ian Graham. Copyright 1977 by the President and Fellows of Harvard College.

Figure 7. Woman dressed in latticework skirt with shark head and pendant shell belt ornament. Posed frontally, she cradles an open serving bowl in her arms. Naranjo Stela 24. Ian Graham and Eric von Euw, *Corpus of Maya Hieroglyphic Inscriptions, Volume 2, Part 1, Naranjo.* Peabody Museum of Archaeology and Ethnology. Courtesy of Ian Graham. Copyright 1975 by the President and Fellows of Harvard College.

The second problematic issue exposed by the debate over the gender of this costume is the weakness of the central assumption that texts always provide captions for the images they accompany. This assumption guided Proskouriakoff in her initial identification of portraits of women in Classic Maya art, and it has informed all subsequent scholarship. But, clearly, texts can as easily complement or supplement images as define them, an argument Flora Clancy, drawing on Roland Barthes's notions of relay and anchorage, has made for Classic Maya sculpture.[21] When secondary codes are added to a narrative in the attempt to narrow the range of interpretative possibilities, as in the accompaniment of Classic Maya images by text, these codes may constrain interpretation in one of two ways. They may invoke associations with other material absent from the image, what Barthes called *relay*; or they may directly comment on the circumstances depicted, providing *anchorage* for the image in question. In order to use the different forms of information provided by Classic Maya representations, we must examine whether texts relay or anchor the images they accompany.

The final issue raised by the debate about the gender of figures wearing the net skirt goes directly to fundamental assumptions about identity in Classic Maya society. Unselfconsciously, Maya scholars have assumed that human beings belong to two natural sexes coincident with two natural genders, and that these nonoverlapping categories will always be separated clearly. Because visual representations in Classic Maya settlements were active media for creating such paired, dichotomous genders, this assumption has produced very little interference with visual analyses, becoming an issue only in respect to the net skirt. But in readings of Maya texts, the assumption of two natural categories of people has had a profound distorting effect.

From Proskouriakoff on, students have learned to identify the names of women in texts by the presence of the *na* head. All other names and titles have been assumed to be those of males. The absence of a complementary sign for *na* to indicate male gender has been addressed by the identification of the phonetic sign *ah* as a marker of men's names and titles. In Maya languages, *ah* is paired and contrasts with *ix*. The two signs are often misleadingly glossed "he" and "she," although linguists identify them as primarily markers of agent (*ah*) and object (*ix*) of action.[22] In deciphering Maya inscriptions, the *ah* and *na* signs have been treated as if they constitute a pair, marking male and female names, respectively, when there is in fact no basis for this contrast in any documented Maya language, and the contrastive pair in which *ah* functions (with *ix*) is only secondarily a marker of gender.

Michael Closs has dramatically illustrated the confusion that could result from this flawed logic in an analysis of texts naming the mother and father of a noble person. In these texts, the mother is twice given the title "One who writes": once with *ah* and once with *na* as a prefix. Taken out of context, the first version of her scribal title would normally be interpreted as indicating a male actor. Both the use of *na* and the structure of the text—naming the noble person as "child of the mother"—make it clear that this individual was a social woman.[23] Without such unique circumstances, it is impossible to be certain how many other individuals named as *ah* might have been female.

Rather than featuring a mass of clearly defined men complemented by a few named women, Classic Maya texts refer to individuals whose gender status is rarely specified, and then most often when the subject is of the nobility, a noble woman, a *na*. As in the case of Formative Period representations of identifiable women, it appears that in Classic Maya textual discourse one gendered performance was particularly at issue: that of women whose status had important implications for their house. These select women, uniformly young adult, often explicitly named as mothers although rarely categorized as wives, are the ones whose gendered performances are depicted in monumental art in the segregated spaces of the Classic Maya regal-ritual cities.

The Representation of Gender at the Monumental Scale

Classic Maya imagery of gender presents two distinct strands, one manifest in monumental images, the other in small-scale ceramic images.[24] Monumental images, presumably commissioned by reigning nobles and others close to them, adorn noble house compounds and monumental architecture in the form of wall paintings, stuccoes, and carved-stone panels, and as free-standing stone sculptures, they mark the segregated spatial settings in which nobles carried out ceremonies.

The initial effect of costume in monumental images is to cover the body of women while simultaneously revealing the body, and hence sexual status, of men. Robes, like long versions of the present-day *huipil*, obscure sexual identity, replacing the body with a densely ornamented textile surface (Figure 6). Only the head, hands, and feet protrude from the enveloping cloth. In contrast, male figures wear garments that almost completely expose the arms and legs, with the upper body only partially covered by jeweled collars. The adult male (or better, not-female) sexual identity of these figures is signaled by their exposed chests, which lack any indication of breasts. The explicit marking of men's sexuality is reinforced by the occasional depiction of facial hair, both mustaches and beards, as on Yaxchilan Lintel 42 and Naranjo Stela 7. Where women's clothing covers the entire body with a uniform textile surface, men's costume prominently

Figure 8. Two male figures in the act of capturing two male prisoners shown wearing rope around their necks and wrists. The man on the right (viewer's left), posed frontally (as indicated by the position of the loincloth), wears a cape of strips of bark paper. The figure on his left, shown in profile, wears the same bark-paper cape and holds a lance in one hand. Yaxchilan Lintel 8. Ian Graham and Eric von Euw, *Corpus of Maya Hieroglyphic Inscriptions, Volume 3, Part 1, Yaxchilan.* Peabody Museum of Archaeology and Ethnology. Courtesy of Ian Graham. Copyright 1977 by the President and Fellows of Harvard College.

features long loincloths, focusing attention on the genital area even while covering it (Figure 8). When a triangular hipcloth is added to this costume, the long narrow loincloth is placed over, not under, it. In one unique instance, on Copan Stela C, the loincloth is ornamented with an image of male sexual organs, depicted with the same graphic convention used in a royal title in texts. Classic Maya monumental costume thus distinguishes noble men as sexual beings while de-emphasizing the sexuality of noble women.[25]

This gendered costuming cloaks women's bodies with layers of cultural imagery. In contrast, costume associates men with the forest through the use of almost unaltered natural materials, absent from women's dress: pendant rows of shell tinklers; jaguar pelt hipcloths with dangling tail and jaguar paw boots and gloves; other animal skins, heads, and claws; flaps or strips of bark paper; and unspun puckered cotton "armor" (Figures 6, 8, 9). The use of unspun cotton contrasts markedly with the laborious spinning of cotton thread and its incorporation through weaving in women's textile garments. While the distinctive elements of women's costume are woven

Figure 9. Two male figures holding hafted personified axes (manikin scepters) and wearing round shields on their wrists. The figure on the viewer's right, posed in frontal view, wears a belt covered in jaguar skin. At the center front of this belt is an ornament composed of a frontal maskette and three celt-shaped pendants, repeated at the side of the belt. The loincloth behind the central belt ornament has vegetation motifs along the sides. Yaxchilan Lintel 3. Ian Graham and Eric von Euw, *Corpus of Maya Hieroglyphic Inscriptions, Volume 3, Part 1, Yaxchilan.* Peabody Museum of Archaeology and Ethnology. Courtesy of Ian Graham. Copyright 1977 by the President and Fellows of Harvard College.

textiles, the result of several steps of intensive labor that transform natural materials into cultural forms, Classic Maya men's costume incorporates forest products in a less-transformed state.

Monumental images represent only a few gendered performances that are not common to the entire class of nobles or to specific political offices. Only figures with loincloths hold lances, the weapons used in battles (Figure 8). Figures whose bodies are covered by the garments of adult women hold pottery dishes or wrapped cloth bundles (Figures 5, 7). The elements of each image metaphorically relate noble status to the ritual actions that are being performed. Each image also condenses a narrative sequence through metonymic links. Male figures who hold the shield and spear, accompanied by kneeling or prostrate bound captives, imply their triumph in hand-to-hand combat (Figure 8). Men are shown engaged in ritual and political action in receptions, warfare, dancing, and sacrifice (Figure 9). When female figures hold cloth bundles and pottery dishes, their actions in food and cloth production (explicit in small-scale images discussed below) are implied, but the surface message is their cooperation in ritual performances in which these materials are consumed. I argue that the selection of these two forms of women's labor for reference in monumental images stems from the political importance of these productive activities in relations between rulers and the noble and commoner houses that supported them. As Julia Hendon notes, textile production actually took place within noble house compounds at Copan, and probably at other Maya centers as well.[26] Small-scale images provide more explicit evidence for the importance of these forms of labor as subjects of negotiation and interpretation of gendered performance in nonreigning houses.

Gender and Labor in Small-Scale Representations

Pottery vessels and figurines are intimate media. Their production is likely to have involved a greater number of people than the production of monuments, and was probably not under central political control. Pottery vessels and figurines were used in burials and caches within house compounds, and most were disposed of in trash deposits created by residents of these groups.[27]

Figurines of female subjects from sites across the Maya Lowlands depart from the scope of monumental imagery.[28] They show women in the acts of producing food and cloth, fostering animals, and nurturing children. Depictions of weavers are particularly prominent in the western lowlands (Figure 10). Figurines of women grinding corn and offering food in

Figure 10. Classic Maya figurine of weaver. Collection of the National Museum of the American Indian (formerly Heye Foundation). Photograph copyright Justin Kerr, reproduced by permission.

pots, or holding infants, are found in both eastern and western lowland sites. Others show women holding small animals, an image that has been related to women's roles in raising animals.[29] Accompanying these female figurines are others depicting men enthroned or as ritual deer hunters, warriors, musicians, and participants in ritual sacrifice. There is much greater overlap between these male figurines and monumental images than is true for female subjects. A major difference in the subjects of figurines is the isolation of individual males, such as musicians, engaged in actions shown only as incidental or secondary in monumental art.

Figurines offered a unique opportunity to focus attention on individual subjects at an intimate scale. Cynthia Conides argues that standing female figurines from the western Maya Lowlands mirror conventions of monumental art, singling out individual women similar to those included in multifigure scenes executed at the monumental scale in the same region. Her argument is particularly convincing for figurines like those from burials on Jaina Island, which depict the same range of actions as seen in monumental art while they give greater prominence to male and female characters who are secondary in monumental compositions.[30] Since these figurines presumably circulated among a smaller group with more direct, intimate knowledge of the identity of the person represented, the lack of written texts naming the person would not have impeded control of interpretation of the images.

The divergence in the range of action represented by figurines of women in this small-scale, intimate medium indicates a disjunction in discourses about women's roles in Maya society that were officially acknowledged (and became the topics of monumental art) and those that occurred in the confines of noble house compounds. A similar, and perhaps more pointed, disjunction is obvious in a third medium: scenes painted on Classic Maya pottery vessels.

The range of male performances noted in figurines is equally evident in painted pottery. One survey of Late Classic painted ceramic vessels from the Maya area illustrates numerous scenes with anthropomorphic figures engaged in identifiable actions. Most of the figures on vessels are males engaged in ritual dancing, warfare and capture of prisoners, a deer hunt, or the reception of visitors in a throne room. Explicitly female figures are most often shown as attendants in throne reception scenes. In a separate study of over two hundred Maya polychrome vases, female figures pictured were described primarily as assistants for male figures engaged in rituals. That other images of women were present in pottery painting is hinted by a sherd from the site of Lubaantun, Belize, depicting a woman grinding corn on a metate, but the quantitative contrast between pottery vessels and figurines remains striking.[31]

The vessels in these surveys, found in burials and caches in noble house compounds, carry images related to their political ceremonial use— images in which the actions highlighted are most often those of select males, rulers (usually male), and deities (usually male). Despite this built-in skewing of subject matter, some of these vessels present scenes in which women are engaged in politically charged performances. One such vessel, from Tayasal, shows two women with wrapped garments facing a male figure, all three on the same ground line, separated by a bowl of the type otherwise used to serve tamales. One of the women is turned frontally, the convention used in Maya images to signal the focal person. On a vase from Tikal, a woman dressed in a long *huipil* holds out a mask to a male figure dressed as a warrior, presumably for a ritual performance. Both of these persons are shown in frontal view, standing on a common ground line. In contrast, the male and female figures on a vase attributed to the Petexbatun region are shown on different levels: the male figure seated on a bench, the female on the lower ground surface in front of him. Yet, again, her body, covered by an elaborate netted, gauze-weave *huipil*, is turned frontally. In each of these examples, the frontal position of the female figure presents that person as a central actor. The composition of the vessels further emphasizes this by leaving enough space between the figures so that only one can be seen at a time.[32]

A similar effect is notable on a cylinder showing a woman in the folds of a supernatural serpent from whose mouth emerges a bust of God N.[33] The isolation of the female figure on one side of the vessel and the god emerging from the serpent on the other creates a dynamic linkage between invocation by the woman and appearance of the deity, between apparition and reaction to it, that gives both figures equal weight as causal in a spiraling sequence of action. Pottery cylinder vessels created a compromise between monumental art and three-dimensional modeled figurines by exploiting the possibilities of painting on a curved surface. Where the simultaneous appearance of several figures in one flat plane always creates an implicit ranking, polychrome painted cylinders can present multiple focal figures, each framed separately, like the isolated subjects of figurines. The scenes on cylinders, never visible all at once, require sequential reading and make manifest the active role of the viewer in constructing narratives from still images.

Narratives of Gendered Performance in Classic Maya Society

To understand the images on Classic Maya monuments, chains of connected implications that radiate temporally and logically from the represented moment must be explored through readings of their narratives. Arguably, the most static and least determined narrative media are figurines, where individual human subjects are highlighted one by one, unac-

companied by texts. Figurines present moments that can only be understood as segments of the actions of individuals. A male in feathered
costume holds a spear and shield. He has dressed for battle or for the formal
celebration of victory; he will meet in hand-to-hand confrontation with his
counterpart or join other captors in the dances and sacrifices that mark the
conclusion of a raid. Another man stands in front of a drum, one hand
poised in the movement of playing the instrument. He is engaged in the
music accompanying a ritual, perhaps a dance like that of warriors returned
from battle. A ruler seated on a throne gazes out from his raised seat, perhaps waiting for the entry of visitors to the court, perhaps sending warriors off to battle, perhaps witnessing a ritual dance. Each of these figurines
presents one participant in social action as the focus of attention, a spur for
the formation of private representations and new public representations (in
Dan Sperber's sense; see Chapter 1).

Because of the lack of coherence between different representational
media, the female figurines manufactured in the same styles do not lend
themselves to inclusion in common narrative threads as easily as male figurines, with their overlapping sets of associations. A weaver works a thread
into her brocade. She has already warped her loom, she is partly through
her weaving; when she finishes, she will have a length of cloth appropriate for a *huipil* or a cloth bundle to shroud sacred objects. Another woman
grinds corn on a three-legged metate. She has soaked the kernels in lime
water in an *olla* to soften their hard coats and carried the jar of kernels to
the grinding stone. She captures the *masa* up in a bowl, ready to form into
tamales to steam and serve covered in chile sauce in a shallow dish, or to dis-
solve in more water to form *atole,* served up in bowls. Each of these figurines
presents individual action as focal. But unlike male figurines, the narratives
that unfold persistently focus on this single human subject. These narratives appear out of context, and it is perhaps this lack of determination that
causes the makers of some figurines to violate the unique characteristics of
this medium to link the female subject physically with other figures. In its
most dramatic form, this impulse results in the creation of a figurine fusing
a female and male figure.[34] More commonly, female figures hold smaller
figures, interpreted as children. The ultimate disposition of the maize being
ground is suggested in one figurine by the presence of such smaller figures
around the metate, in another, by the hand of a small child reaching into a
bowl and touching one of the round, tamale-like forms.

Figurines link the gesture of holding or offering pottery vessels, seen
in monumental images, to women's production of foods in both everyday

and marked performances. The juxtaposition of figurines to monuments reframed the exclusively political and ritual meanings that monumental images and texts sought to communicate. Pottery cylinders also highlight food preparation and serving, through their actual form and use as serving vessels, through the depiction of scenes involving food consumption, and through texts on the pots themselves that refer to presentation of specific foods in these vessels.[35] But the multifigure compositions on polychrome vases place food serving and consumption in narratives in which women's roles in food production are muted, subordinated, or absent. The pictorial images on the walls of these pots have as their explicit subject sequences from myth, ritual action, or political ceremonies. When scenes do involve the presentation of food, in images of mythical or political receptions of visitors by enthroned dignitaries, women's participation is usually reduced to the offering of a plate of maize breads or the pouring of a bowl of drink by a woman whose position, costume, and gestures present her as dependent on a major male figure. While the products of spinning and weaving are lavishly displayed on these pots in men's and women's costume, in hangings that demarcate the spatial settings of the reception rooms, and in coverings on the raised seats occupied by featured characters, none of the pots depicts the image of the weaver found in free-standing figurines.

Nor do these pots present images of the contributions of most other members of society. The focal males, seated on thrones, are attended by subordinate *males* as well as, and more often than, females. The narratives on pictorial pottery are those of the elders of the noble house, of their interaction with other houses, and the mythological traditions and ritual actions supporting the claims of the house to noble status. The multifigure compositions typical of these vessels present the members of the group acting together in support of its representatives. Although most of the persons depicted, males and females alike, have subordinate roles, the composition acknowledges the interdependence of house members while according sequential prominence to focal figures, sometimes including women. The wrap-around form of the vessel allows the focal individuals to be singled out visually from the larger group of participants and makes of these men and, more rarely, women both the causes and consequences of house action.

Gendered Performance in Monumental Spatial Settings

The presentation of unified action is taken to its extreme in the monumental media that ornament the spatial settings for political ceremonies

Table 3. EXAMPLES OF PAIRED IMAGES OF MEN AND WOMEN
ON OPPOSITE SIDES OF CLASSIC MAYA MONUMENTS

Monument	Front	Back
Calakmul Stela 9	male	female
Calakmul Stela 88	male	female
Coba Stela 1	female	male
Pechal Stela 1	male	female
El Zapote Stela 5	male	female
Tulum Stela 1	male	female
Cancuen Stela 1	female	male

built in and adjacent to noble and reigning house compounds. In the single frames of monuments, all figures are visually linked in one scene, in a single set of relations, and one figure is marked as focal by frontal posture, elevated position, or greater ornamentation of costume and regalia. The female figures depicted are as little differentiated from focal males as possible. Women wear ornaments indistinguishable from those of men on their head, hands, and feet, the only body parts visible, protruding from the enveloping robe that covers any anatomically distinctive body parts.

In monumental media, women seldom appear as sole subjects, and instead are usually paired with images of men. Paired images are commonly placed in consistent spatial relations, creating gendered directions in their spatial settings.[36] The axes of spatial differentiation include up and down, front and back, outer and inner, right and left, and north and south, dividing the performative spaces attached to the compound of the ruling house into significant contexts for differential action.

The simplest spatial arrangement for such paired figures is placement on the opposite sides of a single stela (Table 3). Double-sided stelae were commonly set on the periphery of a plaza with the female image facing away from the open space, toward a nearby building, and the male figure facing toward the open space. When paired figures were on the same side of a single monument, right-left orientation was employed (Table 4). Paired figures could also be separated on two stelae set side by side, with profile faces gazing at each other, the female figure often on the left side of the male figure. A third axis of distinction for paired figures was defined by the placement of male figures in elevated settings above female figures. Monuments from Piedras Negras, such as Stelae 14 and 33, embody this pattern, with the male ruler seated in an elevated niche or on an elevated throne and a woman standing at ground level. The separation of paired figures on different monuments can obscure such patterning. At Naranjo, monuments on the north and south sides of a plaza depict the enthroned male ruler on an elevated platform opposite a woman, named as his mother, standing on a ground line. These stelae replicate the composition represented by single monuments at Piedras Negras.[37]

The spatial settings defined by the placement of paired male and female images were marked as stages for the performance of genders with cosmological symbolic associations, reiterated in the features of the costumes these actors wore. In Classic Maya monumental images, women stand at the center of a peripheral field of symbols worked onto the surface of the robes that conceal their bodies. The draping of these robes is carefully depicted, with folds shown spreading along the ground and edges turned over. Multiple layers are indicated by the protruding hems of inner garments. These conventions serve to emphasize the distinction between

Table 4. EXAMPLES OF PAIRED IMAGES OF MEN AND WOMEN IN RIGHT-LEFT ORIENTATION ON CLASSIC MAYA MONUMENTS

Monuments	Viewer's Left	Viewer's Right
Tikal Stela 25, sides	female	male
Tikal Stelae 1 and 2	female	male
Calakmul Stelae 28 and 29	female	male
Calakmul Stelae 52 and 54	female	male
Calakmul Stelae 23 and 24	female	male
Naranjo Stelae 28 and 29	male	female
Naranjo Stelae 1 and 3	male	female
Cleveland and Kimball stelae	male	female
Copan Stelae A and H	male	female
Yaxchilan Stela 1 (main figure faces S)	female	male
Yaxchilan Stela 4 (main figure faces N)	male	female

the woman's unseen body and the layers of cloth in which she is contained. As Walter Morris notes, the cut neck hole of the robe establishes an axis in the textile through which the woman's head emerges, and the patterned surface spreads out from this point.[38] Men's costume reverses this emphasis on horizontality. The male body forms a vertical axis emphasized by the folding and overlapping of the minimal textile surfaces of the loincloth and hipcloth.

The designs on the surface and edges of women's robes reinforce the presentation of women's costume as bounded surfaces. The simplest female robes are ornamented only along the edges, defining the textile surface as a bounded plane centered by the woman's body (Figure 5). Complex edges are also common on more ornamented robes, where bottom and side edges may be differentiated. A fringe of T-shaped flaps along the bottom can be provided with internal dots resembling frontal faces, while side edges are finished with a fringe that Karen Bruhns identified as feather work, accompanied by a narrow panel of "sky band" designs (Figure 6). In other Maya monumental images, such as the lid of the Sarcophagus at Palenque and the elevated niches on stelae at Piedras Negras, sky bands outline rectangular areas that are condensed images of the entire cosmos.[39] As an edge motif on women's clothing, sky bands mark the surfaces of robes as similar images of the bounded cosmos.

The surface of women's *huipiles* is often covered by diagonal rows of diamond-shaped fields. The motifs form a pattern marking the textile as a continuous surface extending out from the human figure at its center. A minority of *huipiles* have rows of motifs that are symbols of entryways into the earth in other Maya images: quatrefoils and a stepped motif with spirals enclosing a cross. These rows of symbols again equate the surface of the textile with the surface of the earth, both pierced by such openings. These symbols are sometimes incorporated in male costume, serving as a point of connection between the horizontal surface represented by women's costume and the vertical axis embodied by male figures in monumental images (Figure 6).

Monuments depict women wearing multiple layers of robes, each successively more removed from the orienting axis provided by the body (Figure 5). In many monuments located in exterior spaces, the outermost layer is an overgarment of beaded latticework (Figure 7). The diagonal latticework of diamond-shaped spaces in this formal robe recalls the design construction of many *huipiles*. The latticework robe or skirt and cape is depicted as composed of interlocking beads, usually interpreted as jade. At the center of the belt is a pendant, the frontal head of a fish monster (*xoc*) with an open mouth above a bivalve shell. Both the formal beaded garment and the similarly patterned diagonally woven cloth robes echo a convention for the representation of the surface of the earth as a cross-hatched diagonal pattern, particularly associated with the emergence of a maize deity.[40] Hence the structure of women's woven robes and these iconographic details associate female costume with the horizontal surface of the earth. The belt ornament that forms part of this costume symbolically extends this horizontal plane to its intersection with the bounding ocean waters. Joyce Marcus has noted the prevalence of water symbolism, not found in male costumes, on female figures at Calakmul, citing both the belt ornament and headdresses ornamented with water birds and fish.[41] At Copan, the figure on Stela H wears this costume and shares its location on the eastern side of the Great Plaza with two other stelae depicting figures dressed in the costume of GI of the Palenque Triad, distinguished by fish fins and shell ornaments, and with altars in the form of fish-scaled monsters.

The typical costume of male figures paired with images of women wearing the net skirt features a belt ornament composed of a jade maskette with three pendant celts (Figure 9). This ornament usually covers a loincloth that is a collapsed image of the central world tree with jeweled serpent branches and a trunk marked with a deity face. I compare the jade maskette on this belt with the decapitated heads depicted as corn cobs in Classic Maya iconography, and with the decapitated head of Hun Hunahpu, hung from a tree in the underworld in the myth recorded in the Postclassic Quiche Maya Popol Vuh.[42] Like the structure of male costume, these iconographic associations relate this costume to the central vertical axes in Maya images. Figures wearing the world-tree costume are consistently placed in upward, northern, and right-hand directions with respect to paired figures wearing the beaded net garment.

These spatial relationships are heightened by the use of a "Quadripartite Badge" as a headdress with female costume. Composed of a bowl marked with the glyph for sun, surmounted by a cut shell, a square-nosed serpent head, and crossed bands, the Quadripartite Badge was originally identified as a mask carried on the tail of the reptilian cosmic monster. In this position, a stingray spine replaces the square-nosed serpent. This form, rare as a female headdress, is depicted at Palenque in the Temple of the Cross and on the Sarcophagus Lid, at the base of world trees whose branches end in square-nosed serpents. By substituting the square-nosed serpent for the stingray spine, the Quadripartite Badge in female headdress represents the entire world-tree image in condensed form.[43]

The abstraction of the world tree as its serpent-headed branches is employed both in women's headdress and in the apron that distinguishes formal male costume. The relative placement of the world-tree image at waist level in male costume and at head level in female costume puts male and female figures in the same high-low spatial relationship seen in other compositions. The same relative positioning is indicated by the placement of a quatrefoil motif on the backs of men's sandals, associating their feet with the surface that covers women's bodies in other images. Formal paired male and female costumes represent men and women as complementary halves of a single spatial whole, the flat plane of the earth's surface and its central vertical axis.

Figures wearing the net-skirt costume make fewer distinctive gestures than other figures in monumental art. They often mirror the actions of a paired male figure. When they engage in complementary actions, the items they hold overlap with the regalia used by male figures: the double-headed bar, shields, staffs, and manikin scepters. In such paired compositions, a pottery bowl and a cloth bundle are the only items uniquely held by the female figure. Holding and offering ceramic bowls and cloth bundles are common gestures of female figures wearing other costumes as well. Pottery bowls and opened cloth bundles held by females in monumental images are shown as containers of ritual implements, such as bark paper, stingray spines, ropes of thorns, and ritual lance heads, emphasizing the participation of these noble women in common sequences of ritual action. But the gestures of female figures are simultaneously portrayed in alternative narrative sequences stemming from the performance of the kinds of labor explicitly represented in contemporary figurines. The cloth of the bundles, the end product of weaving, and pottery serving vessels, containers of maize foods, are metonymically linked to small-scale images of weaving and maize grinding. In monumental-scale images, this reading is muted: the context of the presentation of bowls and bundles is ritual action, and the consequences implied by these actions are political and cosmological.

The actual enactment of rituals in the spatial settings defined by the placement of such monuments further implicated the gestures inscribed on them in shared sequences of political ceremony. The repetition of the same gestures by male- and female-costumed figures emphasized the differences between distinctive embodied genders, one with its sexuality concealed, the other exaggerating masculinity. Variation in gesture between paired figures highlighted action, and suggested a necessary interdependence of individuals of these distinct genders. But the complement to the male lords whose bodies are revealed, and whose faces sprout beards and mustaches, is not clearly a woman, but rather an ambiguous figure whose performance of gender is removed from sexuality and its products. Unlike contemporary small-scale images of women, which reveal breasts, depict infants suckling, and even suggest fondling preliminary to sexual intercourse, the idealized image of the noble woman is one of maximal possible overlap with the noble male.

It is male figures whose sexuality is displayed in Classic Maya art. In the Naj Tunich cave paintings the only body seen is a male one, sometimes with an exaggerated erect penis.[44] The prominence of imagery of manipulation of the penis in ritual contexts contributes to a sexualization of masculinity. The explicit or implicit site of male bloodletting in Classic Maya art is the penis. A painted polychrome vessel from Dumbarton Oaks shows a principal male figure engaged in piercing the penis.[45] A pictograph of male genitalia was used as a Classic Maya title from Copan in the east to Bonampak in the west.[46] Though not displayed in a state of arousal, this pictographic title constituted a decisive display of male sexual status in a writing system and language that did not otherwise provide a clear means to differentiate the sex or gender of the subject of texts.

The de-emphasis in monumental scale images of female biological characteristics and the narrowing of performance to ritual action stressed the cohesion of rulers and nobles in their efforts to construct and exercise power. The most vivid representation of such solidarity was the depiction of nobles performing an encompassing gender. It is this, I argue, that is signified by variations of the net-skirt costume, whether worn by males or females: an encompassing gender that has associations with primordial times, creative forces, and the orderly organization of space and time through subdivisions and cycles that transcended and unified bodily differences of all kinds.

In its simplest form, the net-skirt costume consists of a short kilt of bead lattice revealing the legs, an uncovered chest without modeled breasts, and a fish-and-shell belt ornament. This costume, without the loincloth or facial hair that clearly signals male sexuality in other images, is worn by the maize god in mythological scenes. While commonly treated as a male deity, the sex of maize supernaturals is indeterminate in Mesoamerican mythologies. Maize is both male and female, often cycling through different genders as it grows and matures. A second supernatural being depicted wearing this costume, the moon deity, has a similarly varying gender related to the lunar temporal cycle.[47] The version of the net-skirt costume worn by historic women varies only in the provision of a longer skirt and the use of features of composition to block the view of a chest that might otherwise be expected to exhibit adult female breasts. I suggest that human females also participated in temporal cycles during which their gender was perceived to vary, a point I return to below.

Variations of the net-skirt costume in monumental art are primarily found in images identified in texts as men. The short kilt could be combined with a loincloth, with the mask and three celts replacing the shark-and-shell belt ornament. At Piedras Negras, this costume is found on the portrait of a warrior. On Tikal Stela 1 such a figure holds the double-headed serpent bar across its chest. A ballplayer from the central step of the Hieroglyphic Stairway of Yaxchilan Structure 33, whose chest is covered by a ballplayer's protective wrapping, combines the short beaded kilt with a different loincloth. Texts accompanying each of these images refer to the actions of historic male rulers, their sexuality metonymically represented by their loincloth. The actions in at least two of these examples are related to performances in which Classic Maya women were not depicted as actively involved: warfare and ballplaying.

A second alternative combined a long beaded skirt with the mask and three pendant celts, with a loincloth hanging over the skirt. These two variations, the shorter kilt and loincloth and the longer net skirt and loincloth, are contrasted in the composition of the stuccos on the piers of the Temple of the Inscriptions at Palenque, suggesting that they were slightly different in their significance and perhaps their use in performances. The long net skirt with loincloth was commonly worn by figures identified in texts as men, as in stelae at Xultun and Copan Stela H. These images are closest to depictions of noble women wearing the net skirt at contemporary sites like Naranjo, overlapping completely in gesture, pose, and spatial orientations.

The gendered performance inscribed by these images is not inherently bound to male or female sexuality, but neither is it the deliberate effacement of sexual status seen in Formative Period nude, sexless figurines. The reference of the loincloth to male genitalia asserts one sexual status. But these costumes themselves are less concerned with sexuality and its bodily marks than with the cosmological spatial setting of Maya mythology, replicated in the built environment of the spatial settings for ceremony in which these images appear. Persons wearing the net skirt are enacting the central placement of the body in space, and the world-tree loincloth specifically identifies the bodies of men wearing it as the central vertical axis. Combined, these costumes present performances that encompass space, both horizontal and vertical, while simultaneously encompassing sexualities.

At Copan, the human figure on Stela H wears a long net skirt, combined with the shark-and-shell belt ornament, over a jaguar kilt, otherwise found only on male actors. The gender and sexual identity of this figure has been widely debated. Proskouriakoff, followed by Marcus, noted that Stela H was paired with Stela A through shared calendrical records and suggested that the two stelae represented the ruler and his wife, while acknowledging that she could find no kinship statements on Stela H to record the name of this proposed woman. Recent epigraphers, confirming the absence of a phrase naming a woman on Stela H, have proposed instead that it depicts the male ruler also shown on Stela A, and as a consequence have rejected the identification of Stela H with female gender. Stela H is one of the monuments in which male rulers portrayed themselves in mixed costume to evoke their ability to transcend gender difference and to re-create a primordial condition of dual gender.[48]

Such encompassing gender performances embodied great cosmological power because of their association in Mesoamerican thought with creator gods and times, a point I return to below (Chapter 5). The identified deities who appear dressed in versions of this costume in Classic Maya images—the maize god, moon god, and GI—are characters in events of early creation, and particularly of the establishment of orderly temporal, spatial, and social relations. They are featured in Maya mythologies referred to in monumental texts, forming part of the cumulative strategy of attempting to constrain the freedom of interpretation of representations by metaphorically linking narratives in multiple media so that associations of one directed understanding of associations in another.

Such strategies are amply evident in the Group of the Cross at Palenque.[49] Here the texts of the temples construct layers of reference linking monumental and social time. In each of the three temples of the group, primordial mythological events inscribed on one side of the central image are echoed by legendary historical narratives on the opposite side. Personal time is embedded in each of these monumental scales through the provision of references to life events: birth, a life-cycle ritual for young men, bloodletting, assumption of royal titles, and death. The narratives in texts on the interior are further constrained by the framing texts outside the sanctuary and on the exterior of each temple, texts that place the construction and dedication of the temples within ceremonial cycles. Embedded in texts, the images inscribed in these temples are open to multiple readings, but each strains toward the stories related in the texts through relations of anchorage and relay. The sequences of movement between temples and the living performances implicit in fixed facilities and caches would have further channeled the reading of any one of these temples. In the midst of this highly structured spatial setting, a figure wearing a net kilt and a shark-and-bivalve-shell pendant stands simultaneously as the portrait of a historical ruler, an echo of the actions of the primordial goddess named in the text, and as a performer enacting the persona of the maize god springing forth from the mythical maize mountain literally inscribed in the eastern temple itself. Holding out an unwrapped cloth bundle, this figure is described in the text as the mother of the gods, which is a social, not simply a biological, role.

Gender and Power in Classic Maya Society

The human actor whose performance was inscribed in Palenque's Temple of the Foliated Cross encompassed gender as a cycle from parents to offspring, ancestors to descendants. Noble women wearing the net-skirt costume at Palenque and elsewhere participated in the same performance of encompassing gender. The prominence of this costume as the formal public garb of royal women is a final step in the erasure of sexual difference in monumental images in favor of a unified noble identity, one based on the common claim of Classic Maya rulers to unite in themselves all the social differences that divided their people. Royal women may have most literally enacted such unification as the persons who moved between sites in royal alliance, and whose offspring united the ruling houses of potentially warring centers. Monumental texts repeatedly record these two modalities of inter-city linkage—warfare and marriage alliance—as major historical topics, and of the two, marriage alliances take place between more distant places.[50]

Joyce Marcus noted the high visibility of women in secondary centers of the Classic Maya world. Women wearing the net-skirt costume were often described in texts as mothers of rulers, who had married into the ruling house from other, more powerful sites. The noble woman on Naranjo Stela 22 was the mother of the heir to the rulership of the site, and she appears to have acted as his regent. She is explicitly named as kin of the ruling family of Dos Pilas. The prominence of women wearing the net-skirt costume at sites like Calakmul testifies to the complementary movement of women from secondary centers to a major city-state, helping to build the latter's political power base through alliances. Such women were almost literally re-creating primordial conditions, reestablishing royal houses or establishing them for the first time.[51]

The most abundantly documented presentation of a woman performing such a founding role is the case of the mother of Pakal, the great ruler of Palenque.[52] This noble woman is named by Pakal as his predecessor as ruler, and she is shown dressed in the net-skirt costume handing her son a headdress marked with the *ahaw* icon as he sits on his jaguar throne. Much of the structure of the texts in Pakal's Temple of the Inscriptions is designed to memorialize this woman and place her rule in deep monumental time, and her portrait is repeated on the sides of his sarcophagus. No contemporary texts or images from her proposed reign are known, but the texts and images created by her son present her as the sole source and origin of his legitimacy. Succeeding rulers at Palenque employ the same compositions and historical narratives but provide portraits of both parents passing on regalia to their sons. While much attention has been focused on the presumed anomaly of Pakal's inheritance from his mother in a patrilineal society, her femininity is in fact subordinated to her performance of the primordial encompassing gender. It is the performance of this encompassing gender that is shared by her male successors and enacted in the Temple of the Foliated Cross, a performance also represented by succeeding females who became part of the royal house of Palenque and endowed their children with the same capacity.

Even when they are not portrayed in the full formal regalia of net skirt, shark-head-and-bivalve-shell belt ornament, and Quadripartite Badge headdress, royal women's textile costumes both deflect attention from distinctive physiological features and cloak them in cosmological spatial images. At Piedras Negras, women dressed in this fashion are explicitly depicted in narratives supporting the ascension to power of male figures named as their sons. James Fox and John Justeson have argued that the women given such prominence at Piedras Negras represented a few major lines of descent that they describe as controlling succession to power through the transmission of specific rights.[53] Presented in the idiom of corporate descent groups, their analysis becomes clearer if reframed in terms of the model of house societies. What Fox and Justeson are documenting is the active negotiation of power at Piedras Negras between a few powerful houses, none of which had a decisive advantage over the others. Through successive generations, the reigning house drew mothers for its children from alternating powerful noble houses, balancing them against each other in potentially fragile support of central authority. Through the entry of noble women as mothers of succeeding generations of rulers, the potentially disruptive noble houses were made kin to the ruling house, a relationship formally marked by the prominence given noble house daughters who become royal mothers in the texts and images on monuments at the site.

The women depicted dressed in full robes on Yaxchilan lintels, memorialized by temples in which these carved panels were set and represented as subsidiary figures in the upper panels and on the sides of stelae in the plazas of Yaxchilan, occupied the same central place in the transaction of power between noble houses. Several authors have examined the political dynamics evident among the rulers of Yaxchilan and their kin through marriage.[54] The women depicted on the lintels are named as mothers of the heir, titled as members of powerful noble houses whose male representatives serve as allies in battle, and shown as powerful practitioners of rituals invoking visions of spirits. One woman is shown manifesting a spirit in a location that is named with the specific signs for a place elsewhere noted as the location of a primordial goddess (Figure 11). Her transcendence of the difference between the local and the supernatural location is not unique. Another extraordinary Yaxchilan lintel, whose text is carved in mirror-image orientation, shows a figure dressed in encompassing robes engaged in a similar vision (Figure 12).

This figure may represent a dual-gendered ancestor. The image depicts a kneeling figure swathed in the typical robe of Classic Maya women, tied at the waist by a strip of cloth similar to a loincloth. This ambiguously costumed figure faces a warrior emerging from the jaws of a serpent, and blocks of text distributed around the serpent have been interpreted as naming both the warrior and the kneeling robed figure. Carolyn Tate notes that this text contains the name Lady Xoc in the last four glyph blocks. The first glyph block contains the sign for "Lady" preceding a "founder" glyph, presumably relating the woman named to the "founder." David Stuart identified a text on another Yaxchilan lintel, unaccompanied by an image, as naming "Penis Jaguar," presumably male, as the founder at Yaxchilan (Figure 13). The main text of the lintel attributes the actions shown to the contemporary male ruler of the site. The main and secondary texts describe the actions pictured as both those of the male ruler and of a noble woman connected to the lineage founder. The image portrays a kneeling figure in a hybrid costume that combines male and female diagnostic items of clothing, a performance by the contemporary ruler in emu-

Figure 11. A woman, shown in frontal view, holds an open basket full of ritual implements as she manifests a vision of an ancestral spirit conveyed via a serpent. The text over her head describes the location of her action with a place-name otherwise used for actions by primordial goddesses. Yaxchilan Lintel 15. Ian Graham and Eric von Euw, *Corpus of Maya Hieroglyphic Inscriptions, Volume 3, Part 1, Yaxchilan*. Peabody Museum of Archaeology and Ethnology. Courtesy of Ian Graham. Copyright 1977 by the President and Fellows of Harvard College.

lation of the lineage founder, inscribed as a male/female duality who could be performed in ritual action by noble male/female pairs or specially costumed males.[55]

Although ruling houses at these and other Classic Maya sites did record the actions of noble women in founding and refounding ruling

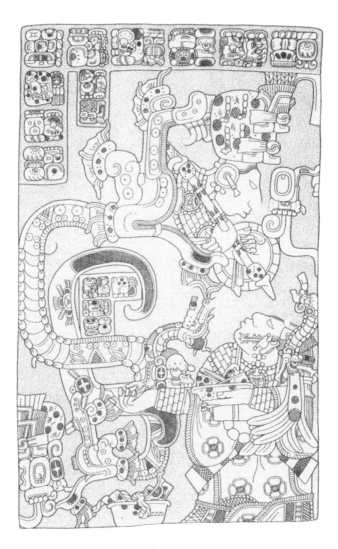

Figure 12. A kneeling frontal figure faces a warrior spirit invoked through a vision serpent. The kneeling figure wears a long robe tied with a sash ornamented like a loincloth. Yaxchilan Lintel 25. Ian Graham and Eric von Euw, *Corpus of Maya Hieroglyphic Inscriptions, Volume 3, Part 1, Yaxchilan.* Peabody Museum of Archaeology and Ethnology. Courtesy of Ian Graham. Copyright 1977 by the President and Fellows of Harvard College.

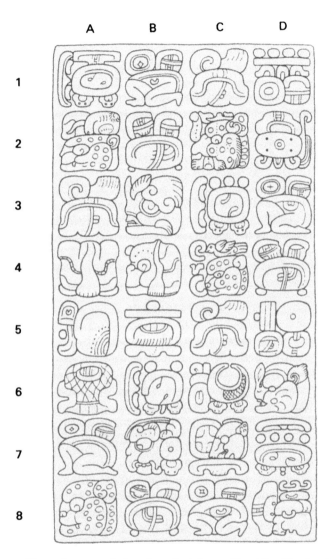

Figure 13. Text at A2 names the founder as Penis Jaguar. Yaxchilan Lintel 11. Reproduced with the permission of Ian Graham, *Corpus of Maya Hieroglyphic Inscriptions*, Peabody Museum of Archaeology and Ethnology, Harvard University. Copyright by the President and Fellows of Harvard College.

families, the images they inscribed de-emphasize distinctive aspects of female-gendered performance seen in other media in favor of a common enactment of ritual action and an encompassment of distinctions in gender. While historical female figures engage in distinctive gestures, holding cloth bundles and pottery serving vessels, more explicit reference to women's roles in producing cloth and the food contained in such bowls are muted in monumental images. This disjunction may represent the interests of ruling houses to play down the potential economic independence of other noble houses as a strategy of political centralization.

In similar situations in which the interplay of gender and political centralization has been examined, the control of women's labor has been identified as a crucial point of tension between emergent rulers and their powerful rivals. In her analyses of historic Tonga, Christine Ward Gailey demonstrates that control of women's labor became a subject of contention between men attempting to create centralized power and other men resisting efforts at centralization that would erode their own status.[56] Like the structure of the Classic Maya world, the economy of Tonga was based on agriculture, and control of labor was critical. Without sufficient labor, fields could not be maintained and planting and harvesting would not take place in a timely fashion. Without sufficient labor, houses could not support the efforts of craft specialists to develop their skills in the production of items of wealth and display. Without sufficient labor, neither the foodstuffs nor the regalia necessary for ceremonies confirming and building political status would be available. As did Classic Maya women, Tongan women not only provided basic subsistence work but also participated in specialized industries that underwrote the display of status.

In response to the efforts of some houses to transform temporary advantages of power and status into permanent ones, members of other houses resisted by continuing to assert their own privileges. Women became a center for this struggle, and houses increased their efforts to control the women who were the labor force, the holders of special knowledge and titles, and the means through which alliances could be forged. Other centralizing house societies known ethnographically and historically exhibited similar intensification of control of women: early modern Europe, the Northwest Coast, and Indonesia each share aspects of this development.[57] Annette Weiner's descriptions of how women's control over their production of goods necessary for ritual results in power and status in Oceania has particular relevance for the Classic Maya.[58] Women's production of textiles and food necessary for ritual, inscribed in the imagery of small-scale ceramic figurines and painted pots, created a similar opportunity to claim credit for the enactment of ritual for Maya women and the houses to which they belonged. Although the political contention involved is actually between houses, women's independent action becomes a symbol of resistance to centralization. By representing female figures in common ritual action, Classic Maya rulers presented noble women as part of a unified ruling house, supporting the common claims to power of that house.

What is lost in monumental representations is the recognition of unique contributions by women both as a group and as individuals. Gailey argues that with political centralization, the separation of control of production from kinship groups erodes the status of female producers, particularly when potential independence of kinship groups based on women's production is perceived as a threat to centralized political authority. This kind of conflict seems evident in the contrast between Classic Maya monumental and small-scale images of gender. Gailey's analysis would suggest that successful centralization of Classic Maya society inevitably produced an erosion of women's status. The example of Inka expansion shows the importance of considering internal differentiation within complex societies. The Inka transformed indigenous concepts of gender complementarity in cosmology into an ideology of gender hierarchy. They extracted textiles produced by non-noble women through a tribute system, and even exercised direct control over women weavers who were moved to administrative centers as *aclla*, or ritual virgins. Yet Irene Silverblatt stresses the continuation of the ideology and practice of gender parallelism, under which Andean women's status and power were maintained outside the narrow confines of the Inka administrative structure.[59]

The recognition of women's production recorded in Classic Maya small-scale images could reflect a higher status for women in nonruling noble house compounds, where they could claim credit for the products of their labor. Figurines made women's production a topic for social reflection, a permanent commemoration of fleeting action. The patterns of everyday performance by men and women in Classic Maya society are overwritten by the abundant inscriptional media through which factions attempted to direct discourse about status. Postclassic Maya sources document the persistence of women's status in the face of political centralization.

CHAPTER FOUR

Transforming Gender

CLASSIC TO POSTCLASSIC MAYA

Classic Maya society is today perhaps best known for its instability, resulting in the abandonment of the major Maya city-states and their conversion back to tropical forest before they came to the attention of European and North American society once again in the late eighteenth and nineteenth centuries. What is less often stressed is that the collapse of Classic Maya states was far from unique; within a few centuries, between A.D. 700 and 1000, the major political centers of Classic Period Mesoamerica fragmented, failed, and were replaced by the ancestors of the states observed by Europeans in the sixteenth century. Monte Albán was abandoned as Lambityeco, Mitla, and Zaachila rose to power in Oaxaca; Teotihuacan fell as Xochicalco and Tula flourished; and in the Maya Lowlands, Chichen Itza emerged as the center for the formulation of a new model of political power. Standing at the temporal pivot between Late Classic polities and Postclassic states, Chichen Itza serves as a historical link in the development of more fixed concepts of gender and the definition of more bounded spheres of political action. By shifting the bases of economic support for the state from noble houses to "predatory elites," [1] the new political economy of the Postclassic Lowland Maya facilitated the creation of a distinction, previously absent in Maya society, between "domestic" and "public" spheres, and marginalized women's participation in the new public domain. Despite the success of this new form of statehood, more diverse gender relations persisted outside the strictly controlled spatial settings of the new centers.

The Maya World on the Eve of Collapse

The collapse of Classic Maya society is identified archaeologically with two developments: the abandonment of centers in the southern lowlands between A.D. 800 and 1000, and the end of the tradition of Classic Maya art and architecture associated with those centers. Participants in a landmark conference about the Maya collapse at the School of American Research (SAR) in 1970 defined a new chronological period, the Terminal Classic, to encompass the events associated with the collapse. The Terminal Classic Period began with a sharp drop in new monument dedication at around 9.18.0.0.0 (A.D. 790). Changes in ceramic complexes begun at this time were complete by about 10.0.0.0.0 (A.D. 830). By 10.4.0.0.0 (A.D. 909) the last dated stelae were dedicated, and the Terminal Classic Period ended within approximately forty years of this date.[2]

The decline in the tradition of Classic art and architecture is associated with population declines at some centers, and their experience has been taken as typical for the characterization of a "collapse" in the ninth century. At Tikal, the Terminal Classic was marked by a severe loss of population (a decline of up to 90%) both in the center and in the peripheries. A Terminal Classic nobility continued to live in the Central Acropolis palaces, but no substantial new construction projects were undertaken at the site. The continuation of patterns of ceremonial behavior, including the placement of a newly carved stela and altar on 10.2.0.0.0 (A.D. 869), suggests that the remaining population of Tikal was striving to maintain Classic customs. Changes are also evident in ritual practice, notably an upsurge in the burning of incense within domestic groups, in addition to the previously favored ritual locations. The looting of burials and caches to obtain material for new ritual deposits was a sign of the reduced circumstances of the nobility. Simpler monochrome (red and black) slips were substituted for skilled polychrome painting on serving vessels. T. Patrick Culbert identified population decline as the underlying cause of the gradual breakdown he described for Tikal. The large Classic population of the site created stress on the local agricultural system, leading to attempts to diversify food sources and intensify production. Evidence of declining nutrition and increasingly poor health in the Late Classic Period at Tikal suggested that the depopulation was caused not simply by out-migration but by increased mortality as well.[3]

But even in the central Petén, there is variation both in depopulation and in the degree of political disintegration. Recent demographic studies provide estimates for the Petén Lakes region population decline ranging from ca. 90 percent to ca. 60 percent. The decline for the Tayasal-Paxcaman zone between the Late Classic and Early Postclassic is estimated at 60 percent. Despite these dramatic population losses, enough of a population was left in place to sustain centers smaller than Tikal. Prudence Rice suggests that diversification in ceramic traditions within the central Petén reflects decentralization, which may have adversely affected large centers such as Tikal but at the same time fostered the development of new, smaller centers. Late stelae at Jimbal (10.3.0.0.0, A.D. 889), Ixlu (10.1.10.0.0, A.D. 859; and 10.2.10.0.0, A.D. 879), and Tayasal were innovative in format and content. Ixlu monuments introduced what Tatiana Proskouriakoff called the "cloud rider" motif, with figures floating in scrolls in the air above the main standing personages. The Tayasal stela depicts a "diving god" figure, accompanied by birds, which may be thematically related. These depictions may reflect a synthesis of preexisting Late Classic lowland themes with new elements typical of sites in northern Yucatan, particularly Chichen Itza. At some of the smaller centers in the Petén, occupation continued from the Terminal Classic into the Postclassic.[4]

Throughout the eastern periphery of the Classic Maya world, sites continued to develop during the Terminal Classic, and some survived into the Postclassic. In the Belize River Valley, monuments from Xunantunich record dates early in the Terminal Classic Period (10.0.0.0.0 and 10.1.0.0.0, A.D. 830 and 849), suggesting that the site flourished then. Excavations in rural settlements along the river showed no evidence of abandonment during this period. Even after the apparent abandonment of major centers in the Belize Valley in the Early Postclassic, rural settlements managed to survive, and their populations might even have increased.[5]

At Mayflower and T'au Witz in the Stann Creek District of southern Belize, plain stelae associated with Terminal Classic caches document continued occupation of the region. Santa Rita Corozal, a major Postclassic center at the northern extreme of Belize, experienced no population decline during the Terminal Classic. Nohmul, the largest center in northern Belize, experienced a continuous peak in population from the Late Classic through the Terminal Classic and renewed ballcourt construction during that period. Specific buildings at the site suggest connections with contemporary Chichen Itza. At Lamanai, temple and ballcourt construction at a new location within the site during the Terminal Classic was accompanied by the establishment of new residential groups on the site periphery. David Pendergast compares the stucco facade of the Terminal Classic temple at Lamanai to contemporary examples from Altun Ha and Seibal, a group to which Virginia Fields adds the stuccos from Xunantunich's major pyramid. Unlike the other sites, which were eventually abandoned, Lamanai continued as a viable Postclassic center.[6]

It is likely that the southern periphery of the Maya world experienced similar conditions during the Terminal Classic as its neighbors in Belize. Direct contacts existed between these two areas at the time. Carved marble vessels from the Ulua Valley were found in Terminal Classic contexts at Altun Ha and San José in Belize and on Ambergris Cay, an island off the coast. Locally made Terminal Classic ceramics at Cerro Palenque in the Ulua Valley follow the model of Fine Paste types from the Pasión River drainage, recalling Elizabeth Graham's description of similar locally made Fine Paste vessels in Terminal Classic sites in Belize. A new ballcourt was constructed at Cerro Palenque during the Terminal Classic, contemporary with the new ballcourt at Lamanai, Belize. Mercury from a cache in the Lamanai ballcourt has been attributed to sources in Honduras. The continued or renewed importance of ballcourts during the Terminal Classic Period in both regions is a common feature, which suggests similarities in political or religious practices.[7]

Renovation and use of a second ballcourt at Copan also dates to this period. Green obsidian, Plumbate, and Fine Orange pottery in Copan's Ballcourt B suggest extensive long-distance connections to the west, and these materials are also among those used in burial and ritual in the site center during this later period, supplemented by other materials from southern sources. The use of obsidian hydration dating at Copan has allowed more precise chronological assessment of the abandonment of the house compounds at the site, demonstrating that rural settlements and peripheral nonroyal noble house compounds continued to be inhabited after the latest dated monuments were erected in the center. Similar late continuity of habitation is seen at Quiriguá, in the Motagua River Valley of Guatemala. An inscription (9.19.0.0.0, A.D. 810) and the construction of a new palace mark the beginning of a late period during which new long-distance exchange for copper alloy ornaments and Plumbate ceramics occurs. Stone sculpture from Quiriguá attributed to the same period, including a *chac mool* and two carved metates, exemplifies forms innovated for the first time at contemporary Terminal Classic Chichen Itza.[8]

In the western lowlands, the beginning of the Terminal Classic was marked by the introduction of fine paste ceramics, replacing the poly-chrome painted serving vessels of the Late Classic over a relatively short span of time. Based on the distribution of new ceramic types in houses at all levels of settlement at Seibal, Jeremy Sabloff and Gordon Willey proposed that the site had been invaded by a non–Classic Maya group. Richard E. W. Adams interpreted scenes on Fine Paste ceramics at Altar de Sacrificios as evidence for military invasion of this site as well. He suggested that the area witnessed at least two waves of attack, the first producing the intrusive occupation of Seibal, the second, the latest occupation of Altar de Sacrifi-cios. Altar de Sacrificios and Seibal experienced a new florescence of archi-tecture and monumental art of a foreign character accompanying the intro-duction of Fine Paste ceramics. New monuments carved at Seibal during the Terminal Classic have non-Classic features of costume, pose, and depic-tion of the human figure, comparable to art from the Gulf Coast and north-ern Yucatan. These features are also found on the new Fine Paste ceramics and are notable in the monumental representations of Chichen Itza.[9]

The diversity of developments in different areas favor models for the collapse that include multiple factors. Militarism was clearly important, especially in the west. The variation in depopulation between the central Petén and Belize Valley areas suggests that the forces that led to decline in population must have more strongly affected the center than the periph-ery. Demitri Shimkin noted that disease levels would have been increased by the conditions of crowded residence in populous centers, and by the use of thatched roof, earthen-floored houses.[10] Intensive cultivation around centers, and the demand for wood for pottery kilns, lime ovens, and cook-ing and heating, would have depleted the cover available for game ani-mals.[11] The lack of sources of animal protein would have placed newly weaned children at particular risk, and endemic disease could have dis-proportionately affected them, leading to high rates of infant mortality. Combined with increasing labor demands from nobles, these factors would have severely affected the ability of commoners to survive. A declining com-moner population would in turn have compromised the ability of the Clas-sic Maya to continue to support large-scale construction projects.

Although Shimkin's discussion was speculative, based as it was on general observations about the nature of life in tropical-forest, pre-industrial urban settlements under conditions similar to those of the Clas-sic Maya, data from human skeletal remains supported many of his obser-vations. In the populations from Altar de Sacrificios and Seibal, there was evidence for nutritional deficiencies, including lack of adequate amounts of vitamin C and of iron. These nutritional deficiencies resulted from a diet in which corn and beans were the primary staples, and little fruit or meat was available. The effects of nutritional stress were sharpest for children near the age of weaning, as Shimkin had suggested. While these observations applied in general to the entire sample, regardless of chronological period, Frank Saul also noted a decline in human height in the Late Classic at Altar de Sacrificios, a pattern previously documented for Tikal. Such a decline in stature might imply that nutritional stress increased during the Late Classic, supporting models in which agricultural capacity was overburdened immediately before the collapse.[12]

The decipherment of Late Classic texts has documented other specific sources of strain on the sociopolitical fabric of Classic Maya society.[13] The degree of investment in monuments and architecture is itself an indication of the weakness of political centralization in Classic Maya society, which required constant reinforcement and novel presentations of arguments for legitimation for each new ruler. The number of unique Emblem Glyphs in use increased throughout the Late Classic as new independent centers were established. As the numbers of centers multiplied in the Late Classic, the demand for labor also increased. Rulers refer to the taking of war captives as a source of personal distinction throughout the Maya area, and capture is recorded as a step in legitimation of succession at sites like Bonampak, Palenque, and Piedras Negras. An increase in the number of centers striving to maintain their independence throughout the Classic Period in a society in which warfare was a means to enhance prestige would have increased the frequency of war. As the number of centers grew, increased competition for the loyalty and services of commoners may have added an additional motivation for more intense conflict. Successful exploitation of the possibilities of militarism may have decreased the necessity for expending labor on large-scale architecture and new monuments. The abandonment of this system of political justification may have accompanied the evolution of new, less laborious means of accomplishing the same ends.

New images on Terminal Classic monuments reflect changes in sociopolitical organization necessary to support conditions created by raised levels of warfare. Alliances between lords of distinct sites may be indicated by monuments with pairs of apparently equal protagonists in the Petén and Usumacinta River drainage.[14] More prominent depiction of warriors in many sites may reflect the emergence of permanent military forces and the promotion of leadership in warfare to greater importance. The logical candidates to serve as members of new, permanent military forces were nonroyal members of the nobility. Nonroyal nobles were featured in late texts at Copan, Palenque, and Caracol, suggesting that rulers at these sites were forced to share their prerogatives in order to retain the loyalty of their subordinates.[15] It is probably not coincidental that many of the late inscriptions that mention nonruling nobles record battles in which these individuals distinguished themselves. The captures of individual rulers in battles would have been crises requiring political responses. As warfare proliferated, disruption of political life due to losses may also have risen. At the same time, demands for greater privileges by nonruling nobles had to be met. When circumstances led to disruption of political authority, some of these individuals may have founded new centers. Declining material conditions would have decreased the incentives for commoners to stay associated with older centers, and perhaps have increased their willingness to affiliate with break-away noble houses.

George Cowgill suggested that internal warfare between independent Maya states might have been a trigger of Classic Maya collapse, comparing the Maya to Chinese and Greek civilizations.[16] He noted that models of the collapse based on population growth simply *assumed* that population size would grow without justifying this assumption. He suggested that military competition provided an incentive for rulers to actively encourage population growth. Cowgill argued that increased militarism need not have been sparked by competition for control of resources, but might be an outcome of attempts to create larger political realms by combining independent states into an empire. The prevalence of warfare in the Late Classic created conditions in which new forms of militarism arose. In the Petexbatun area, Arthur Demarest and his colleagues have explored the evidence that a lord of Dos Pilas extended traditional warfare to a kind of conquest warfare, forming a multisite confederacy of conquered centers.[17] Demarest argues that this unleashed a new ethic of warfare and paved the way for more aggressive campaigns of conquest during the centuries that followed. The process of conquest in the Petexbatun region follows the lines Cowgill outlined for ancient Greece, with a period of attempted military conquest ending inconclusively with the breakdown of the Petexbatun confederacy. Successful conquest warfare may have been achieved during the Terminal Classic by Chichen Itza, which emerged as a dominant power in the northern lowlands.

Chichen Itza and the Transformation of Classic Maya Society

The Classic Maya collapse can be seen as a series of responses to a deterio-
rating situation as centers proliferated, some grew too large to sustain their
populations, and a growing population of nobles strove for greater status
both within established centers and by founding new settlements. Abandonment of established centers by the commoner population, either to
affiliate with newly established centers or to seek better conditions for agriculture in the hinterland away from centers, led to inadequate labor to continue construction in less flexible, older centers. Eventually, such sites were
completely abandoned. Meanwhile, newly established or reestablished sites
drew on new ideological concepts, some of which were presented in the
traditional stela format.

The nobles of many centers founded or revived during the Terminal Classic used ceramics and styles of costume that distinguished them
from Classic nobility. Most prominent among these new luxury goods were
Fine Paste ceramics. Far from being a marker of invasion, in many places
these were locally made and replaced local polychromes. Other new luxury
goods, including Plumbate ceramics, polychromes with serpent designs,
green obsidian, and copper ornaments, were introduced in many of the still-
viable Lowland Maya centers during the Terminal Classic Period. Consumption of these luxury goods reflects the formation of a new wealthy
nobility whose social identity was tied to noble houses beyond the southern
lowlands, in the northern lowlands, Gulf Coast, and highlands. Rather than
localized dynasties defining their legitimacy in terms of descent, the rulers
of the new centers formed a class distinguished from the commoners they
ruled by origin traditions, daily practices, and intermarriage.[18] Representing themselves as warriors, they presumably based their claims to authority
on military prowess. The strength of this claim to political legitimacy seemingly did not require the regular reinforcement represented in Late Classic
sites by the construction of pyramids to lineage ancestors and the erection
of monuments recapitulating the descent and succession of the local lord.

The kinds of changes outlined above for the Terminal Classic Period
correspond to certain features of sociopolitical organization described for
the sixteenth-century Lowland Maya. Anthony Wonderley has suggested
that Postclassic Lowland Maya nobles could make little direct demand on
the labor of the inhabitants of their own sites. He argues that while the
local population provided tribute and acknowledged the authority of ruling
nobles, they resisted the kind of exacting demands that had been imposed

on Classic Period polities, employing instead a contractual rhetoric that defined limits of obligation as the measure of good nobles. Nobles were expected to defend the local population against raids by other sites and lead raids on other sites. They provided imported goods, obtained through successful raids and long-distance exchange relationships that they maintained with the rulers of distant sites, to the local population. The local populace took part in raids on other sites and subsequently shared in the spoils of these raids. But the direct labor they provided was limited and did not underwrite extensive construction projects. Nobles relied on captured prisoners as a source of additional labor. Though numerically it likely occurred on a small scale, the transformation of prisoners captured through raiding into persons without civil privileges would consequently have been a crucial part of strategies through which nobles could support themselves. Wonderley's discussion is compatible with other views of Postclassic Maya political economy that emphasize the importance of tribute extracted from conquered states and point to a diminution in the perception of nobles as sacred.[19] The institution of a contractual rhetoric emphasizing a mutual obligation between nobles and commoners must initially be based on seeing nobles as subject to the evaluation of those they rule. The tactics of raiding that Wonderley describes as a "predatory" mode of production would have been most successful in those instances when, as an outcome of conquest, a conquered place became incorporated as a tributary, resulting in a stable source of support for the conquering group.

The picture Wonderley paints has many of the features that characterized Lowland Maya society during the Terminal Classic Period. A network of noble houses, joined together through long-distance exchange, emerged during this period and continued to function throughout the Postclassic. Individual centers were locked in endemic warfare, fueled initially by political aims. The raids conducted by Postclassic city-states had as their goal not merely the acquisition of captives for ritual sacrifice but also the appropriation of the labor and resources of the losing site. Similar developments may have begun with the ultimately unsuccessful Petexbatun conquests of the lord of Dos Pilas. The lack of major architectural projects in Postclassic Maya states indicates that the labor nobles could draw on was used for other purposes. The construction of large architectural programs to legitimate the claims of rulers was superseded by the authority conferred by military service in defense of the embattled community. The first place where this model of sociopolitical organization seems to have been established in the Maya Lowlands was the great city of Chichen Itza (Figure 14).

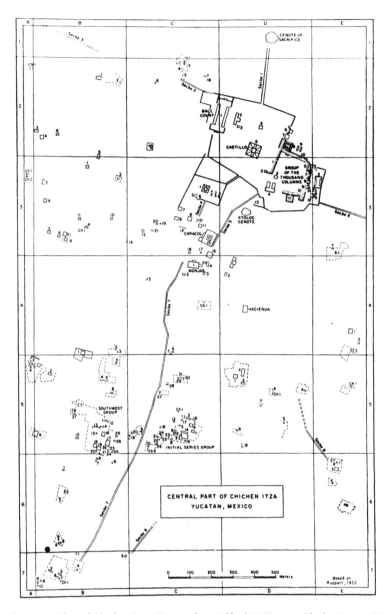

Figure 14. Plan of Chichen Itza. Figure 1 from Alfred M. Tozzer, *Chichen Itza and Its Cenote of Sacrifice: A Comparative Study of Contemporaneous Maya and Toltec.* Memoirs of the Peabody Museum of Archaeology and Ethnology, vols. 11, 12. Copyright 1957 by the President and Fellows of Harvard College. Used by permission.

Chichen Itza is distinguished from its contemporaries in the Maya world of the very late Classic by an innovative use of visual imagery, in preference to text, on architectural forms executed at a very large scale. As Mary Ellen Miller has observed, the forms used at Chichen Itza are all within the canons of Classic Maya visual representation. They appear to be very different because of deliberate choices made in the style of representation, choices that are related to the redefinition of political and social order that allowed the site to flourish in a period when other Lowland Maya centers were in decline.[20]

Chichen Itza provided new settings for gendered performance by a population of as yet undetermined size. A new separation of domestic space from arenas for the assembly of large numbers of people was marked spatially and through the use of distinct styles of architecture and visual imagery. At the heart of the site is a raised platform separated from the groups of house compounds that made up the residential sectors of the site. Some house compounds, with architectural features including ballcourts, are linked to the great platform by raised walkways. The space of the great platform itself is demarcated both by the edge of its supporting platform and by the placement of a series of monumental architectural features, none of which apparently served as residences. The largest group of such residences linked by raised walkways to the great platform, those immediately adjacent to the south side of this platform, are believed to have been the residences of the ruling nobles of the site.

In the closest proximity to the great platform of any architectural complex at the site, these palace compounds are nonetheless separated from it to a degree not previously seen in Maya settlements. The range-type buildings that were the palace structures of Chichen Itza form rectangular courtyard groups like their analogues at Classic Maya sites, and they are decorated in the Classic Puuc architectural style of northwest Yucatan.[21] Older studies of the site argued that these buildings were an earlier Maya settlement that was replaced by new buildings constructed on the great platform by Mexican invaders. This view is now rejected by most scholars who suggest a partial or total overlap in the period of use of both groups of buildings.[22] Instead of representing two phases of occupation, the different architectural styles evident at Chichen Itza may mark an attempt to differentiate public and private spatial settings and associate them with distinct histories inscribed in the form of buildings, the representations ornamenting them, and the texts carved on them.

The Monjas, the Iglesia, the Akab Dzib, and the Casa Colorada palaces and their associated patio groups are the dominant architectural features of south Chichen. Buildings in these clusters include such normal features of residences as benches and the below-ground water-storage facility known as the *chultun,* and they yielded numerous complete grinding stones during excavation. Like their Classic Period analogues, these noble house compounds also incorporated architectural settings for specialized ritual. Both the Monjas group and the Casa Colorada have ballcourts attached, with architectural reliefs in the same style as ballcourts on the great platform. Wendy Ashmore describes a repeated pattern at Classic Maya sites, including Copan and Tikal, of locating special-purpose architecture north of palace compounds. The Mexican-style Temple of the Wall Panels at Chichen Itza is located north of the southern palaces, in the same relative location that the temples of the North Acropolis and Great Plaza had with respect to the palaces of Tikal's Central Acropolis.[23] In fact, the entire northern edge of the noble residence zone at Chichen Itza was occupied by buildings forming a specialized architectural assemblage.

The northern edge of the palace district at Chichen Itza included all the architectural forms and functional complexes found in Classic Maya sites. The Caracol, a probable night-sky observatory, was located on the east. The Casa Colorada ballcourt (running north-south) and Monjas ballcourt (running east-west) delimited the western and southern edges of an open plaza. The north side of this complex was occupied by the Ossuary, a nine-platform pyramid like Tikal's Temple I or Palenque's Temple of the Inscriptions, which contained a series of burials. This pyramid, with its feathered-serpent stairway facing a low, four-stairway platform and a *sacbe* leading to the Cenote Xtoloc, and accompanied by a colonnaded hall, provided the model for the much larger buildings on the great platform.[24] But while the Ossuary and its surrounding structures were embedded in the palace district, just like the comparable building complexes at Tikal and Copan, the buildings of the great platform were abstracted from the residential domain and set apart as a formal public space.

The formal space of the great platform is arranged around a north-south axis defined by a vastly expanded version of the Ossuary and adjacent structures. The north-south axis runs from the Caracol to the Cenote, with the Castillo, or Temple of the Feathered Serpent, at the pivotal position. A second east-west axis is defined by the structures east, west, and immediately north of the Castillo: the Great Ballcourt complex on the west, the Temple of the Warriors on the east, and the Venus Platform immediately north of the Castillo. Three distinct spatial arenas for performance, none associated with residences, were created through the orientation and juxtapositions of these monumental architectural complexes on the great platform.[25]

The Great Ballcourt, a greatly exaggerated version of the north-south oriented Casa Colorada ballcourt in the palace district, provided a processional space within which movement wound downward from the Upper Temple of the Jaguars and outward from the alley.[26] This was also a gendered space in which male and female supernaturals and human beings were depicted in narrative scenes that inscribed distinct forms of publicly celebrated male and female action. Nine shrines or temples were placed within this architectural complex in such a way as to mark five elevations spiraling around the ballcourt alley, from the Upper Temple of the Jaguars at the highest elevation on the southwest, to the Lower Temple of the Jaguars at ground level on the eastern exterior side of the complex.

The buildings on the eastern side of the great platform present equally expansive versions of the colonnaded halls that formed part of the palace district of Chichen, again abstracted from residential use. A pair of temples (the Temple of the Warriors and the Temple of the Big Tables) with floor plans identical to that of the Upper Temple of the Jaguars marks the northwest edge of this complex. This pair of temples features gendered imagery in the form of a public inscription of male-female complementarity among supernatural beings. The eastern edge of the complex was defined by the ground-level Temple of the Little Tables, sharing the same floor plan. A series of colonnades originally formed long galleries on the west and north sides of the Court of the Thousand Columns framed by these temples. On the southern side of the Court of the Thousand Columns was located a unique building. Misleadingly named the Mercado by archaeologists, it consists of a central sunken courtyard surrounded on all sides by colonnaded galleries, a gallery-patio plan also found in the palace district and in other house compounds.[27]

The Court of the Thousand Columns complex presented a setting for performance contrasting markedly with the Great Ballcourt complex. In place of a processional spiral from inside to outside, from upper to lower levels, the colonnades provided formal sitting areas, long benches lining the eastern and northern sides, each with a raised dais at one end, ornamented with low-relief sculpture. Movement here was from peripheral enclosed spaces, including ballcourt and sweatbath complexes located on the north, east, and south, to a central open plaza. The gendered imagery inside this complex emphasized the actions of human actors, all apparently male, playing the ritual roles that in Classic Maya sites were carried out by noble men and women acting together.

In the construction of the great platform, buildings not used for everyday activities—ballcourts, nine-terraced temples, and the gallery-patio structure—were extracted from their setting within the noble house compound and reoriented to form a decisively new architectural setting. It is in this new public setting that abundant carved and painted human images and narrative scenes inscribed a new history and mythology for Chichen Itza, and it is here that we can see transformations of the gendered performances of Classic Maya centers to the forms recorded by Spanish observers in the sixteenth century.

The Inscription of Gender in the Public Spaces of Chichen Itza

Both the beaded-skirt costume and the gesture of holding a dish are prominent at Chichen Itza. They were identified as characteristic of male priests in Alfred Tozzer's authoritative account of the significance of the site's art. More recent scholars, following Tozzer, have identified only one figure, an old, almost nude woman, as a possible depiction of a human female. This is a remarkable poverty of images at a site where historical texts record the parentage of the ruler only in a female line, giving names for both his mother and her mother.[28] Clearly, noble women were politically important to the ruling house of Chichen Itza in the same way that such women were at Naranjo, Palenque, Calakmul, Piedras Negras, and Yaxchilan: as assets in advancing claims of political status. But unlike at these Classic centers, there appears to be no imperative at Chichen Itza to depict the participation in ritual of noble women as counterparts of male nobles and rulers. Figures make the same gestures as Classic Maya women and wear related costumes, but they are portrayed either as sexually male or as supernatural females. These changes accompany an expansion of military imagery through the construction of colonnades depicting warriors, the carving of multiple-figure compositions of warriors in low relief on exteriors and interiors of buildings, and the painting on selected building interiors of narrative scenes of warfare recording new images of battle against the general populace.

Two different groups of images at Chichen Itza are linked to inscriptions of female-gendered performance in Late Classic monuments. Low-relief carvings in one temple depict explicit breasts on supernatural beings wearing skirts, including the net skirt. These standing figures support fram-

A   B   C   D

Figure 15. Photographs of the four sides of the north column on the Lower Temple of the Jaguars, Chichen Itza, showing the female supernaturals on each side: (a) east face; note exposed breasts, net skirt, elaborate pendant hanging over chest, and wide collar; (b) north face; note skeletal mask or face, feathered belt, skirt with crossed bones and disks; (c) south face; note exposed breasts, skirt with sets of crossed bones and eyeballs; (d) west face; note net skirt. Photographs courtesy of Peabody Museum, Harvard University, from the Carnegie Institution of Washington collection. Copyright President and Fellows of Harvard College.

ing panels with upraised hands. Figures wearing the same costumes and in related poses, standing or reclining with upraised hands supporting other panels, occur in several other public buildings, on carved columns and carved and painted murals. Breasts are clearly shown on some of these figures, and I argue that they are all depictions of the same supernatural female performance.[29]

Elsewhere in the site, standing or seated figures wearing similar skirts hold out open serving bowls. These figures are shown with an exposed chest lacking breasts whenever the view of the chest is not obscured by the arms. At Chichen Itza, explicit depiction of breasts on an uncovered chest is a trait unambiguously identifying females, both supernatural and human, a major change from Classic Maya conventions. Unlike Classic Maya monumental art, the Terminal Classic art of Chichen Itza is concerned to identify adult genders with specific sexual characteristics and to present the public actions of the nobility as almost exclusively the work of men.

SUPERNATURAL FEMALES AT CHICHEN ITZA

The archetype for images of female supernaturals is provided by four figures carved on the faces of a square column that supports the north side of the doorway of the Lower Temple of the Jaguars (Figure 15). Two are dressed in beaded skirts and two wear skirts with round disks and crossed bones. At least one of the figures wearing crossed bones in her skirt has a skeletal head. These figures each display a bare chest with clearly delineated breasts. Each figure supports, with her hands held above her head, a depiction of a cleft hill from which spring warrior figures and plants, and stands on a watery plane marked by water lilies, cormorants, turtles, and fish. In parallel compositions on the southern column on the opposite side of the threshold, male figures with lines of age on their faces, wearing turtle and snail shells, webbed loincloths, and hair nets, make the same gesture as these female figures. The male figures have long been identified as representations of supernatural figures that hold up the surface of the earth.[30] The female figures are clearly counterpart supernatural beings. In this temple, differently gendered supernatural actors perform complementary cosmological actions in compositions of common action like those constructed in Classic Maya historical monuments commemorating ritual performances by human nobles.

Other images reinforce the complementarity between male earth-bearer figures and the skirted female supernaturals. Earth-bearer figures with the diagnostic loincloth, often wearing a turtle shell or snail shell, commonly occur in small panels at the base of columns throughout the site, and less commonly in similar panels at the top of columns. They make the characteristic gesture of raising hands to sustain the frame above them. The central, larger panel of these columns depicts warriors and other nonsupernatural figures engaged in historical, legendary, or ritual performance. In a few instances, the figure in one or more of the earth-bearer panels on these columns wears the beaded skirt or a skirt with disks instead of the shells, hair nets, and loincloths. While most of these small figures stand in profile, their arms covering their chests, a few are drawn in postures that reveal a chest with marked breasts like the larger versions in the Lower Temple of the Jaguars (e.g., Figure 16).

A cluster of skirted earth-bearer figures were carved in the Temple of the Big Tables (Structure 2D-7) north of the Temple of the Warriors. Viewed from the plaza, the temple is a shorter version of its more highly decorated counterpart to the right. A single stairway leads from the plaza to a summit antechamber, originally with serpent columns supporting the doorway. A centrally placed inner door opened into a rear chamber that once held a series of benches supported by three-dimensional carved-stone figures with raised arms.

Each face of the four columns supporting the roof of the inner chamber and three faces on each door jamb of the inner doorway were carved with a main figure framed by upper and lower earth-bearers. All figures on the columns and jambs on the south, the right-hand side for someone approaching the building, are typical male earth-bearers. Most figures on the two northern columns and the northern door jamb also represent male earth-bearers. But the eastern face of these two columns and the corresponding door jamb, surfaces that would be visible to the left as a person entered the inner chamber, depict figures wearing long skirts shown either as netted, ornamented with crossed bones, or with dangling beads. Eduard Seler originally suggested that these skirted figures were females, based on their costumes and positions.[31] The upper and lower figures on the interior columns stand with raised arms and reveal clearly marked breasts, while the lower figure on the outer door jamb reclines with arms above the head (Figure 16). (The upper figure on this door jamb was not recovered.)

Paired male and female earth-bearer figures are featured in a third set of images, on the inside of temples opening onto the interior alley of the Great Ballcourt. The carved and painted scenes inside these buildings are divided into registers, like those on columns, although the main regis-

Figure 16. Female earth-bearer figure on the interior doorway of the Temple of the Big Tables, Chichen Itza. Note net skirt and exposed breasts, visible just above boundary of top carved block. Photograph courtesy of Peabody Museum, Harvard University, from the Carnegie Institution of Washington collection. Copyright President and Fellows of Harvard College.

ter is much wider, occupying entire walls. The main registers of two well-preserved sets of murals, in the North Ballcourt Temple and the Upper Temple of the Jaguars, depict scenes of ritual and warfare.[32] In the base panel below these narrative scenes, male earth-bearers wearing the diagnostic hair net, shell, and loincloth kneel, supporting the upper frame with raised arms. Reclining between them with knees upraised are figures wearing long blue-green skirts covered with disks.[33] Although the details are

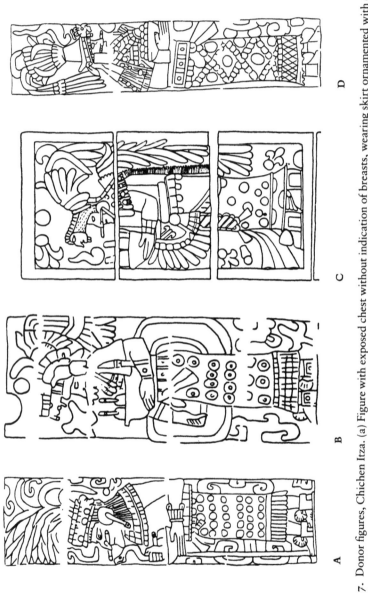

A   B   C   D

Figure 17. Donor figures, Chichen Itza. (a) Figure with exposed chest without indication of breasts, wearing skirt ornamented with disks and wide collar, and holding flat open bowl and serpent staff. Temple of the Chac Mool (buried phase of the Temple of the Warriors), column 4S. (b) Figure wearing disk skirt, holding wide bowl obscuring chest. Northwest Colonnade, column 39S. (c) Figure wearing hip cloth and frontal belt ornament over disk skirt, holding flat bowl, with chest obscured by arm. Northeast Colonnade, column 4E. (d) Figure wearing net skirt and cape, holding open bowl obscuring chest. Temple of the Warriors, column 12N. Figures 656, 669, 670, and 672 from Alfred M. Tozzer, *Chichen Itza and Its Cenote of Sacrifice: A Comparative Study of Contemporaneous Maya and Toltec.* Memoirs of the Peabody Museum of Archaeology and Ethnology, vols. 11, 12 (1957).

worn, early copies suggest that at least some of these figures had exposed female breasts, and they have been identified by several authors as images of a goddess.[34] The postures of the earth-bearer figures exemplify the same spatial relations embodied in Late Classic formal costumes: the female costume oriented as a horizontal plane, while the male body and costume establish vertical axes.

"DONOR" FIGURES AT CHICHEN ITZA

At Chichen Itza, earth-bearer images depicting supernatural beings are part of framing conventions used to place scenes of human action in cosmological contexts. Other figures with features similar to the female earth-bearers are located in quite different settings and contrast in gesture and pose. They occupy the main field of murals or columns, a position devoted to presumed human actors (whether historical or mythical) everywhere except on the columns of the Lower Temple of the Jaguars. These human figures wear long skirts with disks, beaded latticework, or crossed bones, and hold in their hands open serving bowls. Alfred Tozzer identified over twenty of what he called "donor" figures, and compared their costumes and gestures to Classic Maya images that he believed were male priests, now understood as portraits of noble women.[35] Donor figures appear interspersed with warrior figures in three locations in the great platform. Several appear on columns and paintings in the Temple of the Warriors and in the Temple of the Chac Mool, which preceded it and is preserved inside the later building (Figure 17a, d). Some are found on colonnades in the Court of the Thousand Columns (Figure 17b, c). Figures in these locations on the eastern side of the great platform all wear a skirt with circular spots, oval beads, or bead netting. In the third location with donor figures, on the western side of the great platform, figures wearing skirts with crossed bones are found in registers on the interior vault of the North Ballcourt Temple (Figure 19).[36]

Despite the costume and gesture they share with Late Classic images of women, the donor figures are identified as sexually male by their exposed chests lacking female breasts. Exposed breasts *are* depicted on the sole recognized human female, on the central panel of a low-relief column in the Temple of the Warriors, as well as being prominent features of supernatural female earth-bearers. The contrast is clear and suggests that at Chichen Itza ritual actions previously carried out by human women were the concern of persons marked explicitly as not-female, as men.

Gendered Performance at Chichen Itza

The architectural settings of donor figures are not random. The Court of the Thousand Columns is a spatially expanded version of house compounds of Classic Period sites, enclosed on all four sides by buildings. The Mercado, the gallery-patio structure on the south side of this group, produced grinding stones and hearths, evidence of food preparation, and has been interpreted as a probable analogue of later Postclassic noble residences.[37] Charles Lincoln has related specific features of the gallery-patio structure to accession rituals featuring bloodletting.[38] In Classic monuments like the murals of Bonampak, such rituals were depicted as taking place in and around the residence of the ruler, with the active participation of women of the royal family. This participation is not acknowledged in the imagery of Chichen Itza, which depicts actions formerly carried out by noble women as a performance by anonymous male functionaries, the donor figures.

Accession ceremonies are the focus of the setting of other groups of donor figures at Chichen Itza. Interior carvings in the North Ballcourt Temple are complex narratives that Linnea Wren and Peter Schmidt have identified as depictions of accession rituals, beginning with the mortuary rites of the preceding ruler (Figure 18).[39] Donor figures wearing skirts with crossed bones appear on the south interior roof, among images of rituals for the dead ruler. On the north roof vault, figures holding bowls and wearing long skirts are more eroded, but at least one has two preserved rows of disks on the skirt. They participate in activities that take place around images of ground-level buildings identifiable as residences by their architectural features. Wren and Schmidt interpret these as acts of blood sacrifice forming part of the accession sequence for the new ruler, the same kinds of activities in which royal women participated in the Bonampak murals.

The north wall of the North Ballcourt Temple is occupied by a multi-figure scene interpreted as the central act of investiture of the new ruler. In it, twelve figures seated on pillows flank a central standing figure, while in another register other figures stand on either side of a vacant throne. An image of a palace building at the lower right shows one figure seated on a pillow inside the house facing a second seated on floor level. The depiction of seating rituals links the North Ballcourt Temple with the images featuring donor figures in the Temple of the Chac Mool and its successor, the Temple of the Warriors. Both versions of this temple featured permanent seating platforms on east, north, and south walls of the interior room. Preserved painted decoration on the south bench in the buried Temple of

Figure 18. Group of four donor figures participating in mortuary and accession rituals. All wear skirts with crossed bones and disks like those on the Lower Temple of the Jaguars north column, north face. South roof vault inside the North Ballcourt Temple, Chichen Itza. After Wren and Schmidt (1991; fig. 9.7). Drawing by Linnea Wren after Peter Schmidt. Reprinted with the permission of Cambridge University Press and Linnea Wren.

the Chac Mool shows a series of skirted donors seated on jaguar cushions (Figure 19). The counterpart northern bench had a series of seated warrior figures.

The images in the North Ballcourt Temple associate accession ceremonies with precisely the kind of palace buildings replaced spatially and functionally by the Court of the Thousand Columns. The Temple of the Warriors was connected to this courtyard by a long colonnade. The north and west colonnades that outline the Courtyard of a Thousand Columns are greatly enlarged versions of Classic palace structures, long multidoor-wayed buildings with built-in benches. In addition to their contrasting size, the long benches in the colonnades are placed, not in an interior room, but in an antechamber formed by the columns supporting the roof, visible from within the courtyard. The architecture of the interior, private, domestic space of the Classic palace literally becomes a more public, visible, exteriorized site for action at an expanded scale. The practice of domestic food production in the courtyard is attested by artifacts from the Mercado. But the images associated with this expanded palace compound present men as the subjects offering food-serving bowls and dressed in costumes linked with the supernatural females at this site, and with noble women in earlier sites.

Figure 19. Seated donor figures from the south bench, Temple of the Chac Mool (buried phase of Temple of the Warriors), Chichen Itza. Each figure sits on a jaguar-skin-covered cushion, holds an open bowl containing conical objects, and wears a wide collar and a broad-rimmed hat covered in plumes. The figure on the viewer's left wears a disk-ornamented skirt, and the figure on the viewer's right wears a skirt covered with asymmetric oval designs. The chests of both figures are exposed with no breasts depicted. The left-hand figure may be aged, as suggested by the wrinkle lines on the face, while the right-hand figure, which holds a rectangular shield, is shown with a youthful face. Figure 671 from Alfred M. Tozzer, *Chichen Itza and Its Cenote of Sacrifice: A Comparative Study of Contemporaneous Maya and Toltec.* Memoirs of the Peabody Museum of Archaeology and Ethnology, vols. 11, 12 (1957).

The gendered performances of donor figures explicitly complement those of the other figures that crowd the walls of Chichen Itza's new public spaces. In the Temple of the Chac Mool, images of donor figures seated on jaguar thrones are portrayed opposite images of seated warriors, dressed in jaguar-skin costume and holding serpent-handled axes. Warrior figures occupy the other faces of columns with donor figures. Explicit scenes of battles and capture painted in a narrative style adorned the interiors of the Upper Temple of the Jaguars and the Temple of the Chac Mool. Three-dimensional modeled figures of warriors literally support the raised benches in the interior sanctuaries of the Temple of the Warriors and its analogues, the Upper Temple of the Jaguars, the Temple of the Little Tables, and the Temple of the Big Tables. Processions of bound captive warriors adorn the raised dais of benches in the Court of the Thousand Columns. The redundancies between these images present warfare and its outcomes as the primary valued, and male-gendered, performance in the public spatial settings of Chichen Itza.

The warrior imagery of the site presents an extremely varied complement of individual performers, singled out in the colonnades by the isolation of one figure on each side of a rectangular shaft. These warriors have unique costume details and, in some cases, pictographic signs that have been interpreted as marking their membership in specific noble houses brought into military alliance at Chichen Itza.[40] Narrative panels in the Lower Temple of the Jaguars depict processions of warriors and figures whose features suggest supernatural identities. Among them are the leaders also featured in the painted murals of the interior walls of the Upper Temple of the Jaguars, the Sun-Disk, Feathered-Serpent, and Cloud-Serpent captains. The vivid details of the battles shown in this temple, including the construction and use of siege engines, assaults on walled towns, and hand-to-hand combat, have been taken as signs that these recorded historical battles. But Clemency Coggins has also related the sequence to astronomical cycles.[41] The nonnatural depictions of the captains, floating in space above the action, and the parallels of the actions of conquest with solar cycles suggest that these scenes may constitute a visual representation of the kinds of legends of conquest represented by much later political histories like the Highland Quiche Maya *Popol Vuh*. As in the *Popol Vuh*, the inscription of representations of legendary battles at Chichen Itza accompanied an emphasis on conquest warfare in which men played uniquely prominent roles.

The prominence of warfare permeated the site, from the monumental scale and time of inscribed practices to the personal time and scale of embodied performances. The display of (male) captives in processions in the reliefs on benches in the Court of the Thousand Columns accompanied the display of physical trophies — the skulls of decapitated victims — on the Ballcourt Skull Rack, and the disposal of bodies in the Cenote. The processions and decapitations depicted in low relief on the interior walls of ballcourts provided a mythical narrative underlying these practices, just as the murals and low reliefs in the Upper and Lower Temples of the Jaguars provided legitimation for military raiding. The Great Ballcourt Stone, originally located in the Great Ballcourt alley, depicts heart sacrifice, also inscribed on gold plaques destroyed and thrown into the Cenote, attributing these sacrificial actions to supernatural eagle warriors.[42]

Women have no place in the inscription of the sequence of activities surrounding raiding and human sacrifice that dominates the material remains of the public sector of Chichen Itza. Even the gesture of offering serving bowls that characterizes the donor figures was separated from associations with food serving by embodied practices. Bowls of the same shape were the most numerous category of materials recovered from the Cenote. These vessels contained shaped copal resin, some ornamented with jade artifacts. Among them are examples in which the copal resin has been formed into a human figure.[43] The close connection of the burning of incense with the processing of human bodies is further emphasized by the presence in the Cenote of a human skull transformed into an incense burner.[44] Ruth Krochock has identified the contents of bowls held by donor figures as copal shaped into forms like those found in bowls in the Cenote.[45] Like the noble women who offered similar bowls of ritual regalia at Classic Maya sites such as Naranjo and Yaxchilan, the male donor figures performed this action dressed in a costume that centered them in cosmological space and associated them with primordial time and encompassing gender. Their presence replaces noble women in a public landscape transformed into a celebration of male prestige gained through warfare and captive sacrifice.

The masculinization of this arena did not erase all avenues to renown for noble women at Chichen Itza, but it did severely restrict the scale of recognition granted to women. While the great platform stands as a prominent public arena for the large-scale glorification of warfare, the more intimate confines of noble house compounds continued to serve as locations for political and ritual action, alliance through marriage, and negotiation of status through recounting of descent. Noble women continued to be prominent links through which such status was traced. Texts in the Maya writing system were placed primarily in interior locations at Chichen Itza, most notably on the lintels of buildings in noble house compounds. The ritual actions of both noble men and noble women were recorded, particularly their participation in the dedication of parts of these buildings themselves.[46] The apparent ruler at the height of Chichen Itza's existence, who carried the royal title Kakupakal, recorded his kinship through his mother and her mother, suggesting the houses of these women were important allies. But the actions of noble women no longer were subjects for either monumental representation as part of noble action or small-scale inscription to commemorate the contribution of their labor to the independence of their kin. Fundamental changes in political economy had taken place.

Raiders, Traders, and Noble Women at Chichen Itza

The Chichen Itza murals graphically depict attacks on villages and the binding of captured residents of those villages, including figures dressed in female costume, some carrying what appear to be children. David Freidel proposes that these and other innovations in the art and architecture of Chichen Itza reflect a reorientation of the goals of warfare to "conquest, territorial consolidation, and defense of large-scale states." The intense use of warfare as a means to expand political domains was a key development during the Terminal Classic Period. Studies of Classic Maya warfare, based on the representation of battles and their outcomes in texts and images, have emphasized the apparent limitation of its impact to more or less temporary loss of prestige. In some instances, such as the expansive warfare practiced by Dos Pilas and the domination of Naranjo by Caracol following a defeat, Classic Maya warfare resulted in textual and iconographic evidence of political subordination, but most analysts have viewed these as exceptions. More typical are the situations represented by the continued independence of Copan from Quiriguá and Palenque from Tonina after the captures of rulers of the first sites by warriors from the second.[47]

David Webster correctly warns against mistaking representations of warfare in texts and images as exhaustive testimony for its functions and meanings; nevertheless, the *contrasts* between otherwise comparable kinds of documentation (monumental images in comparable spatial settings) suggest that a real shift in the ideology of warfare is represented in the Terminal Classic at Chichen Itza.[48] Classic Period raids may well have resulted in the acquisition of goods or land, but these were not the effects commemorated in monuments. At Chichen Itza, the conquest of other communities was a subject of practices of inscription, a subject that included marking the captivity of noncombatant men and women (Figure 20). Models of political economy of the later Postclassic states of Yucatan suggest that these anonymous captives were destined for slavery.

Anthony Wonderley's description of Postclassic Lowland Maya nobility as "raiders and traders" employing a predatory strategy for economic and political continuity, using land and slaves seized in raids on neighboring communities for broader economic support, also can characterize Chichen Itza. For sites like Chichen Itza that successfully used conquest

Figure 20. Warriors sack a town, forcing inhabitants, including women, away. Mural from west wall, south section, Upper Temple of the Jaguars, Chichen Itza. Detail from figure 60 from Alfred M. Tozzer, *Chichen Itza and Its Cenote of Sacrifice: A Comparative Study of Contemporaneous Maya and Toltec*. Memoirs of the Peabody Museum of Archaeology and Ethnology, vols. 11, 12 (1957).

warfare, the new political economic regime helped resolve the instability inherent in dependence on the economic production of autonomous houses characteristic of Late Classic Maya polities. In the process, noble predation may also have eroded the grounds for whatever recognition women in noble houses received because of the key importance of the products of their labor.

The insistence on revealing biological sexuality in the practices of inscription of Chichen Itza can be seen as a step in an overt writing-out of women from participation in political-religious ceremony. Images that expose the flat chest of ritual participants wearing the net skirt and carrying bowls are as much a sign of not-being-female as they are of being male; it is a sign constructed by the contemporaneous presence at the same site of exposed chests marked as female through the provision of breasts. That women continued to be jurally important to the nobility is obvious not only from the textual record at Chichen Itza but from the emphasis placed in the sixteenth century on noble affiliation through both the mother and the father. But these practices of textual inscription were available only to the literate few who understood Postclassic Maya script.

In Postclassic Yucatan, spatial arenas of action were redefined in terms of differing permissible levels of participation by men and women. Classic Maya ruling men and women are depicted as coparticipants in ceremonies that took place within the royal household and in the monumental spaces framed by the palace and its attached temples, ballcourts, and plazas. Terminal Classic Maya women are inscribed at Chichen Itza as anonymous figures taken captive in villages under attack or as named noble mothers and grandmothers not shown as actors. In their stead, human males carry out complementary actions in ceremonies set in the newly expanded nonresidential reception halls and the precincts of temples. The conversion of women's action within the Classic royal house compound to men's performance of formerly female ritual tasks effectively created a public sphere from which most women were excluded. Sixteenth-century Spanish accounts of Yucatec Maya settlements document the existence of such separation, but they also show, as archaeological studies of Chichen Itza have not, that it was challenged by other practices in more intimate settings.

Sixteenth-Century Yucatec Women: Rereading Bishop Landa

The single most extensive Spanish source on late Lowland Maya society is Diego de Landa's *Relación de las cosas de Yucatán*. The annotated English translation by Alfred M. Tozzer, whose footnotes provide a wealth of comparative data, has been particularly influential on students of gender among the ancient Maya.[49] Unfortunately, the same footnotes provide intrusive and often misleading commentary, particularly on the status of women. Maximizing the utility of this source requires rereading it without the filter of Tozzer's early-twentieth-century interpretations.

The prominence of women in Classic Maya monumental images has seemed anomalous to many observers who have relied on Landa. Some statements directly contradict Late Classic and even Postclassic images, such as the assertion that women did not let blood, an action common to noble women in Late Classic images and performed by goddesses in Postclassic codices.[50] Although he describes women as coparticipants in household-level ritual, Landa says that only specific older women took part in ceremonies within the temples, where they offered special textiles and bowls of prepared food. Landa makes it clear that the key factor in women's participation is the site of ritual: "To the other festivals, *which took place elsewhere,* women could go and be present there."⁵¹ During the sixteenth century, Maya societies of Yucatan maintained a distinction between the household compound, where women's participation in ritual continued to be a *required* complement to that of men, and a public arena in which women's participation was tightly limited.

By privileging the temple as the site determinative of women's status, scholars relying on Landa have arrived at extremely negative assessments of the status of women in Postclassic Yucatan. Participation in ritual within the confines of the temple was highly restricted: "Nor did they allow them to go to the temples for sacrifices, except on a certain festival, at which they admitted certain old women for its celebration. . . . All the men assembled in the temple, by themselves; since in no sacrifice or festival, which they celebrated in the temple, could women be present, except the old women who had to dance their dances." The participation of these old women in the dances was in fact crucial to New Year's ceremonies held in the temple. They "danced clothed in certain garments" and held offerings in their hands as they danced.⁵²

The ceremonies in the temples involved specific products of women's everyday labor: "They offered other gifts of food" and "a cloth without embroidery, which the old women should weave, whose duty it was to dance in the temple." These are the same materials whose production was a marked element in Late Classic monumental and small-scale images of women. Landa distinguishes the spatial setting of the house compound from the temple, noting that women participated fully in rituals set away from the temples. Every ritual included feasting, described as a communal activity and implicitly based on the conjunction of men's agricultural labor and women's labor in cooking. "They ate with dances and rejoicings, seated in couples or by fours." The specific role of women in ritual was to offer "presents of cotton stuffs, of food and drink and it was their duty to make the offerings of food and drink," products of women's transformative labor.⁵³

Landa records a series of specific ritual feasts observed by specialists in different occupations. "The physicians and the sorcerers assembled in one of their houses with their wives," and after purifying their divination tools, "taking the bundles on their backs, all danced a dance called Chan Tuniah. The dance ended, the men sat down by themselves and the women by themselves," and took part in a feast. Similar ceremonies were recorded for other specialist groups: "the hunters came together in one of the houses of one of their number and brought their wives with them like the rest," engaging in the same sequence of purification, dancing, and feasting.[54]

Though Landa presents the participation of women as incidental support for their husbands, he also provides abundant indications that women were themselves specialists of various sorts and recognized for their activities, although Landa does not always recognize these occupations as specialized. Weaving, conducted in groups at special locations, dental modification and tattooing, raising birds for their feathers and animals for meat, and curing, especially related to childbirth, are specific occupations Landa noted for women. That the work of women was not categorically differentiated from the work of men, as less central to their identity, is suggested by the inclusiveness of a ritual in the month of Yaxkin conducted "to anoint with the blue bitumen, which they made, all the appliances of their pursuits, from the priest to the spindles of the women." Women participated in house-level occupational rituals as practitioners of these crafts, not simply as supporters of men.[55]

The centrality of labor to individual and collective identity is implied by the inclusion of all workers in the ritual dedication in the month of Yaxkin. It is further reinforced by the description of a second feast in this cycle, in the following month of Mol, which involved all the children who did not yet practice their adult crafts. The unusually detailed description of this feast makes clear that the rituals taking place in the house compounds involved parallel male and female practitioners. "For this feast they collected all the boys and girls of the town; and instead of smearings and ceremonies, they struck each of them on the joints of the backs of the hands, nine slight blows; and to the little girls, the blows were given by an old woman, clothed in a dress of feathers, who brought them there, and on this account they called her Ix Mol, that is to say, the conductress. They gave them these blows, so that they might become skillful workmen in the professions of their fathers and mothers. The end of this ceremony was a good drunken feast, the offerings having been eaten, though there is reason to believe that that devout old woman took with her the means to get drunk at her own house, so that she might not lose on her way the feather of her office."[56]

Most scholars have followed Tozzer in assuming that this woman, described as a ritual specialist, was anomalous. This discounts the references in Landa's text to women's participation in house rituals (by relegating women's participation to support roles) and in centrally administered temple ceremonies (by treating the women who participated as exceptional because they were of a defined age status). But the feast in the month of Mol is simply the best described of a series of life-cycle rituals, distinguished from the agricultural-calendar ceremonies held by different groups each month and the New Year's ceremonies conducted under centralized control primarily by their association with the gradual socialization of children within the house. These ceremonies were primary settings for the performance of gender by men and women, adults and children alike, and their description in sixteenth-century sources provides an invaluable source of insight on the production of gender and gender ideology in late prehispanic Mesoamerica. While the Postclassic Maya states of Yucatan provided little space for women to exercise authority in the newly defined public spaces of governance and religion, in the traditional rituals and acts of socialization within the intimate confines of the house compound, women and men both had significant parts in reproducing specific forms of embodied social existence in succeeding generations.

Prehispanic Maya Childhood and the Performance of Gender

Throughout his text, Landa records changes in details of costume that took place at particularly significant points in the life of Maya boys and girls. Adult hairstyles are contrasted with those of boys and girls. Males painted their body black until they were married, when they began to add tattoos. Landa notes the attention adult women paid to the hairstyle of marriageable girls, and describes a specific hairstyle "in four or two horns" used by "little girls, until they reach a certain size."[57]

Children's development was subdivided into intervals marked by explicit ritual actions. Four to five days after birth, following their first bath, babies were placed in their cradles, where boards were used to form the head into the desired profile, and a dangling ornament was used to induce the eyes to cross, both effects considered attractive. Cradled infants were taken to a diviner who determined their life chances and decided on their childhood name. During the first three years of life, Landa claims that children wore no clothing, but were provided with gender-specific ornaments. For the boy, this was a white bead on the head; for the girl, a shell hanging at the waist from a string, suggesting Postclassic spatial associations of male and female with higher and lower positions like those noted in the Classic Period.[58]

After the first three years of life, children underwent a ritual Landa compared to baptism. During this rite, called "second birth" in Yucatec (*caput sihil*), the ornaments marking infantile gender status were removed. Each child burned incense for the first time. An adult threatened to strike the children on the forehead nine times with a bone implement, and four ritual assistants threatened to strike the children nine times with flowers and smoking pipes. The participants drank the intoxicating beverage *balche,* which was brewed from honey. Landa reports that at age four to five, in other words, just after this rite was carried out, boys and girls began to wear versions of adult clothing. Landa also says that at this point children ceased using the name they were given by the diviner immediately after birth and were referred to by their father's name. Socially, the child was reborn into the house of its father through this ritual, marking the successful investment of the efforts of house members in sustaining the new life.[59]

In his description of rituals tied to the agricultural calendar, Landa provides hints that there were other ceremonies during childhood that might have occurred after the "second birth" and before the transition to independent adult status, and he best describes the feast in the month of Mol. The ritual actions on this feast echo those of the "second birth," with a more explicit linkage to adult labor than Landa recorded for the previous feast.[60]

According to Landa, the ritual of second birth, carried out at the latest by age twelve, was a prerequisite for marriage. He says that boys of "marriageable age," presumably those who had passed through the ritual of second birth, did not associate much with married people, but instead lived together in large, open young men's houses. Marriage, at about age twenty, marked full adult status. In addition to changes in body ornamentation, this transition was registered by another change in name, which Landa describes as the use of both the father's and the mother's name. Socially, the adoption of a name from the mother's house would both reassert the claims of her kin on her children and reflect the wider network of kin on whom the new adult could draw. While Landa gives no description of the ceremonies accompanying marriage, they may have included some formal recognition of such kinship links as mother's and father's houses joined to support marriage negotiations.[61]

These very late textual descriptions of multiple stages of childhood and rituals of transformation to adulthood bring into focus the extraordinary emphasis in earlier Maya representations on a single age status, that of young adults, to the exclusion in Classic Maya monumental images of any other age. While Chichen Itza's monumental images do include elderly supernatural beings and toothless old men and women, they are overwhelmed by the representation of young warriors and ritual participants. Postclassic painted manuscripts, calendrical almanacs with scenes of patron deities, are almost equally innocent of indications of age. All female images in these codices seem to represent either young-adult status or extreme old age.[62] These are the same age statuses that were noted as relevant to public ritual performance in Landa's narrative, but the range of development from birth through youth that he described is unmatched by any visual images from Terminal Classic or Postclassic Periods.

Even in the more extensive range of images created by Classic Maya societies, variation in age is extremely limited and serves to reinforce an emphasis on the young-adult age in which marked, dichotomous gender was at its peak. When infants or children are represented in Classic Maya figurines, they appear as dependent figures in compositions with women, where, I have argued, they serve to create a narrative of the provision and consumption of food and the social reproduction of the house. Among these figurines are examples in which the kinds of age-related costume cues described by Landa may be observed. A child, hand in hand with an adult in a figurine from Chiapas, is nude except for an apparent neck pendant. Another child, held astride the hip in a Classic Maya figurine from the Petén, wears only a plain cloth over the head.[63]

In contrast, other Classic Maya pottery figurines represent children costumed identically to the adults with whom they are shown.[64] In Classic Maya monuments where texts identify participants as children, accompanying images use the same convention of simply scaling down adult representations. Some of these monumental images accompany texts explicitly recording age-related rites of passage. Differences between children and adults are downplayed in the accompanying images in favor of presenting children as small-scale adults, emphasizing the performance of a status these Classic Maya youths shared with adult members of their house. This status itself was produced through the house-based rituals that were the occasion for recording differently aged persons in an inscriptional record otherwise dominated by a timeless young adulthood. Classic Maya life-cycle rituals, though rarely recorded and only attested for a minor cross-section of the nobility, are evidence for a long history of the practice of ceremonies like those recorded by Landa in his descriptions of sixteenth-century Yucatan. The persistence of such life-cycle rituals is not casual. It resulted from their crucial role as a medium through which embodied social positions were reproduced within the intimate confines of the house compound. The few examples recorded in Classic Maya monuments provide a glimpse of the socialization of children in a setting where childhood was otherwise deliberately erased and subordinated to the unified interests of the house, the nobility, and the state.

Age, Gender, and the Performance of Power

The rare Classic Maya monumental texts and images that represent or refer to children document ceremonies to which young men were subjected at around age six or seven, and in the early teenage years. The political motivation for recording these rituals was their importance as part of the justification of the claims of an heir to succeed a preceding ruler, and in most cases the images and texts were created when the child who was their subject had already become an adult and had assumed a central political position. This selectivity of subject should not obscure the likelihood that other members of Classic Maya society underwent fleeting versions of the same ritual performances that were not inscribed in monumental, permanent media. To the extent that Classic Maya rulers claimed to be exemplary of the social practices of the general populace, their transitions from childhood to adulthood would have been enhanced versions of common ritual events.

The most explicit ritual of childhood represented in Classic Maya images is recorded in the mural paintings inside three rooms of a palace at Bonampak. The first scene in the sequence shows a small-scale figure, held by an adult male on a platform raised above a group of higher-status adult males. The child wears a long robe, and green paint suggests jade ornaments, including ear spools. Mary Ellen Miller argues that this scene began a series of rituals culminating in the capture and sacrifice of prisoners by the father of the child, affirming the designation of the child as successor to the father. The text associated with the murals does not provide a clear record of the age of the child when these events took place.[65]

Mary Ellen Miller and Linda Schele compare the Bonampak mural scenes to the program of public art in the Group of the Cross at Palenque. Short texts inserted in the images on three temples in this group have been interpreted as a record of rituals sponsored by a ruler to designate his successor. The texts in the Group of the Cross record the ceremony as occurring to the child when he was about six years old. The rituals noted began with the display of the child from a pyramid, which Linda Schele and David Freidel identify as the Temple of the Inscriptions at Palenque. There, stucco reliefs on the exterior piers between the doorways depict standing adult figures holding a child, the same action represented in the first of the Bonampak murals. The texts in the Group of the Cross at Palenque suggest that the ceremonial sequence was completed by a sacrifice, on behalf of the child, of a prisoner captured in a raid, corresponding to the events shown in the second of the Bonampak murals. Of the three episodes in the Bonampak murals, only the final dance is not paralleled in the Palenque texts.[66]

Linda Schele noted that events of the same kind were inscribed in texts at Naranjo concerning the five-and-a-half-year-old boy who later succeeded to power as the ruler Smoking Squirrel. A pyramid event recorded on Tikal Stela 31, featuring the Early Classic ruler Curl Nose, may be another parallel passage.[67] As gendered performances, the events recorded or depicted at Bonampak, Palenque, Naranjo, and Tikal involve the assumption of adult male costume and participation in the most distinctive adult male activity of the Classic Maya nobility, warfare and the capture of prisoners. These public affirmations of the designated successor to a ruler are the most concrete instances of young men's rituals among the Classic Maya, singling out the period around age six as a focus in the transition to adult age and gender status.

Other texts at Palenque record an as-yet-undeciphered event that occurred to boys of about the same age, perhaps the more general record of a rite of passage itself rather than of the incorporation in political action of a ceremony marking a transition to adulthood. Like the sequence of rituals for heir-designation, the "deer-hoof" event may be associated with the first performance of significant aspects of a noble male adult gender.

The verb for this event, which depicts a hand holding a deer hoof, is recorded at least four times at Palenque.[68] A "deer-hoof" event is recorded in a mythological text concerning events around the beginning date of the current era, in 3114 B.C. The birth of the subject of this deer-hoof event, a supernatural being designated GI', was recorded as happening eight years before the deer-hoof event, placing the latter action at the same stage of childhood in this being's life as historical heir-designation ceremonies. The texts record GI' subsequently engaging in personal blood sacrifice and establishing a building, a temple or a house, in the northern world direction.[69] Each of these is an action ascribed to adult males in historical Classic Maya texts. Although GI' is never explicitly named as the parent of the three gods whose later births are celebrated in the individual temples of the Group of the Cross, scholars like Schele and Freidel assume GI' had that role in the oral traditions reflected in these texts. The mythological texts dealing with GI' may have provided a cosmological precedent for the transformation from childhood to adult status. The political importance of the transformation to adulthood of the historic ruler who commis-

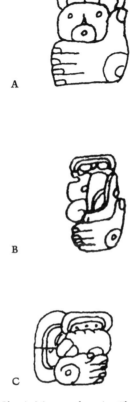

Figure 21. Comparison of Classic Maya verbs using "hand" as the main sign, with the object held in the hand indicating specific meaning: (a) T533:670, *ahaw;* (b) T617:670, God K or smoking mirror; (c) T294:670, deer hoof.

sioned these temples was inscribed through the caption texts accompanying images of the historical actors they commemorated, which record the heir-designation sequence.

While the "deer-hoof" glyph itself remains undeciphered, it is one of a set of verbs in which the hand is shown in the same fashion, but the object held varies. These include the verb for taking office as *ahaw* and for taking the name of God K as a title (Figure 21). In each of these other verbs, the assumption of a formal role is represented by a hand holding a costume element that was worn as regalia signifying that role. The "jester-god" headband worn by the highest political official, the *ahaw,* is indicated by an *ahaw* face in the hand.[70] The "manikin-scepter," depicting a personification of God K as a hafted ax with a mirror in the forehead, held by individuals engaged in ritual sacrifice, is represented by a mirror in the hand.[71] Deer hooves were also represented as regalia, although much less commonly depicted than the jester-god headband or manikin scepter. For example, a relief panel from Jonuta, in the same region as Palenque, shows a figure seated on ground level in front of a stepped platform.[72] He wears the deer hoof in his headdress. Texts in front of the figure give his personal names and titles, none of them unique to this context.

If the deer hoof was iconographically distinctive, like the *ahaw* image and the mirror from the forehead of God K, it may have been associated with the ritual of deer hunting. As Mary Pohl has shown, ritual deer hunting was an important activity marked in iconography and in practices of the distribution of meat at Classic Maya sites.[73] Pottery vessels showing deer hunts have significant connections to others depicting warfare. Like warfare, deer hunting appears to be exclusively a male activity in Classic Maya images. It is possible that participation in deer hunting was a mark of transition in age and gender status, as it was for certain North American societies.

The Tewa of the United States Southwest practiced a sequence of rituals to transform children into adults that provides a useful analogy for Mesoamerican ceremonies. Following a key ritual of transformation between ages six and twelve, Tewa children were eligible to become members of ritual societies and to receive insignia appropriate to the society they joined. Only Hunt society membership was limited to boys, and only Women's society was limited to girls. The members of the Hunt society had as their specific duty rituals related to hunting, of which "the sweeping of deer earth navels" was symbolically central. Led by the head of the Hunt society, any men who were hunters could assist in this ritual, which marked the beginning of the hunting season.[74] Other North American Indian groups associated adult male authority with the deer hoof itself. Rattles made from the deer hoof were the insignia of the Dog Society of the Hidatsa, an age-graded male society whose members socialized, took part in common rituals, and together enforced order in camp.[75] In these and other North American Indian cultures, hunting and adult male identity were closely linked and given form in ritual performance using specific regalia of the hunt. The deer hunts of Classic Maya imagery may have had a similar relationship to conceptions of adult male gendered performance embodied in deer-hoof regalia bestowed in the ceremony recorded with the deer-hoof event glyph, whose earliest mythological subject was a supernatural being born before the beginning of the current era.

A

B

C

Figure 22. Examples of the "deer hoof" sign at Palenque: (a) "deer-hoof stone building," from the Tableritos; (b) "deer-hoof event," from the Palace Tablet; (c) "deer-hoof event," from Temple XVIII.

Other references to the "deer-hoof event" at Palenque are placed in historical time. One text records the completion of a temple whose name incorporates the signs for deer hoof, stone, and building (Figure 22a).[76] According to the text, this "deer-hoof stone building" was dedicated on the thirteenth anniversary of the boyhood heir-designation rituals described in the Group of the Cross, when the boy who had undergone those rituals would have been about twenty. The dedication of a temple commemorating the date of those rites, named "deer-hoof building," suggests an identity between the heir-designation ceremonies inscribed in the Cross Group and a basic life-cycle rite, the deer-hoof event.

Two later instances of the deer-hoof event were recorded at Palenque. The Palace Tablet records a deer-hoof event a year before the deer-hoof temple dedication, twelve years after the heir-designation sequence recorded in the Group of the Cross (Figure 22b). The subject is the younger brother of the heir, a person who eventually took power as ruler of the site after his older brother. A final example of the deer-hoof event was recorded on Temple XVIII, the only source of information about an even later ruler at the site (Figure 22c). It records his birth and a deer-hoof event, in this case when the boy was already fourteen years old. This may be a late enactment of an age-graded ritual held at intervals of several years, like the Tewa ritual mentioned previously. Participants in such periodic rituals range in age from the minimum age required (in texts using the deer-hoof verb, about age six) to the minimum age plus the number of years in the interval between ceremonies, for candidates who were not quite old enough when the ceremony was held and were required to wait for the next cycle.

The time period between about six and fourteen years of age is also the only episode of youth marked in Classic Maya monumental images in which young boys are repeatedly shown assuming adult costume and pose. Linda Schele and Mary Ellen Miller have suggested that Relief Panel 2 from Piedras Negras, whose subjects they estimate were young men of about age twelve, represents a rite of passage related to war.[77] The panel shows a group of kneeling figures in front of the standing ruler. Standing behind the ruler is a smaller-scale figure who has been described as his son. The main event sign in this inscription represents a spangled helmet similar to those worn by warriors in other Classic Maya images. Schele and Miller suggest the scene is one of initiation of the son of the ruler into warfare. They argue that the kneeling figures are drawn at the same scale as the child, implying that the young men formed a cadre of newly initiated warriors, an age grade. While the text accompanying the image does not clearly identify the age of the figures, this interpretation is certainly consistent with sixteenth-century Aztec accounts of the beginning of training in warfare in the early teenage years (discussed in the next chapter).

The Piedras Negras lintel, and other images like it, show smaller-scale figures dressed in costumes that share all the attributes of those of an adult male with whom they are paired. On Ucanal Stela 4, two male figures stand on a bound prisoner while holding identical manikin scepters, a shared image of conquest implying ritual sacrifice (Figure 23). On Yaxchilan Lintel 2 both figures hold staffs, ornamented with birds, that were apparently used in ritual performances associated with solar observances at this site (Figure 24).[78] The smaller-scale figures are presented as socially adult, but still dependent, graphically illustrated by their smaller

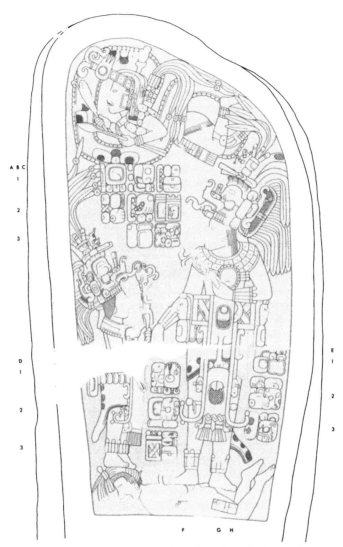

Figure 23. Two figures stand on a prone bound captive. The frontal figure, on the viewer's right, wears a jaguar-skin kilt, a belt with masks, and a long loincloth, and holds a manikin scepter. The half-scale figure on the viewer's left wears an identical costume and carries an identical scepter. While the long bead projecting from the taller figure's ear spool is clearly delineated, the shorter figure's ear is largely obscured by his hair. The shorter figure wears a simple rounded haircut, whereas the taller figure has a carefully shaped stepped hairstyle. Although the text does not clarify the relationship between these two figures, they appear to be a male adult and child, perhaps father and son. Ucanal Stela 4. Ian Graham, *Corpus of Maya Hieroglyphic Inscriptions, Volume 2, Part 3, Ixkun, Ucanal, Ixtutz, Naranjo.* Peabody Museum of Archaeology and Ethnology. Courtesy of Ian Graham. Copyright 1980 by the President and Fellows of Harvard College.

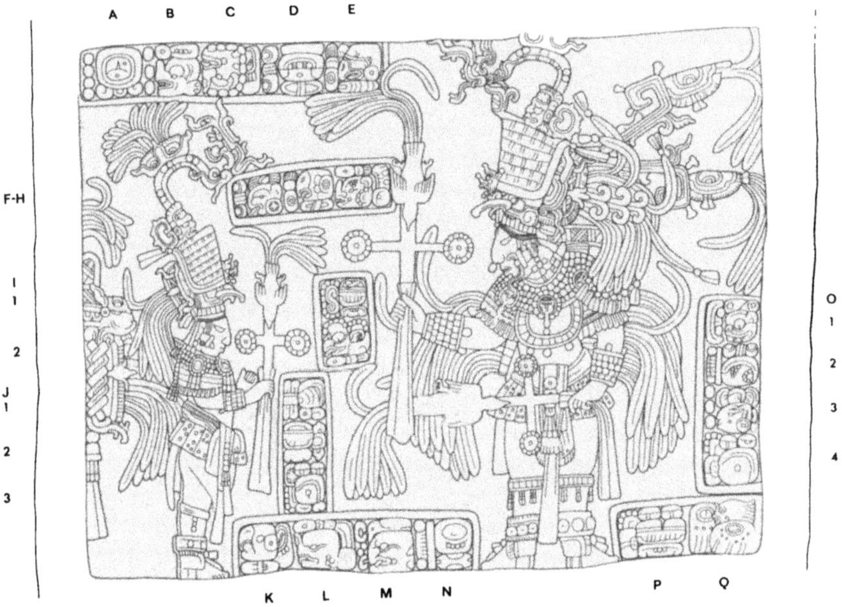

Figure 24. Two figures dressed in identical costumes featuring kilts made of strips of bark cloth hold cross-shaped staffs with bird ornaments. The figure on the viewer's right is named in the text as the ruler of the site, Bird Jaguar. The shorter figure on the left is named Chel-Te, the personal name used in youth by a later ruler of Yaxchilan, presumed to be the son of Bird Jaguar. He wears ear spools identical to those of the adult figure and has his hair cut in formal stepped outline. Yaxchilan Lintel 2. Ian Graham and Eric von Euw, *Corpus of Maya Hieroglyphic Inscriptions, Volume 3, Part 1, Yaxchilan*. Peabody Museum of Archaeology and Ethnology. Courtesy of Ian Graham. Copyright 1977 by the President and Fellows of Harvard College.

scale and their pairing with another figure. Without the presence of the paired adult figure, there would be no cues to show that the smaller figure was not fully adult.

Like these other scenes of ritual performance during the youth of boys, the images in the Group of the Cross at Palenque depict one figure as smaller in scale (Figure 25). Linda Schele and David Freidel have argued that, in an exception to the general practice of showing the young child as smaller, this figure is the deceased father rather than the son and heir. They reject arguments by others for the identification of the smaller figure as the child undergoing rituals associated with heir designation.[79] The personal appearance cues in the image itself, however, provide support

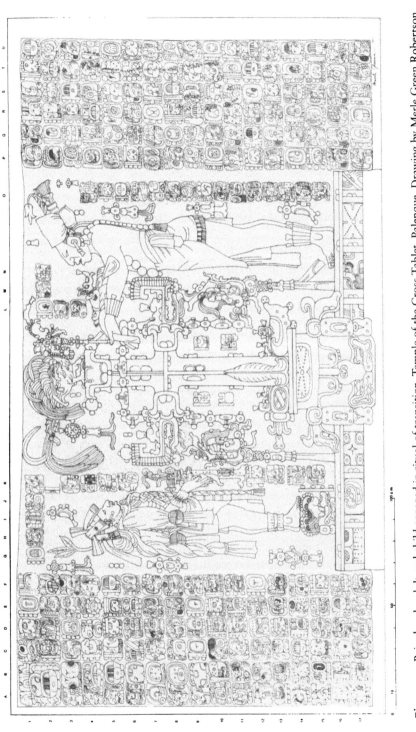

Figure 25. Paired male adult and child engaged in ritual of transition. Temple of the Cross Tablet, Palenque. Drawing by Merle Green Robertson, published as Figure 9 in *The Sculpture of Palenque, Vol. 4: The Cross Group, the North Group, the Olvidado, and Other Pieces*. Princeton: Princeton University Press, 1991. Courtesy of Merle Greene Robertson.

for a more consistent interpretation of contrasting scale as an indicator of relative age in Classic Maya images. The carefully detailed costume of the smaller figure lacks the ear flares shown on the adult figure. Instead, the ear is shown pierced and held open by long rods. This feature conforms to expectations from sixteenth-century documents about the importance of changes in costume in marking gradual transitions in childhood, and to specific age-related patterns of ear-spool use documented in burials as early as the Formative Period and continuing into the Postclassic Period (see Chapters 2 and 5). An unpublished suggestion by Floyd Lounsbury that the boy was handling the objects representing political power that "he would one day wield as king" strongly recalls central actions in rituals of transition in the lives of children described for the Postclassic Maya and their Aztec contemporaries.

The key characteristic of the feasts held in the months of Yaxkin and Mol in Postclassic Yucatan was an intimate tie between work and adult gender. Far from an innate biological essence, Postclassic Yucatecan Maya society treated gender as emerging through performance, marked by the provision of distinctive costume, and given substance through a series of rituals of transition over the life of a person. Textual and representational inscriptions from earlier Classic Maya societies, though selective in their emphasis on boys of ruling families, suggest a similar process of creation and control of adult identity through the definition of proper dress and action and their marking in ceremony. Although textual sources are unavailable for Formative Period societies, material practices manifested similar processes of performance and constraint, including the development of crucial media of costume such as ear ornaments, that continued to shape gendered performance into the sixteenth century. The wealth of documentary sources from the sixteenth-century Central Mexican Aztec, or Mexica, illuminate most clearly relationships between the formation of gender and other aspects of personal identity effected through ritual, and the way such formalized performances were manipulated by the state and resisted by houses, by factions within houses, and by individual people.

CHAPTER FIVE

Becoming Human

BODY AND PERSON IN AZTEC TENOCHTITLAN

Although Christopher Columbus touched briefly on the coast of Honduras in 1502, it was two decades after his initial voyage to the Americas in 1492 before Europeans began to enter the Mesoamerican world. When other Spanish expeditions followed an ill-fated crew—shipwrecked in 1511—to Yucatan, they were turned back by Postclassic societies used to resisting invasion by neighboring groups of noble raiders. It was only after moving up the coast to the Gulf of Mexico, the edge of the Aztec tribute state, that the Spanish in 1519 were able to advance into Mesoamerican territory. Here, within the largest, most powerful, and most secure state in the region, the Spanish were received cautiously but without the automatic military rejection that Yucatec Maya states gave to the newcomers. The succeeding conquest, aided by disease, native allies, and internal weaknesses of the Aztec polity, was the last opportunity Europeans had to record observations of an intact Mesoamerican society. The fall of the Aztec state alone disrupted economic and political organization throughout Mesoamerica, and diseases spread from the initial points of Spanish entry into the region beyond the active campaigns of conquest. When the Spanish finally brought much of Guatemala, Honduras, and Yucatan under military control in the 1530s and 1540s, the societies they saw had already experienced massive population loss and consequent political, social, and economic turmoil. And by this time, the Spanish already had a model for understanding the newly conquered peoples of the region, provided by their experience of Aztec society. While the sixteenth-century ethnohistoric records for the Maya world are schematic, sometimes overly dependent on information from Central Mexico, and reflect societies already in decline, Spanish sources on the Aztecs promise the possibility—if approached critically—of coming closer to a native Mesoamerican reality. Nowhere is that promise more intriguing and frustrating than in understanding Aztec concepts of gender and sexuality.

Tenochtitlan on the Eve of Conquest

Hernán Cortés, Bernal Díaz, and other firsthand witnesses of preconquest Tenochtitlan, capital of the Mexica state government, stressed the size of the city, its orderly administration, and the wonders of its great marketplace. They are uniformly silent about details of everyday life, and their comments on religion and ritual are informed by Catholic concepts of infidelism. But beginning immediately after the conquest of Tenochtitlan, Spanish clerics worked to record vocabularies and accounts of Aztec society that provide partial information about virtually every aspect of life in the metropolis. These sources have formed the basis for generations of scholarship on Aztec society, but relatively less has been known about the edges of the tribute state: outlying provinces, their capitals, and villages. Recent archaeological work has added significantly to our knowledge of these parts of the Aztec world.[1] Nevertheless, Tenochtitlan still dominates our awareness of the Aztecs.

By limiting my discussion to what we can say about life in Tenochtitlan, I hope to accomplish two goals. First, this discussion takes the inhabitants of a specific place in time as its subjects. The previous chapters have necessarily had recourse to abstractions of various sorts in order to deploy fragmentary explanations of different data sets from specific sites, to move toward a representation of possible past realities that remain undocumented at any one site. For Tenochtitlan, I can come as close as possible to demonstrating crosscutting tensions, understandings, and actions *within* a single Mesoamerican society at one place and time. Second, by using Tenochtitlan as a focus, I can show how access to textual representations changes the kinds of issues that can be examined. Studies of gender using monumental art, figurines, and the archaeological traces of activities at individual residential sites have established a rich body of suggestive interpretations for the Aztecs that are on a par with, or even more developed than, those developed from similar materials for other earlier Meso-american societies. But Aztec archaeology is unique in also having at its disposal rich information about ideologies that can only be suggested for earlier Mesoamerican groups. The long history of discussion of these textual sources has tended to deploy them primarily as proof of a highly dichotomized, normative set of gender identities and relations, sometimes represented as uncontested. My argument in the pages that follow is that this image partly reflects European assumptions, and partly the persuasive intent of patrons of the textual sources, nobles and state officials, to present an orderly and controlled view of the Aztec world.[2] I treat texts as another body of inscriptions, one characterized by abundance of detail. In some cases, this leads me to read these texts quite differently than others have.

Tenochtitlan itself was a city as large as any in Europe at the time. With over 150,000 inhabitants, the city sprawled across reclaimed land and its island core in the southwestern end of the Valley of Mexico. Stone causeways connected the city with the mainland, and aqueducts brought fresh water from the shore to the city. Canals provided a means of transport using canoes, supplementing the system of paved streets throughout the city. On the city's edge were the *chinampas,* highly productive agricultural fields maintained by annual renewal with organic-rich soil dredged out of the canals. While the ultimate owner of all land was the state, in the person of the *tlatoani,* control of land use was divided between governmental units, nobles, and groups of commoners. The lands of the nobility and government entities, worked by slaves and tenants, included land gained through warfare and granted to specific individuals by the ruler. The division between nobles and commoners, Edward Calnek notes, was not strictly speaking a class distinction. Instead, he describes a situation much like that Joyce Marcus presents for the Postclassic Maya and Zapotecs, in which there was an unbridgeable difference between nobles and commoners. Calnek notes that the status of noble (*pilli*) was marked by a claim of genealogical connection to a past ruler, while commoners (*macehualtin*) were the diverse mass of subjects, of varying occupations and material means, who could not make such claims.[3]

At the center of the populated quarters of the city was a walled precinct of temples and administrative buildings. At the city center the ruler had his palace, with guest quarters for visiting dignitaries. Here also individual administrators and members of warriors' societies had their meeting places, and some religious specialists and functionaries serving the palace maintained their residences.[4] The walled temple precinct was a public space of the kind exemplified at Chichen Itza, providing formal settings for the performance of ceremonies of governance and the rituals of state religion, abstracted from the residences of the population.

Filling in the rest of the city were the house compounds occupied by commoners and nobles. For most individuals in Tenochtitlan, life was centered on their own house, or *calli,* and the people who inhabited it and neighboring houses, which together made up what Bernardino de Sahagún called the *calpulli* (literally, "great house"). Some contemporary scholars argue that in using the term *calpulli* for the subdivisions of Tenochtitlan, Sahagún and other early chroniclers were falsely conflating the much less complex social organization of the countryside with that of the state capital. These scholars identify the term *tlaxilacalli,* a state administrative ward, as the more appropriate Nahuatl term for the subdivisions of Tenochtitlan. As Susan Kellogg notes, the *tlaxilacalli* and the *calpulli* identified by Sahagún and other early chroniclers had identical names. The former provided the framework for tribute payment and labor service to the state. The latter was defined by common ritual practice, shared craft traditions, and asserted identity, including connections with patron deities and traditions of origin, features that Elizabeth Brumfiel compares to the self-identification of an ethnic group.[5] I argue here that these identity-based divisions of Tenochtitlan can profitably be examined from the perspective of the model of houses, particularly in comparison with examples in which houses exist in highly stratified polities, such as feudal Japan. This perspective may help clarify a number of contradictory features of the social subdivisions of Tenochtitlan that Sahagún's informants labeled *calpulli,* which were the social units responsible for the initial training of children in appropriate ways of being, including gendered performance.

An intense debate centers on the degree to which *calpulli* were structured by kinship. While Arturo Monzón concluded that the *calpulli* represented clans, most other authors have found the evidence for kinship as a structuring principle weak. Kinship organization in Tenochtitlan stressed bilateral descent and the formation of cognatic kindreds. Edward Calnek observes that any person could construct a claim of connection through named individuals of either sex in three ascending generations to affiliate with multiple lines of descent, a construct he identifies with the *tlacamecayotl,* or "rope" of kin. He suggests that the decision to claim connection to one or another *tlacamecayotl* might be based on residence or other strategic interests. By claiming such multigeneration links, the residents occupying particular districts of the city were able to present their connections using an idiom of kinship. But while cognatic kindreds like these appear to have formed the skeleton of most of the residential wards Sahagún called *calpulli,* these residential units also integrated dependents with whom kinship links were not asserted.[6]

It is more useful to consider what we know of the actual relations of *calpulli* members than to attempt to classify this unit. The noble males who provided information for Bernardino de Sahagún's *Historia general de las cosas de Nueva España* consistently placed everyday life and individual development within the context of these residential districts.[7] Each person born in Tenochtitlan had potential rights in the estate of the *calpulli* of which their natal house was part, including the agricultural land held and used by its members, the communal buildings they used, and the exercise of skilled occupations that were traditional monopolies of certain *calpulli.*[8] The most detailed description of such an occupational monopoly, and hence the source for much of our understanding of how any *calpulli* worked, is the discussion of specialist traders, the *pochteca.*[9] The identity of the members of this *calpulli* was tied to the practice of long-distance exchange under the patronage of specific deities, an identity reinforced in rituals marking the initiation and end of each trading journey. Sahagún's informants detailed a specific oral tradition about the origins and history of this *calpulli* that must have been taught to children as they grew up. Children were ordinarily sent for training to specific schools based on their residence in a particular district. Although the *pochteca* had unique supernatural patrons who were venerated in their own temples, they also took part in the wider municipal ceremonies through which the Aztec state bound together the population of Tenochtitlan.[10]

For most everyday matters, one's individual house compound and its inhabitants were the social group of most relevance. But as Susan Kellogg notes, on various social occasions, and during life-cycle rituals in particular, wider groups of people were drawn together. Sahagún describes many of these social ceremonies as involving rituals performed in the *calpulli* temple. The *calpulli* maintained its own temple for common ritual practices, both those tied to the agricultural calendar and others related to the life cycle, as well as its own common schools for youths, and in some cases apparently supported temple schools where, among other things, craft skills were developed. Each residential district was named. As the *tlaxilacalli,* the residential district was responsible as a unit for satisfying the central government's tribute demands. As the *calpulli,* the named residential district had its own patron deities, origin traditions, and ritual practices.[11]

On the surface, *calpulli* or *tlaxilacalli* conform well to the general model of the house. They were enduring social units with their own estates, both material (buildings) and immaterial (origin traditions, patron deities, craft skills and knowledge, rights to determine land use), perpetuating themselves by the transmission of their estates and name through recruitment not limited to kinship but relying heavily on it. At the same time, these analogues of the house in Tenochtitlan raise significant issues. How does the deployment of a house differ in a highly centralized, economically stratified state? Alan Sandstrom and John Chance both suggest that the apparent contradictions in previous studies of the *calpulli* might be resolved by the use of the house as a model. While most of the examples considered by Claude Lévi-Strauss were nonstate societies, the medieval French *maison* that gave its name to the concept was part of a centralized state. Roxana Waterson has demonstrated the utility of examining the tensions between the house society structure and centralizing state dynamics in her discussion of feudal Japanese society. Like Tenochtitlan, the feudal Japanese system was highly stratified. The Japanese *ie* was a unit that operated at both the peasant and noble strata. Between the twelfth and the sixteenth century, nobles integrated *ie* of their followers in a hierarchical relationship, using the metaphor of "stem" and "branch." Branch *ie* included sections of a kin group that had their own estates but recognized the authority of the stem lord, and also nonkin client *ie,* sometimes even noble *ie* that sought advantages by affiliating themselves with a more powerful group. Noble Japanese houses were thus tied to specific commoner houses, and provided the formal articulation between these commoner houses and the state. Waterson notes that during the Tokugawa Period, while power was centralized in the hands of the shogun, scholars believe that for most people the primary relationship was with the lord of their stem *ie*. The *ie* was the focus of agricultural, mercantile, and craft production; the center for ancestor ritual; and the mediator between its members, other *ie*, and the state. The powerful centralized Tokugawa bureaucracy used the ideology of the *ie* to legitimate the government as a kind of higher-order *ie*. Following the restoration of authority to the emperor in the Meiji Period, *ie* ideology was again used to present the imperial line as the sole stem house, with all others branch houses described as children of the imperial parent.[12]

As in the Japanese feudal system, the head of the *calpulli*, the person responsible to the central government, was a noble appointed by the state. But this official administrative role did not displace the significant position that elders had in the *calpulli,* particularly with respect to the socialization of children, evident in the orations recorded by Sahagún, especially those on the occasion of life-cycle rituals. The social unit that Sahagún called the *calpulli* corresponds to other Mesoamerican houses in two crucial ways. Its members lived in proximity to each other, and that proximity was formalized as a basis for mutual identification through the permanent establishment of temples hosting distinctive rituals drawing together residents, especially rituals of the life cycle. Like other Mesoamerican houses, *calpulli* were also the groups allocating rights to agricultural fields to member house compounds. Ultimately, the ruler held all rights to the land, but these rights were delegated not to kinship groups, marital couples, or individuals, but to the *calpulli*. As in other house societies, the word for the unit itself, whether *tlaxilacalli* or *calpulli*, is derived from the word for house: *calli*.

While members tended to occupy spatially segregated areas within Tenochtitlan, failure to reside in these precincts did not result in loss of house identity. Particularly important exceptions to the general rule of residence in the house district were those individuals who took up residence elsewhere in Tenochtitlan to pursue opportunities created by their own distinctive abilities. For example, some skilled feather workers, *amanteca*, resided in the royal palace. Such attached specialists had learned their craft in the social context of a residential ward, most of whose members continued to produce their craft work in that spatial context. Other house members became religious specialists and lived in communal residences. Some of the young men abstracted from their natal house compounds during their training for war remained dedicated to battle after their initial training and continued to live in the house of youths as senior officers.[13] Nonresident members increased the prestige of their house of origin and gave it a stake in institutions integrating the capital city.

These ties to the overall political system balanced other tendencies that could have made *calpulli* potential foci of division within the Aztec state, as Classic Maya noble houses had been and as feudal Japanese *ie* were. Because the *calpulli* was grounded in a residential district where members carried out common activities, its members tended to marry within their own local group, achieving an ideal of house societies: minimizing the loss of people and property that inevitably results when members marry out. *Calpulli* controlled instruction in craft skills and the distribution of rights to work land, providing for an independent economic basis. The ritual observances of the *calpulli* drew together all its members (resident and nonresident) in locally maintained temples. The youths of each were trained in schools maintained and administered at the level of the residential ward (*tlaxilacalli*).[14]

The day-to-day life of children growing up in Tenochtitlan, consequently, was most strongly structured by the house of origin. A child was welcomed into the world by its house affiliates, was cared for within a residential ward occupied by fellow members, regularly took part in shared rituals honoring the unique house deities, learned its traditions and history within schools run by the house, and passed through major life crises with the ritual aid of the house. Contact with the wider arena of the city and state was also mediated by the house, as children participated in the economic activities that helped the group provide required tribute goods. Until boys and girls reached the age to be sent to the temples or enter the House of Youths, their most direct experience of the state would have come from forays into the city market and participation in the citywide festivals that marked the common agricultural calendar.[15] The market and the calendar were major forces that bound commoners and nobles of different houses together as Tenochca, people of Tenochtitlan.

European observers, beginning with Cortés, were awed by the scale and level of activity of the great markets of Central Mexico.[16] These European commentators found the markets easy to understand, since what they saw conformed well to European ideas of commerce. In markets, producers and resellers provided goods whose values appeared to be determined by the give-and-take of haggling, with certain standards of value serving both as a means to set exchanges and as real currency. Market judges patrolled to make certain that no false weights or measures were in use and that currencies offered were not adulterated. All of this was transparent to European eyes, untroubled by the great differences between Mexica and European commercial transactions. Thus the European commentators did not dwell on the nature or potential significance of standards of value: for instance, the high value placed on a natural raw material, cacao, otherwise used to create a beverage for ceremonial occasions, or the widespread use of lengths of woven cloth, products of women's labor in the household compounds, as a measure of value. Nor did the Spanish commentators focus their attention on the role of the marketplace itself as a social arena for contacts between members of individual houses.

The vocabulary recorded in early Nahuatl dictionaries provides an alternative way to view the significance of trade, the market, and currencies for the Mexica speakers of this language. These terms provide a useful means to begin to define the moral value of exchange.[17] Three separate groups of Nahuatl words are associated with the Spanish terms *mercado, mercar, mercaduría* [sic]/ *mercadería,* and related entries in the sixteenth-century dictionary compiled by Fray Alonso de Molina (Table 5).[18] Published in 1555 and 1571, this source reflects the effects of Spanish colonial reorganization, but comparison between the Spanish-Nahuatl and Nahuatl-Spanish sections provides guidance in interpreting Aztec concepts of exchange. One set of terms for the act of trading, things traded, people who engage in trade, and for coinage corresponds to two Nahuatl roots. These terms do not portray the marketplace as the location for exchange. Instead, they center on setting prices, meeting prices, and paying for goods with coinage. "To substitute something in place of something else" is the core definition of one of these roots. The other is based on the term *to buy.* A second set of terms is based on the names of the groups that other sixteenth-century documents tell us were responsible for long-distance exchange. The actions of these groups (the *pochteca* and the lesser-known *oztomeca*) are defined in circular terms, distinguished in the Spanish glosses by the verb *tratar.* No association with money is evident. The terms themselves denote specific social groups whose essence is participation in such long-distance exchange.

A third set of terms for trading, goods, and the trader as one who sells is listed as separate entries in the dictionary. Related terms include words for the marketplace itself but not a word for currency. These definitions incorporate concepts of moral value, centering on the exchange of one thing for another with which it is equivalent, and including the use of proverbs as moral guidance. The same root forms the basis for the verb for *to marry.* This vocabulary is one infused with moral value, and these are the terms associated with the marketplace as a location, not the terms based on money exchange.

The vocabulary documents an economy in transition under colonial administration. Based on the concept of setting a price as the substitution of values, but lacking any moral connotations, the first set of terms describes trade mediated by money. That this system was the Spanish colonial economy is made clear by the definitions of the terms for money, which describe metal coins. These exchanges are not associated with the marketplace. Instead, the marketplace is the locale for the establishment of moral exchange relations, a scene of social activity, the site of *ferias,* and a place through which to walk. Exchange in the marketplace is described as giving something for something else of equal value and is related to marriage, which established a relationship of equivalence between two groups of kin. Money is not mentioned.

The morality of exchange in the marketplace is underscored by words

Table 5. NAHUATL VOCABULARY FOR MARKETS AND EXCHANGE FROM FRAY ALONSO DE MOLINA (1970)

to trade	tlacoa tlacouia	patiyotia				
thing traded	tlacouhtli (comprada)	tlapatiyotilli				
trade for another	tlacouia					
trader	tetlacouiani					
moneda (money)	tlacocoualoni					
goods			nanauhtli nanauhyotl (heritable)	tiamictli tiamiquiliztli	tlanamaquiliztli	
trader (one who sells)				tiamicqui	tlanamacani	puchtecatl
marketplace				tianquiztli tianquizco tiamicoyan	tlanamacoyan	
to trade (tratar)						puchtecati puchtecauia (also: oztomecati)

for breaches of the moral relationship involved. Selling for more than fair price is described with a term that also means to envy or be angry at someone, and is also defined as trickery. Selling something for less than its worth is described with a term also used for taking away a privilege or office, or reducing the tribute offered. The embedding of economic activities in social relations is equally clear in the accounts recorded by Bernardino de Sahagún, which make explicit the role of the nobility in ensuring the morality of exchange.[19] The market is described as the location of exchange. Noble market officials ensure just exchange, setting equivalencies of goods. The climate of the market was one of moral exchange, and the marketplace itself was the primary scene of moral relations between houses, mediated by the nobility. In market exchange, two standards of value were salient: cloth, the product of the work of adult women within the house compounds throughout the city and empire; and cacao, the raw material for the sacred beverage whose ordinary use was limited to the nobility, and whose use by commoners was limited to specific ceremonial occasions, including those marking marriage alliance.[20]

Counterposed to the moral domain of the marketplace, the rituals of the agricultural calendar provided another setting for participation in the life of the city for members of the individual *calpulli*. Sahagún provides detailed descriptions of key ceremonies for each of the eighteen months of the calendar, in which the leadership of the nobility and religious specialists and the participation of warrior societies are prominent features. Preparation and consumption of feast foods within the residential district is a constant feature of these ceremonies. At the same time, the activities of these festivals engaged the populace in movement from the residential neighborhoods to the walled temple precinct at the city center, physically unifying the space of the city through the movement of its inhabitants as participants and spectators.[21]

Exemplifying the segregation of a public spatial arena like that which distinguished Chichen Itza and other Postclassic Lowland Maya sites, the sacred precinct of Tenochtitlan was walled, cardinally oriented, and connected by gates to major roads.[22] Within the walled precinct, the dominant building was the Templo Mayor, whose terraces supported twin temples dedicated to Huitzilopochtli, the solar warrior patron deity of the Mexica, and Tlaloc, the agricultural patron. At the base of the stairs of these twin temples was a great ballcourt and skull rack. Other temples, platforms, and residences of religious specialists crowded the enclosed precinct, and the halls of the warrior societies were placed at either side of the main temple.

To a singular extent, the layout of the main sacred precinct was in-

scribed as the setting of the central mythical struggle between Huitzilopochtli and his elder siblings, the Huitznahua, headed by their sister, Coyolxauhqui. The great temple was called Coatepec, or Serpent Hill, the place in
myth of Huitzilopochtli's conception, birth, and conquest. A monumental
image of Coyolxauhqui, dismembered and cast on the ground, was placed
at the foot of the stairway from the temple of Huitzilopochtli, just as the
myth said her body came to rest at the foot of Coatepec. The ballcourt
and skull rack in turn mimicked corresponding locations in myth where
Huitzilopochtli was said to have placed Coyolxauhqui's decapitated head.
These monuments and buildings served as the literal stage for the reenactment of the mythical conflict during the ceremonies in the month of Pan-
quetzaliztli.[23]

A network of other state-sponsored temples extended throughout
the city, providing sites for ceremonial performances and points on procession routes throughout the year. The movement of people through the
streets from site to site—which sometimes involved singing and dancing,
sometimes runners racing through the streets, and on other occasions mock
battles between groups that transcended the individual houses—guaranteed the intrusion of these ceremonial performances into at least the periphery of everyday life in the house compounds. Each of the individual ceremonies combined rituals related to the agricultural round with episodes
echoing the myths of Huitzilopochtli and dramatizations of military conflict and its aftermath, human sacrifice. The imbrication of these different themes in single public performances makes these ceremonies rich, but
sometimes contradictory, sources for Aztec symbolism of gender, social
status, and power. Despite their predominance in the Spanish sources from
the sixteenth century and the visual media at monumental scale—which are
all that remain of the Aztec capital city—these public performances were
in dynamic tension with the everyday practices that individual Tenochca
had already experienced within their house compounds before they ever
participated in citywide events.

The Everyday Performance of Gender within Aztec Houses

Geoffrey and Sharisse McCafferty argue that an ideology of gender complementarity, expressed in the work of men and women within the household,
was central to Aztec society. This ideology was legitimated by traditions of
a primordial dual-sexed creator deity, Ometeotl, a single entity with male
and female aspects, Ometecuhtli and Omecihuatl, from whose union came
all subsequent beings. What such cosmological concepts might mean to

living people can be suggested by examining a parallel case of a "complementary dualism that makes the participation of both male and female elements a requirement for all creative production and a characteristic of overarching power," based on concepts of primordial double-gendered deities similar to Ometeotl. Janet Hoskins, characterizing the Kodi of Indonesia in this fashion, notes that all Kodi are conceived as initially having both male and female attributes. Adult gender is produced through life-cycle rituals that suppress the attributes of one gender and encourage those of the other.[24] A similar process of creation of adult difference from the substance of the child is discernible in sources about Aztec childhood.

Information pertaining to rituals of life transition is fragmented and distributed throughout separate volumes of the work of Sahagún.[25] In several descriptions of calendar ceremonies, Sahagún's informants noted the performance of specific rituals involving young people. There is no guarantee that the ceremonies noted in passing exhaust the range of ritual actions marking stages in childhood, and indeed there is good reason to suspect they leave out those ritual actions not made part of centralized political ceremony. Most of the information available about birth and marriage, both times of marked change in the status of the child, was included to illustrate speeches during these life passages rather than actions. Despite the limitations imposed by the fragmented and selective nature of these documents, they provide a suggestive picture of adult Aztec views of childhood.

In drawing on these sources, I treat the language used in orations concerning children as more than simply poetic metaphors. I argue that these verbal figures reflect fundamental concepts of the nature of infants and adults. I view the Aztec data as much like the situation Janet Hoskins summarizes for the Kodi of Indonesia: "The rites of the life cycle can be divided into two separate complexes. The first . . . is concerned with socializing the new-born child and bringing it into the human community from a previously wild, animal-like existence. . . . The second complex . . . serves to mark gender identity and marital status."[26] What this ethnographic analogy suggests is that, given an ideology of primordial gender dualism, the production of male and female adult genders is not something natural and inevitable; instead, it requires work to achieve adult gender status. This view of the production of gender is far from that assumed in contemporary western European ideology, in which children already have an innate sexual identity and simply need to be taught how to behave as a good exemplar of their sex.

Aztec adults worked to craft new people out of the raw material of infants and children. This raw material was as much vegetal as animal. In speeches addressed to expectant mothers, children were characterized as the thorn that grows from the tip of the maguey leaf and as maguey about to sprout and blossom. Other characterizations as feathers or as chips of flint specifically emphasize the identification of the child with materials that were crafted into valued forms within the household-based productive economy of the Aztecs. Elizabeth Brumfiel notes that crafted goods, like humans, were endowed with *tonalli*, a life force. When the midwife was hired to begin her work, in the seventh or eighth month of pregnancy, she described her job as to "produce, be successful with the precious necklace, the precious feather." The same images recurred, in even more explicit form, in speeches she made after the birth, with the child described as a product made by the gods: "The truth is that through our lord we seem to dream, to see in our dreams, to look into the face of the one who has arrived, the precious necklace, the precious feather, the baby, which has been flaked off here. Our lord the creator, the master, Quetzalcoatl, flakes a precious necklace, places a precious feather, here on your neck, at your breast, in your hands he places a precious necklace, a precious feather, the incomparable, the wonderful, the precious, the priceless, the rare."[27]

In exhorting mothers during childbirth, productive metaphors treating children as growing plants or precious raw material gave way to the master image of production among the Aztecs, that of capture in battle. The woman was urged to "seize well the little shield," and once delivered was told, "You have become as an eagle warrior, you have become as an ocelot warrior. . . . You have returned exhausted from battle." The midwives actually shouted war cries to mark this "capture." These two sets of images are not as disparate as they seem at first glance. Aztec warfare, as one of its effects, resulted in tribute of raw materials and worked goods. The hierarchy between the captor and the captive was explicitly modeled on Aztec parent-child relations. The victorious warrior said: "He is as my beloved son"; and the captive replied: "He is as my beloved father."[28]

The switch from life-cycle rituals that, following Hoskins, *socialize* the newborn and bring it into the human community, to those that *mark* gender identity and marital status, occurred over the first four years of life in the Aztec case. Only the earliest speeches, associated with prebirth and birth rituals, characterize the child as nonhuman. By the time the period of infancy was over, the child was treated as fully part of the social group. Beginning at birth, rituals included imagery and actions designed to introduce the infant to adult gender identity.

The earliest ritual actions performed by the midwife immediately following birth were associated with cutting the umbilical cord and burying it. The midwife made reference in her speeches to the work and the clothing that would be the adult lot of the child. She differentiated between boys and girls in the disposal of the umbilical cord. Addressing the girl child, the midwife said, "And how will you be clad? and how will you be arrayed?" and promised that "there will be work, labor, for daily sustenance. There is sweat, weariness, labor when there is to be eating, drinking, the wearing of raiment." As she buried the girl's cord by the hearth, she said, "You will be in the heart of the home, you will go nowhere, you will nowhere become a wanderer, you become the banked fire, the hearth stones. Here our lord plants you, buries you. And you will become fatigued, you will become tired; you are to provide water, to grind maize, to toil; you are to sweat by the ashes, by the hearth." To the baby boy, whose umbilical was, in contrast, buried on the battlefield, the midwife said: "You have been sent into warfare. War is your task. You will give drink, nourishment, food to the sun, the lord of the earth," and addressing the gods, "He is your possession, your property; he is dedicated to you. For this was he created, to provide you drink, to provide you food, to provide you offerings. He belongs to the battlefield there in the center, in the middle of the plains." The prescriptive nature of these actions is obvious. In a society in which gender was something fluid that required work to stabilize, these actions took on the significance of creating gender difference, not simply reflecting it.[29]

At this point, the child was still described as a sprouting plant, a chip of stone, and even as a wild bird in a nest. A shift in balance toward symbols drawn from the social universe came with the reading of the calendrical fortune of the child's birth date by a male specialist. Since the Aztec used the birth date as a name, this ceremony also marked the first part of the formal designation of the child's name. Name designation was completed by the midwife in the ceremony of bathing, whose date was set by the calendar specialist four days after he read the calendar fortune or, if that were an inauspicious date, a more promising one.[30]

The formal bathing employed a rhetoric of work and clothing to impose conceptions of adult male and female identities on the newborn. The verbal expressions were given material form in this ceremony. The bathing ceremony for the boy used "a little shield, a little bow, little arrows . . . his little loincloth, his little cape," and that for the girl, "the equipment of women—the spinning whorl, the weaving sword, the reed basket, the spinning bowl, the skeins, the shuttle, her little skirt, her little shift." The midwife was the first to address the child by name, urging the baby to take and use the small versions of adult tools present. Once she named the baby, she dressed it in the small versions of adult clothing that had been provided, which were not the habitual garments of infants and would apparently not be worn after this ceremony.[31] This initial act of dressing certainly did not make an adult of the infant, a task that lasted through many long years. But it did begin to treat the child as a social being of the same kind as the adults with whom he or she shared this manner of dress. A sequence of changes in hair, costume, and ornaments that followed gradually created distinct social identity, above all that of simultaneously constituted adult gender and work role.

The verbal descriptions Sahagún preserved of these early rituals (as he says, because they were full of good rhetoric) can be compared to a visual document, the sixteenth-century *Codex Mendoza*, combining pictographic scenes with brief Spanish glosses. The first image, on manuscript page 57, shows a mother with a baby in a cradle linked by a dotted line to an older woman (labeled "midwife") holding the baby over a pottery vessel full of water set on a bed of rushes. Footprints around the mat form a counter-clockwise path, corresponding to the description of the movement of the midwife during the bathing ceremony. Dotted lines link the baby to a shield and spears on one side, and to a broom and spinning basket on the other. The insignia on either side of the mat—shield and spears, and the spinning basket and broom—correspond to the emblems of dichotomous adult genders, used respectively for a boy baby or a girl baby. In addition to the items mentioned in the *Florentine Codex*, the shield and spears of the boy are augmented by tools for woodworking, feather work, scribal practice, and metalworking. In contrast with the account presented by Sahagún, no clothing is shown.[32]

The parallel between this section of the *Codex Mendoza* and Sahagún's account continues with the dedication of the baby in the cradle to train either in the religious schools (*calmecac*) or the secular "house of youth" (*telpochcalli*), represented in the *Codex Mendoza* by the "house of song" (*cuicacalli*), the attached building where young men and women in secular training went to practice songs and dances.[33] Directly below the drawings of the bathing and naming ceremony, the cradled infant is shown in front of its parents. Dotted lines link the cradle to two other figures, identified in the glosses as the master of the *telpochcalli* and the priest associated with the *calmecac*. The either/or convention of the dotted line in this case differentiates not the gender of the child, but the major institutional basis for differentiation of its adult role, which, among other things, implied different experiences of adult sexuality. The verbal description of this event recorded by Sahagún makes clear what the implications of this choice on the part of the parents were and adds important and suggestive information on the ceremony itself.

The assignment of boys and girls to the *calmecac* is described as destining the child to a life of chastity and penitence.[34] Accompanying this promise was a feast, which took place in the temple precincts because the head priest could not enter the house compound. The speeches made on this occasion referred to the distinctive haircut of religious life that would be adopted in adulthood. In the meantime, the child's body was marked by ritual scarification on the hip and chest, and the child was given a distinctive necklace, the *yaqualli*. For a child to be promised to the *telpochcalli*, a feast for the masters of the House of Youths was celebrated at the child's house. On this occasion, "to make it known that he belonged to the *telpochcalli*, the lip was pierced in order to place the lip plug there." The distinction in adult destiny being signaled through ritual was literally marked on the bodies of children. Through ritual the raw material of the child began to be transformed into the social substance of the adult person, the costume and gesture of adult gendered performance.

Life-Cycle Transformations in Aztec Childhood

The use of costume, hair, and body ornaments systematically serves to mark passages from one life stage to another among the Aztec. These systematic distinctions are evident in a section of the *Codex Mendoza,* immediately following the bathing ritual and dedication scene, that presents what purports to be a chronological account of the training of children by parents.[35] Each panel of this sequence features adult male and female figures instructing a young boy and girl. The age of the children is indicated in the Aztec manner by a set of dots, each standing for a single year. The series begins with year three and runs through year fourteen. It presents the gradual replication of adult gendered performance in costume and labor as the central activity in raising Aztec children. The timing of major transitions in childhood in turn may hint at the scheduling of life-cycle rituals that were not systematically identified in Sahagún's texts.

The three-year-old girl and boy each wear the upper garment appropriate to their gender, the blouse and cape they were presented with as babies. A contrast is set up between age three and four by the addition to the girl's costume of a skirt. Although a seven-year-old boy wears a loincloth while fishing, the figures of boys shown inside the home dispense with this garment. At age thirteen, the boy is shown wearing a loincloth in every image, while the girl's blouse and skirt are shown, for the first time, with finished hems like those worn by the adult woman. The hair and facial appearance of the boy and girl are identical, cropped short over the entire head, through age eleven. At age twelve, the girl wears her hair down and long in back. Together, these costume cues suggest one shift around the age of three to four, a second around age six to seven, and a third around age twelve or thirteen. Children at each of these stages required more food, indicated in the *Codex Mendoza* by drawings of tortillas above each scene. Between age three and four rations rise from half a tortilla to a full tortilla. The next change is indicated at age six, with rations augmented by another half tortilla. At age thirteen, the final recorded shift, to two tortillas a day, is indicated.

The subdivisions of childhood indicated by changes in dress and food rations parallel those in the sequence of learning, which is the overt topic of this document. The three-year-old children are not yet being trained. From age four to five, the children begin to be instructed in their adult duties without practicing them. At age six, with increased rations, boys are sent out into the marketplace to glean food and girls begin to spin cotton. The succeeding stage is marked by harsh discipline for infractions of decorum and of expectations about work. The boys and girls given rations of two tortillas a day at age thirteen are fully trained, and they wear the costumes appropriate to youth ready for marriage or training in the *calmecac* or *telpochcalli*.

The transitions suggested by the changes in visual representation of boys and girls in the *Codex Mendoza* are naturalized as simply resulting from biological aging by their presentation in a European format of year-by-year changes. But in Aztec ideology, as recorded in Nahuatl texts, maturation actually results from the effects of life-cycle rituals. Where European ideologies view maturation and personal identity as inevitable expressions of natural essences, Aztec ideology, like other Native American ideologies, viewed personal identity as something that required work to produce and was open to much wider variation. For example, Alfonso Ortiz argues that Tewa children were not seen as fully human until after the completion of three rituals in a series of four life-cycle ceremonies: naming, water giving, water pouring, and finishing.[36]

The *Florentine Codex* does not present a coherent narrative of rituals marking stages in the life of the child such as those ethnographically described for Native American peoples like the Tewa. But reference to such ceremonies was preserved in passing when it complemented a focal topic of Sahagún's work. Embedded among descriptions of calendrical festivals are fragmentary references to life-cycle rituals. These texts present cumulative physical treatment of the child as central to the emergence of a proper adult. In the month of Quecholli, mothers brought infants of unspecified age to the temple Teotlalpan, where they were cradled by the senior women of the temple. This action recalls part of the description of the dedication of the child to the *telpochcalli,* when the masters "cradled it in their arms to possess it, to make it forever their possession, until it reached a marriageable age."[37] Whether the ritual in Quecholli was part of a similar dedication of children to the temple or a more general step in socializing raw infants is ambiguous. But the rhetoric employed, in which holding the child formed a physical attachment, is the same.

Providentially, among the life-cycle rituals for children described in greatest detail, because of its inclusion in the calendrical round, was the occasion that marked the transition from the freedom of the three-year-old to the structured education of the child over age four. This feast was held every fourth year in the month called Izcalli, "when children were grabbed by the neck to make them grow tall." Like the "cradling" of children in Quecholli, the rhetorical aim of this ceremony was, through physical manipulation of the body of the child, to control its maturation. But the additional details available for this feast provide a much more nuanced vision of how the control of maturation was to be accomplished.[38]

As Inga Clendinnen notes, the timing of the feast — every four years — requires that the children participating could not all be the same calendrical age. In essence, the rituals of Izcalli can be thought of as establishing an age class of four years. Clendinnen argues for individual calculation of the four-year interval from weaning, correlated with the ability to walk, so that children from age two or three to age six or seven passed through the ritual together. I suggest instead that the timing of the ritual was uniform and included all those recently turned age four and extended to those who had just missed the threshold during the previous cycle, up to about age seven. A similar practice marked finishing, the fourth life-cycle ritual of the Tewa, in which all children who had reached the age of six during the interval between enactments of this ritual were finished together, forming an age grade spanning four (ages six to ten) or seven (ages six to twelve) years, depending on the major division of the Tewa people to which the child belonged.

The visual sequence in the *Codex Mendoza* portrays socially marked transitions set absolutely by the calendar, not relatively by physical processes, and may be linked to the life-cycle rituals Sahagún described. At age eight, children are for the first time shown subjected to physical punishments, several of them extremely exaggerated. The fundamental punishment at this stage involves the use of maguey spines to pierce the body. A nine-year-old boy is specifically shown with the spine inserted in the ear. The central bodily mark that children received at Izcalli was the first piercing of the ear, linked in ritual with production of blood for sacrificial offerings. The visual representations in the *Codex Mendoza* reflect the creation of age grades of children between the ages of four and eight, who underwent the ritual of Izcalli together and thus entered into the phase of adult life when they were subject to adult discipline and participation in adult forms of ritual observance.

Izcalli rites are described twice in the material gathered by Sahagún. The major actions featured in both accounts are the piercing of the ears of children, dancing with their ritual sponsors, and drinking the intoxicating beverage pulque. After midnight, while it was still dark, ritual sponsors chosen by the parents of the child, and addressed by the kin terms "aunt" and "uncle," carried or led the children to the *calpulli* temple. There, the priests pierced their ears with a bone awl, thread was strung through the perforation, and the children were decorated with feathers.

While Clendinnen and others view the significance of this ritual action as the first instance of bloodletting by the children, I also note that it provides the aperture that was necessary in prehispanic Aztec society for the wearing of ear spools. In the *Codex Mendoza*, ear spools are displayed clearly on a boy of age fifteen shown coming to the *telpochcalli,* and on the girl of the same age shown being married on the same page. A later scene, glossed as a feast held by a newly married boy to beg leave from his peers in the *telpochcalli* for spending his time away from them, shows six young men and the young bride, each with carefully detailed ear spools.[39] Just as the dedication of the infant to the *telpochcalli* involved the piercing of the lip for a labret, but not the immediate use of the ornament, so may the Izcalli ritual have marked the creation of a space on the body to be occupied later by the ear spools of socially adult boys and girls.

The final action in the sequence of piercing is described as the "singeing" of the children, who were held over fires by the old men of the residential neighborhood. This action, also referred to as dedicating the children or "giving them uncles and aunts," may have resulted in additional body markings. The use of fire to mark the body is suggested by a passage concerning constellations associated with the new fire ceremony, itself tied to the month of Izcalli. Sahagún noted in passing that "it was customary that the men make certain burns on the wrist in honor of those stars [the Fire Drill constellation]. They said of him who was not marked by those burns that, when he died, there in hell [sic] they would produce fire on his wrist, drilling it as those do who here drill fire with the stick."[40] Nothing in Sahagún's text clarifies which individuals received these marks, or at what age they earned them, but the passage implies that absence of such marks was both exceptional and an omission that would be corrected even after death.

The return home of the children and their sponsors at dawn began a round of feasting, drinking, singing, and dancing in which the sponsors led the children by the hand or else carried them on their back. In the afternoon, the sponsors again carried the children to the temple and brought with them pulque and special drinking vessels for the children: "And for drinking, for drinking the pulque, there were quite small drinking vessels; only exceedingly small ones. And all were giving pulque to the small children."[41] Everyone continued drinking throughout the day and, after returning to the house, throughout the evening.

The ritual of Izcalli initiated the period of childhood during which the conventional practices of labor and costume through which gender was constituted were intensified. The complex tropes that related children to precious raw materials used for ornaments, referred to in speeches early in the child's life, are particularly suggestive of the importance of body ornamentation as marking changes of status. The layering of body markings and items of costume accrued by progress through life stages in Aztec society substituted a "social skin"[42] for the original skin of the newborn with its explicit marks of biological sex. The adoption of young-adult hairstyle and costume, evident at age twelve or thirteen in the images in the *Codex Mendoza,* followed the complete mastery of adult labor. Aztec bodies were made, and the means through which they were made was repeated decorous action.

The Body and the Person in Aztec Adulthood

Aztec texts related the transformations of a boy's hair to his training and distinction as a warrior.

> At first, while still a small boy, his hair was shorn. And when he was already ten years old, they then let a tuft of hair grow on the back

of his head. And when he was fifteen years old, then the tuft of hair became long. [This was] when he had nowhere taken captives. And if he took a captive . . . then the lock of hair was removed. . . . And when the tuft on the back of his head was removed, he was shorn so that he was left [another] lock: his hair dress kept, on the right side, the hair hanging low, reaching the bottom of his ear; to one side [only] was his lock of hair set. . . . And he who then did not take a captive . . . might not remove his lock of hair. . . . Thus was his hair shorn: it was cut like a ring-shaped carrying pad; they shaved only the crown of his head.

The young man who continued as a specialist warrior was allowed a new hairstyle when he captured his fourth captive on his own. A scene in the *Codex Mendoza* shows the fifteen-year-old boy destined for the *cuicacalli* with the long tuft of hair, and later pages depict specific hairstyles and labrets of warriors with ever greater distinction.[43]

The boy's transformation to an adult is marked by changes in hair and costume that signaled mastery of the stereotypic adult male task, the capture of prisoners in war. Sources for the girl's parallel transformation are much less complete. Distinctions are noted between noble girls with "hair all cut the same length," with the "young girl's lock of hair," and with the hairstyle of women "wound about the head," but neither the ages nor circumstances of the shifts are detailed. The transformation to the woman's hairstyle takes place after the marriage ceremony in the visual documents in the *Codex Mendoza*.[44]

A brief commentary on another ethnic group, the Otomí (characterized in these passages as having "a civilized way of life," despite standing elsewhere as an example of less polished peoples), describes the costume and customs of these people in terms identical to those used for the Aztecs. Changes in male hairstyles follow the same sequence as changes in Aztec boys' hair, from a tuft of hair to long flowing locks. This parallel is important because the section on Otomí women is more detailed than that for the Aztec. "When the women were still young girls, they cut their hair short; but when [they were] grown, when [they were] young women, the hair covered their shoulders. . . . And when one was a mature woman, when perhaps she also [had delivered] her child, the hair was bound around her head."[45]

Ceremonial haircutting or hairdressing forms a central part of women's puberty rituals in a number of Native American societies, from the Tewa of the Southwest United States to the Kuna of Panama and the Tukuna of Colombia.[46] I suggest that references to changes in Aztec and Otomí hairstyle are traces of ceremonies that marked the social maturation of the young in these societies. The hair worn long at the back, described as typical of Otomí young girls when they were grown, corresponds to the "young girl's lock of hair" in the summary of Aztec elite women's appearance. But the gendered nature of this translation is misleading. The *same* Nahuatl term is used to refer to the unbound hair hanging down and marking the young man embarking on his career as a warrior. The image of the fifteen-year-old boy on his way to the *cuicacalli*, and a later image showing the boy undergoing training, shows a long tail of hair visually indistinguishable from that of the young girl between age twelve and marriage.[47] Whereas the boy earns the right to his adult hairstyle through capture of war prisoners, the girl achieved her bound hairstyle after marriage or, I suggest, specifically following childbirth, which was also systematically represented as capture.

The equation between achieving the rank of warrior and delivering a child, and its embodiment in changes in body ornamentation, was underlined in ceremonies in the month of Toxcatl celebrating social transformations in the life of the god Tezcatlipoca. The human actor embodying the god for the feast and sacrifice was ornamented with feathers on the head, a form of body ornamentation first conferred on children during the ear-piercing ceremony in Izcalli. After he was presented with four women who embodied the brides of the god, his ornaments were changed for those of a warrior and his hair was cut in warrior style.[48]

Secular marriage ceremonies did not stress the equivalence of capture and childbirth, but they did involve manipulation of costume. The central act of weddings involved the same articles of clothing originally presented to the newborn baby as signs of adult gender destiny: "And the mother of the man went to give gifts to the bride. She placed a blouse on her, and a skirt before her. And the mother of the woman also went to give gifts. She tied a cape on the groom, but his breech clout she placed before him. . . . And the elderly matchmakers tied them together. They took the corner of the man's cape, they drew up the woman's blouse, then they tied these together." In the scene representing this moment depicted in the *Codex Mendoza*, the bride and groom are joined by their tied clothing. This scene marks the first time ear ornaments are worn by the girl. This feature is first visible in the costume of the boy shown going to the *cuicacalli* at age fifteen, depicted on the same page as the wedding scene.[49]

Aztec childhood was divided by these rites of passage into a series of phases distinguished by different bodily practices. From birth to age three or four, children wore undifferentiated haircuts. Nevertheless, their adult destiny was marked symbolically by the provision of miniature tools and costume, and their bodies were physically prepared for distinctive adult ornaments that would eventually mark them as practitioners of priestly or secular careers. Between age four and eight, Aztec children wore parts of their adult costume. By the end of this period, they had received the ear perforations that would accommodate adult ear spools. By age thirteen, boys and girls adopted a long flowing haircut and were using full adult clothing that distinguished between male and female. Transition to complete adult status was marked by the habitual use of ear spools and adult hairstyles, with the capture of real prisoners through war and metaphorical prisoners through birth marking adult incorporation into the imperial economy. From an undifferentiated beginning, the bodies of children were systematically laden with signs of difference in gender, achievement, and status. The physical differences observable at birth were not alone sufficient to determine adult gender and status, but had to be transformed into socially defined identities through action that actually began before birth, as indicated in the speeches linking sweat bathing by the pregnant woman with the working of raw material into crafted form. Children were literally products of adult action, in the same way that the materials used to mark them socially—items of clothing and ornaments marking statuses—were products of work. Central to the transformation of children into adults were Aztec concepts of sexuality.

Sexuality and Beauty in Aztec Society

Aztec children's bodies were marked for distinct experiences of adult sexuality in ways that could not be changed as easily as setting aside one form of clothing in favor of another. The lips of boys destined to train for war were pierced to prepare them to receive the lip plugs that would signify their successful capture of different numbers of prisoners as young adults. Children dedicated to serve in the temple not only lacked this piercing, but instead were ritually scarred on their hip and chest. For infants with these destinies, body modifications marked not only their intended adult work but their sexual status: children who entered the temples would be celibate, while boys who trained in war enjoyed sexual liaisons with special groups of young women, and eventually might contract permanent marriages. All children's bodies were further distinguished by ear piercing, the setting for a form of ornament worn by all adults, regardless of status.

Hair was a particularly important site for the display of sexual status. Children, both boys and girls, had their hair trimmed short—not quite shaved, but left so short that it followed the shape of their heads—until around age ten to twelve. For young men, the contrast between long flowing hair and elaborate combinations of long locks and shaved areas marked different forms of adult labor but also differences in accepted sexuality. The flowing hair of young men was paralleled by that of young women, whose transition to adult status resulted in the adoption of a style of hair bound up into two horns. Controlling hair marked control of adult sexuality. It does not seem coincidental that the negative stereotype of the female prostitute described for Spanish clerics singled out long, unbound hair as one of the signs of this practice.[50] As a body part that grows out of shape, hair resists static formalizations of appearance. Aztec adults continually reenacted the social creation of appearance out of the raw material of infant bodies in the discipline of their own hair, a discipline that simultaneously marked their sexuality.

The control of adult sexuality was a topic that pervaded the admonitions recorded by Sahagún. Here the social position of his informants, male members of the nobility, undoubtedly affected the kinds of information provided. Unconstrained sexuality was as problematic for the social control that nobles and elders wanted to exercise as it was for the new Spanish religious authorities. This makes it extraordinarily difficult to recover a more balanced view of sexuality from these late text sources. But traces remain even in these texts of ideals of sexual attractiveness grounded in specific gendered performances. The primary context recorded in the Aztec data for moments of beautified gendered performance is the participation by groups of young men and women in ceremonies marked by public processions, singing, and dancing, activities the child first experienced during the rituals of the month of Izcalli: "There the dancing, the singing continued—the songs, in all, spreading the sound, crashing like waves."[51]

These performances were marked by extreme attention to body ornamentation and the social attractiveness it enhanced. The songs sung on these occasions were learned and practiced by the young men and women in the *cuicacalli*.[52] They incorporate sensual references to beautified appearance that are inherently evaluative and reflexive, inviting the performers to rejoice in their own appearance:

> In Tzonmolco, the songs are being sung
> which we have started
> Here's why it's time, to come out disguised
>   (FROM THE "SONG OF IZCOZAUHQUI")

The young men of the Tzonmolco district sang of singing and going out disguised, as the *pochteca* who lived there did on their long-distance journeys in search of luxury goods. These included the feathers the *amanteca* of Tzonmolco turned into elaborate garments worn in the dances as signs of achievement, the yellow feathered capes and eagle robes awarded to successful warriors by the *tlatoani:*

> Huitzilopochtli, leader in war
> whose work is on high, who goes on his way:
> not in vain I take the yellow feathered cape
>   (FROM THE "SONG OF HUITZILOPOCHTLI")

> The Tocuiltec are panting
> eagle robes lie in Huitztlan
> By the young men of Olopan
> my captive lies feathered
>   (FROM THE "WAR SONG OF HUITZNAHUAC")

The dance performances of Aztec youths, embedded as they were in agricultural-calendar ceremonies and formally controlled by the training given in the *cuicacalli,* can also be seen as beautified sexual displays by marriageable young men and women. On the occasions described in surviving Aztec sources, young men were led out from the House of Youths where they were living while training for, and first experiencing, warfare. In the months of Tlaxochimaco and Tlacaxipehualiztli, young men danced ornamented with eagle down on their heads, wearing flower garlands and a cape of flowers, shell jewelry, and the special bells called *oyoalli* on their legs, the same costume worn by the impersonator of the god Tezcatlipoca before his marriage in the month of Toxcatl.[53]

Young women also took part in public dancing. "And when it was Hue Tecuilhuitl, there was dancing which was the particular task of women; old women, maidens, mature women, little girls. The maidens, who had looked upon no man, were plastered with feathers; their faces were painted."[54] The language of some of the songs that have been preserved is imbued with sexual innuendo:

The night is intoxicating
why do you have to be coaxed?
Consume yourself now,
Array yourself in garments of gold
    (FROM THE "SONG OF XIPE TOTEC")

The sleeper, the sleeper
in sleepiness drowses
here now with my hand I turn the girl over
the sleeper am I
    (FROM THE "SONG OF ATAMALQUALOIA")

Many scholars have assumed that the only women taking part in dances were ritual prostitutes. But passages in Sahagún's texts specifically describe young women on some of these occasions as "one's daughters." In the month of Hue Tozoztli, such young women, with painted faces, pasted with red feathers reaching from ankle to thigh and from wrist to shoulder, and with garlands of flowers on their heads, exchanged inflammatory comments with the boys: "Thus the women could torment young men into war; thus they moved them; thus the women could prod them into battle. Indeed we men said 'Bloody, painful are the words of the women; bloody, penetrating are women's words. . . . Indeed we have gone; we have said that we shall not live.' " [55]

That the lively exchanges between the young men and women were, as they appear from the comments and descriptions, sexually charged is further intimated by a riddle that asks, "What are the things that, at their dancing place, they give stomachs, they make pregnant?" This metaphor for the accumulation of thread on the spindle attests to a connection between the dancing of young men and women and their sexual activity. Spinning and weaving served as metaphors for heterosexual intercourse in Aztec society.[56] Public dances and processions were sanctioned opportunities for young men and women to display their sexual attractiveness and test their newly achieved adult status.

This image of young men and women displaying themselves as attractive sexual objects stands in stark contrast to the admonitions preferred by Sahagún. There, good noble girls are described in idealized terms as chaste and contrasted with the bad noble girl who "is a descendant of commoners—a belittler, a rude person, of lowly birth. She acts like a commoner; she is furious, hateful, dishonored, dissolute, given to carnal pleasure, impetuous." The repeated description of the negative stereotype as

common and the relatively low priority of "carnal pleasure" in the list of un-
acceptable traits suggest that what is at issue here is not so much sexuality
itself as decorum, the proper behavior of the noble woman. Other negative
stereotypes of bad noble women strengthen this interpretation:

> The bad little girl is an evil talker, a belittler—inconsiderate, per-
> verse, impetuous, lewd. She shows disrespect; she detests, she shows
> irreverence, she belittles, she presumes. . . . The bad maiden is cor-
> rupt, incorrigible, rebellious—a proud woman, shameless, brazen,
> treacherous, stupid. She is inconsiderate, imbecile, stupid; she brings
> dishonor, disgrace. . . . The bad noblewoman is a gluttonous noble,
> a noble completely dishonored, of little value—a fool, impudent—
> a consumer of her inner substance, a drunkard. She shows concern
> for none but herself; she lives completely for herself; she governs her
> own conduct, assumes her own burdens; she is disrespectful.

Governing her own conduct, the nonideal noblewoman would not be gov-
erned by the wishes and interests of her house or the state. Worst of all,
she is indistinguishable from a commoner: "The bad noblewoman is like a
field worker—brutish, a great field worker, a great commoner."[57]

Commentaries on commoner women, remarkably, share the same
language of dismissal: a bad cook is "a field hand—very much a field hand,
very much a commoner." Although they celebrated specific working skills,
Sahagún's noble male informants still maintained the criteria for decorum
derived from the noble class. Skill at work was an ambiguous thing, particularly so in the case of those women who were most notably independent, medical specialists. Such women could use their skills to support their
own sexual satisfaction: "The bad physician, a counselor, advised, a person of trust, of professional knowledge. She has a vulva, a crushed vulva, a
friction-loving vulva." The language used here is identical to wording de-
nouncing women who engaged in same-sex relations.[58]

These texts also brand as debauched young men who drink and take
drugs too much, and they mention as one of the attributes of such men
that they keep mistresses and are given over to sexual pleasure. Alternative sexual practices are strongly denounced by the noble informants of the
Spanish cleric. Homosexual men and women are described as perverting,
confusing, and corrupting others, and male homosexuals are presented as
objects of ridicule and even of death by burning. The *patlache,* translated
as "hermaphrodite," a female who takes women as her sexual partners, is

denounced in particular for not taking a husband, a breach of social order that "scandalizes" rather than being an affront to nature. Similar language indicts adulterous women who are condemned for "bearing bastards." [59]

The tension that existed between the desire to socially control reproduction and the display and celebration of the sexual attractiveness of young men and women is dramatized by the figure of the "harlot," the *auiani*. Condemned for consuming her inner substance, the *auiani* is described almost as a perpetual youth:

> She parades; she moves lasciviously. . . . She makes herself beautiful; she arrays herself; she is haughty. She appears like a flower, looks gaudy, arranges herself gaudily; she views herself in a mirror— carries a mirror in her hand. She bathes; she takes a sweat bath; she washes herself; she anoints herself with *axin*—constantly anoints herself with *axin*. . . . She paints her face, variously paints her face; her face is covered with rouge, her cheeks are colored, her teeth are darkened—rubbed with cochineal. [Half] of her hair falls loose, half is wound about her head. She arranges her hair like horns.

None of these actions is inherently evil; all are practiced by "good" women in restricted, controlled contexts, specifically those leading to the institutionally favored adult female role: marriage. Her violations of decorum are linked to her lack of a proper place in a house compound.

> She ornaments herself well, places herself at the market, adorns herself at the marketplace. . . . Restless on the water, living on the water, she is flighty; she travels along the road—travels shamefully along the road; she walks as if a part of the marketplace; she walks painted in the marketplace. She walks back and forth many times along the road; she walks circling, constantly. She nowhere finds lodging. She settles anywhere, she sleeps anywhere, she wakes at dawn anywhere.[60]

In Aztec society, to be without a place was the worst condition that could be imagined, and it was the threat of expulsion from the house that lay behind the moral injunctions recorded by Sahagún.

> Already in another's compound, already in the entrance of another's house: With this saying were taught, were admonished one's sons or

the common folk, in order that no one might do an improper, a bad thing; in order not to be driven forth, in order not to be forced to wander to others' compounds, to others' house entrances. He was advised: If you do something evil, you will be driven forth, you will be made to wander in others' compounds, in the entrances of others' houses.[61]

One's house provided a place to live, a way of making a living, and the ritual practices through which life and development were nurtured and memory after death ensured. The elders of the house controlled and limited the expression of sexuality, and the performance of gender was channeled within the house into very narrow acceptable possibilities. The commentaries on alternative behaviors suggest that these strictures were not accepted without resistance, resistance that had an additional political dimension as the centralized state strove to control individual houses and their members.

Resistance in the Aztec Household

The standards of decorum recorded by Sahagún ultimately derived from the nobility, who presented noble behavior as exemplary and the actions of commoners as gross, unrefined, and given to excess. It is among the nobility that the lives of men and women were most severely controlled. Nobles were said to admonish their daughters:

> Seize the broom; be diligent with sweeping. Do not neglect the offering of incense. . . . When it is so, when you have made preparations, what will you do? What will you seize on as your woman's work? Perhaps the drink, the grinding stone? Perhaps the spindle whorl, the weaving sword? Apply yourself well to the woman's task, the spindle whorl, the weaving sword. Open your eyes to the way to be an artisan, to be a feather worker; to make designs by embroidering, to judge colors, to apply colors to please your sisters, your ladies, the noblewomen. Look with diligence; apply yourself to learn how the heddles are provided; how leashes are provided, how the pattern is placed.[62]

The same language is echoed in the descriptions of wedding speeches.[63] The old men of the bride's house said to her:

> Oh my daughter, you are here. For your sake your mothers, your fathers have become old men, old women. Now you approach the

old women; already you begin the life of an old woman. Forever now leave childishness, girlishness; no longer are you to be like a child, no longer are you to be like a girl. Be most considerate; regard others with respect, speak well, greet them well. By night look to, take care of the sweeping, the laying of the fire. Arise in the deep of night.

The old women of the groom's family also spoke to the bride:

My daughter, your mothers, your fathers encourage you here. You are unfortunate; you have undertaken that which is like a heavy burden, a large carrying frame, which is truly heavy, and cannot be lifted.

Following close on the heels of participation as young adults in the public ceremonial processions and dances for which they were ornamented in elaborate costume, and the celebrations in the young men's houses following success in battle, the transition to the hierarchy and control by elders in the house that accompanied young married status must have been difficult. New roles in ceremonial performance allowed some continuation of participation in this public source of affirmation of personal distinction. Some individuals clearly rejected the constraints of proper social action for the practice of the alternative sexualities condemned by Sahagún's noble male informants. But even for those who followed the officially sanctioned path of heterosexual marriage and labor within the house, there was still room to contest the social consensus promulgated by the state in the rituals of the calendar cycle and reinforced in marked ceremonial performances within the house. To the extent that control of adult gender performance was a major component of the overall exercise of control of the people of Tenochtitlan, one form of resistance was to play with gender ideology.

Geoffrey and Sharisse McCafferty argue that a discourse of female gender centering on weaving drew on and inverted an official ideology of male hierarchy. They show that the sexual implications of weaving allowed the skillful performance of this craft to assert overtly suppressed pleasure in sexuality. They suggest that within individual house compounds, everyday performances would have included verbal celebration of sexuality, not only as a service to the reproduction of the state and the house but as individual pleasure. They argue that even the penetration of official gender ideology into the house compound was subverted by this alternative discourse. Women's weaving and spinning tools might be assimilated to the weapons of war, childbirth reframed in the language of capture, and cloth redefined as the standard of value for tribute resulting from military subordination,

but within the house, excellence in spinning and weaving continued to reflect individual achievement in a female gendered performance that was
imbued with sexuality.[64]

Harriet Whitehead has noted a general relationship in native North
American societies between prestigious craft production that reflects on
the individual craft worker, and the presence of alternative gender identities. Although her concern was identifying key features of alternative genders, her argument assumes that possibilities existed for the expression of
individual distinction by recognized competence in prestigious craft work.
In Aztec houses, cloth production provided a site for asserting personal
achievement. Cloth was the ultimate tribute good in the Aztec state. Used
to mark status distinctions in political ceremonies and required in religious
rituals, woven cotton cloth signified civilized existence for the Mexica. The
provision of cloth by one house to another, or to civil authorities, embodied
the recognition of hierarchy but also of mutual obligations. Annette Weiner
has argued that cloth's perishable nature reinforces the continual need to
re-create social relations. By celebrating their work in weaving, women in
Aztec houses simultaneously asserted their sexuality against the social con-
trols that surrounded it and claimed individual distinction against a society
that attempted to advance obedience to the authority of the state and of the
house as the greater good.[65]

Even other less stereotyped and symbolically charged forms of labor
served as means by which women and men in individual houses resisted the
closure of possibilities that was fostered by the state and house authorities.
Elizabeth Brumfiel has called attention to the likelihood that large numbers of women were actively engaged in the kind of physical labor and
commerce that was denigrated by Sahagún's noble male informants. She
demonstrates that basic food production and selling of foodstuffs, a viable
means for individual women and their kin to better their economic position, was intensified in the process of political incorporation into the Aztec
state. Brumfiel also documents intriguing changes in the proportions of
figurines with different images that accompanied the incorporation of rural
communities into the Aztec state. Her analysis suggests that figurines that
depicted women's reproductive activities were prominent in situations in
which the labor of women was an important resource for meeting the demands of political centralization, when women's work would have been an
issue in negotiation of relative political power, as I have also argued for the
Classic Maya.[66]

I suggest that the vehemence of noble male denunciations of behavior not in keeping with noble notions of decorum and control is less a reflection of what the state of affairs *was* in Tenochtitlan than an indication of one of the major sites of tension in this complex state. Official state ideology, expressed in the centrally administered festivals and the monumental images used to create settings for them, went furthest in embodying the violence of control, including control of the diversity of gendered performances with all their divisive possibilities.

Violence in the Aztec State and Official Ideology of Gender

Brumfiel, McCafferty and McCafferty, and others have emphasized the potential for factions and individuals within Aztec society to claim authority over their own lives. The looming specter of Aztec state violence is the implicit background for these studies. Against the ideology of gender complementarity in which Geoffrey and Sharisse McCafferty find the possibility of a positive valuation of feminine gender, a number of scholars have seen only a systematic denigration of femininity and women's status. At base, as Brumfiel and others have noted, this disagreement stems from differential attention to the media for dissemination of ideas fostered by different interest groups within Aztec society. Taken as specifically focused on women, Aztec state violence has been seen as evidence of pervasive misogyny. But placed in the context of violence visited on men and women alike, the same patterns of visual and oral rhetoric instead reflect an attempt to engage an entire people in the pursuit of the ends of a militaristic, expansionist government.

An official Aztec state ideology of celebration of male warriors and of violence toward women has been described by a number of authors. It was inscribed in the iconography of stone sculpture in which monstrous or unnatural female supernaturals are defeated and cut into parts by the militaristic male deities of the Aztec state religion. It is argued that this ideology underwrote a marked gender hierarchy in Aztec society, particularly among the nobility. At its most explicit level, this gender ideology is exemplified by the legend of Huitzilopochtli's defeat of his elder sister, Coyolxauhqui, ending with her dismemberment and beheading. This is the scene commemorated by the monumental relief at the Templo Mayor showing the dismembered goddess at the base of Coatepec, the sacred mountain and temple (Figure 2).[67]

Coyolxauhqui is shown dressed in a loincloth, with eagle down on her head, wearing "little bells called *oyoalli*," ornaments Huitzilopochtli appropriated from her and her brothers after their defeat. Her costume links her to the living actor who performed Tezcatlipoca, the most powerful Aztec deity, in the month of Toxcatl: "eagle down covering his head, popcorn flower garlands and a stole of popcorn flowers, with shell jewelry, and the bells called *oyoalli* on his legs." The Tezcatlipoca impersonator set aside these ornaments when he married, when his hair was cut in warrior style and he adopted warrior ornaments. The feathered head ornamentation shared by Coyolxauhqui and the young Tezcatlipoca was also an attribute of the newborn Huitzilopochtli, who wore feathers on his head and had child's face painting until he defeated his elder siblings. The immature children undergoing the rite of Izcalli also were ornamented with down on their heads. What these deities and human actors shared was a liminal status in their life cycle, poised between childhood and adulthood. Coyolxauhqui, though depicted with an explicit vulva and breasts, is just as prominently marked nonadult as she is female. As an immature person, she was not yet fixed in adult gender. The actions she performed as a warrior were gendered male in the Aztec polity. She is portrayed as a liminal figure, not as an unambiguous adult female, and the danger she posed in myth and image was the threat of nonconformity to her adult destiny.[68]

State-sponsored calendar ceremonies re-created the primordial act of violence in the Huitzilopochtli myth with periodic sacrifices of goddess-embodying actors, a circumstance that has been treated as confirming the existence of an official ideology of violence toward women. At regular intervals throughout the year female actors embodying goddesses were subjected to sacrifices metaphorically linked to each other and to the death of Coyolxauhqui by the common practice of decapitation (Table 6). In the month of Tecuilhuitontli, Huixtocihuatl, an elder sister of the Tlalocs who was said to have angered her brothers (as Coyolxauhqui did her brother Huitzilopochtli), was ritually beheaded after dancing while holding a feathered shield and wearing bells on her legs. In the following month of Hue Tecuilhuitl, the maize goddess Xilonen died, beheaded. Three months later, in Ochpaniztli, the mother goddess Toci, or Teteo Innan, was beheaded and flayed, and priests danced in her skin while wearing her eagle-feathered clothing. The ceremonies in this month recalled the conception of Huitzilopochtli, when his mother Coatlicue was impregnated by a ball of feathers while sweeping the temple.[69]

Two months later, in Tepeilhuitl, women performing the mountain goddesses Tepexoch, Matlalcueye, Xochtecatl, and Mayahuel died, their bodies rolled down the temple stairs, their heads severed and set up on the

Table 6. MONTHS OF THE AZTEC CALENDAR IN WHICH DECAPITATION
SACRIFICE TOOK PLACE*

Month	Person Decapitated
Atlcahualco	
Tlacaxipehualiztli	Male war captives; captors dance carrying decapitated heads
Tozoztontli	
Hueytozoztli	
Toxcatl	Deity impersonator of Tezcatlipoca (principal god); head set up on Skull Rack
Etzalcualiztli	
Tecuilhuitontli	Deity impersonator of Huixtocihuatl (elder sister of the Tlalocs)
Hue Tecuilhuitl	Deity impersonator of Xilonen (young maize goddess)
Tlaxochimaco	
Xocotlhuetzi	
Ochpaniztli	Deity impersonator of Teteo Innan (Toci) (mother goddess)
Teotleco	
Tepeilhuitl	Deity impersonators of Tepexoch, Matlalcueye, Xochtecatl, and Mayahuel (mountain goddesses) and Milnahuatl (mountain god); bodies rolled down temple stairs, heads set up on a skull rack
Quecholli	Deity impersonators of Cuetlacihuatl and two Coatlicues (goddesses of pulque and hunting) and of Tlamatzincatl, Izquitecatl, and Mixcoatl (their husbands)
Panquetzaliztli	
Atemoztli	
Tititl	Deity impersonator of Ilamatecuhtli (old goddess); dance carrying decapitated head
Izcalli	

*After Sahagún (1951).

Skull Rack. Their bodies were then taken to the *calpulli* temples, where they were dismembered. The echoes of the defeat of Coyolxauhqui in the ceremonies of Tepeilhuitl were reinforced by the simultaneous sacrifice of impersonators of the four hundred Totochtin, or gods of pulque, who were analogous to the four hundred brothers of Coyolxauhqui. The following month, Quecholli, the performers of the Huitznahua themselves died, along with three goddesses, Cuetlacihuatl and two named Coatlicue, patrons of hunting and pulque, at a temple called Coatlan. Three months later, in Tititl, the Old Goddess, Ilamatecuhtli, was beheaded after dancing with her white eagle-feathered shield and weaving sword, and her severed head was carried in a dance by a priest dressed as the goddess.[70]

These ceremonies, patterned on the defeat of his sister by the patron deity of the Mexica, seemingly pervade the calendar round with violence toward women, and on their own would seem to support the idea that women in Aztec society suffered from an official devaluation of their humanity. These sacrifices have been used as evidence that the Aztecs conceptualized their military foes as a feminine other, and their women as internal foes.[71] But these analyses, although careful in drawing out implications for officially sanctioned violence against living women, take the experiences of women in calendar ceremonies out of a context that makes it harder to see violence as only directed against women based on their sexual identity.

The same form of sacrifice, display of the dismembered body, and placement of the head on a skull rack was practiced on the performer who impersonated Tezcatlipoca, the most powerful Aztec male deity, in the month of Toxcatl, two months *before* the first sacrifice of a goddess during the annual calendar round. The costuming of Tezcatlipoca on this occasion is described precisely as that attributed to Coyolxauhqui and the Huitznahua in the narrative of their defeat, and identifies Tezcatlipoca with the older brothers of Huitzilopochtli who also resisted him. Three months before this sacrifice, in the month of Tlacaxipehualiztli, Mexica warriors danced with the heads of sacrificed male warriors, prefiguring the sacrificial dance in the month of Tititl at the end of the year, reiterating the performance three months earlier during the previous year. The women playing goddesses sacrificed in the months of Tepeilhuitl were accompanied in death by a performer of Milnahuatl, a male mountain spirit, and in Quecholli by the sacrifice of men performing the husbands of the goddesses, Tlamatzincatl, Izquitecatl, and Mixcoatl. Throughout the year, men performing as the gods were sacrificed as regularly as women playing goddesses. Rather than manifesting an official attitude of deprecation of women, the violence shown in these ceremonies, and recorded in the myths they dramatized, was integral to the Aztec state's promotion of an ideology of military dominance.[72]

In support of their military conquests, Aztec religion offered a mythology in which blood was the crucial fluid that ensured the continued cycles of the sun, daily from night to day and yearly from winter to summer, from barrenness to harvest. In the service of that ideology, both men and women were encouraged to think of themselves as warriors for the state, engaged in complementary actions that supported the expansion of the Mexica domain. The defeated targets of this expansion were the elder-sibling societies that had preceded the Mexica in civilized development within the Basin of Mexico, likened to Coyolxauhqui and the Huitznahua defeated by Huitzilopochtli. Aztec myths related the dispersion of the dismembered body parts of the sister of the god to the creation of a fertile landscape.[73] These myths reinforced the central message of the state, that through military conquest greater order had been brought into being to the benefit of everyone. Violence was central to Aztec state imagery, but it was not preferentially directed against women. As Geoffrey and Sharisse McCafferty argue, the official ideology of gender was based on the complementarity of male and female principles in creation, providing primordial precedent and supernatural sanction for the performance of adult heterosexual roles that were of ultimate interest to the state in ensuring production of material and personnel for expansionist politics.

Gender Complementarity in Aztec Cosmogony and Politics

The primordial dual-sexed creator deity, Ometeotl, provided the model for the unity of complementary aspects that is crucial to Aztec mythology, history, and ritual practice. Numerous scholars have noted the tendency of Mexica to identify opposite-sex complements for their deities.[74] Most of the female counterparts to male deities were glossed as "wives" by the Spanish and are described only in sketchy terms. A closer examination of the scraps of creation traditions recorded suggests that three different kinds of cosmological cross-gender relationships were significant: that of mothers and sons; siblings; and perhaps least important, the husband-wife pairing that the Spanish emphasized. Sibling relations, whether cross-sex or same-sex, were imbued with competitiveness, and repeatedly elder siblings were displaced by younger ones. Indeed, gender seems to be subordinate to seniority in sibling relationships. It is the reversal of seniority that exemplifies Huitzilopochtli's triumph over his sister and brothers, a reversal the Aztecs claimed for themselves in their rise from the last to arrive in the Basin of Mexico to their political dominance of the region.

Relations between primordial mothers and sons, in contrast, were positive, characterized by the support Huitzilopochtli offered his mother when her other children threatened her with death. In the ritual performances accompanying the deaths of Xilonen, Teteo Innan, and Ilamatecuhtli, younger male performers playing their male offspring accompanied and guided the older women. These younger males, essentially analogous to Huitzilopochtli in his relationship with Coatlicue, were all corn gods, emphasizing the idea of cycles linking generations from fertile mother to offspring. The older women in these pairs are simultaneously mothers and warriors, holding shields in one hand and the tools of their gendered labor in the other, like Chicomecoatl, a maize goddess holding the sun shield, Teteo Innan holding a broom and a perforated shield like a spindle whorl, and Cihuacoatl, credited with the invention of the tumpline and digging stick, holding a weaving sword. As Susan Gillespie has shown, mother-son relationships provided a model for Aztec claims of lineal connection to the original ruling houses of the region through royal women from whom they received specific rights and regalia. Of human grandmothers, who occupied positions like these goddesses and legendary women, it was said: "The good great grandmother, worthy of praise, deserving of gratitude. She is accorded glory, acclaim by her descendants. She is the founder, the beginning."[75]

The pairs that the Spanish glossed as husband/wife couples are never explicitly dramatized in mythology as coparents or representatives of different allied groups. Instead, they represent different halves of a whole: like siblings engaged in positive relations rather than conflicts over seniority. While the Tlalocs had an antagonistic relation with their sister, Huixtocihuatl, not unlike that between Huitzilopochtli and Coyolxauhqui, Tlaloc also had a more positive female counterpart, Chalchiuhtlicue, goddess of the still earthly waters. The personifications of the mountains, sources of rainfall, and fertility were conceived of as a male and female set, the four women Tepexoch, Matlalcueye, Xochtecatl, Mayahuel, and the single male Milnahuatl. Tezcatlipoca was accompanied during the month of Toxcatl by four female counterparts, his brides, Xochiquetzal, Xilonen, Atlatonan, and Huixtocihuatl.[76] Paired male and female deities were particularly prominent in agricultural ceremonies. As models of human behavior, such halves of a whole could also exemplify the marital couple, both usually members of the same *calpulli,* working together in different ways to support the goals of their house.

The ceremonies of the shared calendar that united the Aztec state invoked gender complementarity in the reenactment of mythological action and its performance by ritual specialists. Similar cosmological images of complementary action were prominent at the intimate scale of the house compound on the occasion of household rituals, particularly those related to reproduction. Systematic parallels were drawn between childbirth and warfare, projected into the daily cycle of the sun through the complementary fates of those who died in labor, the *mocihuaquetzque,* and those who died in battle:

> Thus is the tale, the consensus of the elders: the brave warriors, the eagle-ocelot warriors, those who died in war, went there to the house of the sun. And they lived there in the east, where the sun arose. And when the sun was about to emerge, when it was still dark, they arrayed themselves, they armed themselves as for war, met the sun as it emerged, brought it forth, came giving cries for it, came gladdening it, came skirmishing. Before it they came rejoicing; they came to leave it there at the zenith, called the midday sun.
>
> And here is the story, the tale, of the women who had died in war, and of the *mocihuaquetzque:* it is said that the women who had died in war and the *mocihuaquetzque* lived there at the falling place, the entering place, of the sun. For this reason the old people, those who went recording things, named the place where the sun entered *cihuatlampa,* because the women lived there.
>
> And when the sun had emerged, when it already had advanced along its course, when those who had died in war, the brave warriors, already came gladdening it, came giving cries for it, when this sun had already advanced along its course, then the women arrayed themselves, armed themselves as for war, took the shields, the devices. Then they rose up; they came ascending to meet the midday sun there. There the eagle-ocelot warriors, those who had died in war, delivered the sun into the hands of the women. And then the warriors scattered out everywhere, sipping, sucking the different flowers.
>
> And the women then began: they carried, they brought down the sun. They carried it with a litter of quetzal feathers; it traveled in quetzal feathers; they provided it a support. And as they bore it, they also went giving cries for it, they went gladdening it, they went gladdening it with war cries. They left it there, it is said, where the sun enters.[77]

The *mocihuaquetzque* were women who died in childbirth. During labor, the midwife urged the mother to complete her capture of her child:

> You have become as an eagle warrior, you have become as an ocelot warrior; you have raised up, you have taken the shield, the small shield. You have exerted yourself, you have encountered, imitated

our mother Tonan, Cihuacoatl, Quilaztli. Now our lord has placed you on the eagle warrior reed mat, on the ocelot warrior reed mat. You have returned exhausted from battle, my beloved maiden, brave woman; be welcome.

And when the baby had arrived on earth, then the midwife shouted; she gave war cries, which meant that the little woman had fought a good battle, had become a brave warrior, had taken a captive, had captured a baby.[78]

If the mother died, her capture incomplete, she was honored as a fallen warrior:

And the midwives, the old women, *titici ilamatzitzin,* assembled to accompany the dead mother. They bore their shields; they went shouting, howling, yelling. It is said they went crying, they gave war cries. . . . And of this *mocihuaquetzqui,* although there was weeping, there was sorrow because she had died in childbirth, when she had really died, it was said she had become a *mocihuaquetzqui.* Her parents and the husband rejoiced therefore even more, for it was said she went not to the land of the dead; she went there to the heavens, to the house of the sun, Tonatiuh ichan.[79]

Through the posthumous support of the sun in its daily movement through the sky, the complementary performance of male and female adult genders was inscribed in the most pervasive visible spatial setting in the Mexica world. Adult heterosexual male and female genders, two halves of a whole, east and west, each dependent on the other for definition, each endowed with parallel roles in Aztec expansion and domination, were given formal recognition in cosmology and enactment in practice at all scales from the intimate to the universal.

The cosmological patterns of gender complementarity inscribed in Aztec myth, ritual practice, and monumental representation were also embodied in the monumental temporal scale of narratives of royal origins of the Mexica. Susan Gillespie shows that official Aztec genealogies relied on the transmission of the right to rule through women, who are specifically treated as links to traditions of creation. These women are variously represented as mothers, daughters, sisters, or wives, not due to confusion in sources, but as the emphasis shifts between the transmission of authority across generations and the combination within a generation of complementary aspects of rulership. Aztec royal narratives represent political power as

subject to continual reformulation and periodic renewal through the interventions of women, whose gender identity could be ambiguous when they
were not playing crucial roles in defining the dual bases of power.[80]

For Aztec rulers, power began with the split between the two aspects
of the creator god Ometeotl, the male and female deities Ometecuhtli and
Omecihuatl. In the exercise of authority in the Aztec state, governance embodied the creative duality of Ometeotl in the offices of *tlatoani* and *cihuacoatl,* both held by men but gendered complementary male and female.
The *cihuacoatl* was an institutionalization of bodily practices of costume
and action through which biological males performed normally female-
gendered actions. The images of skirted figures with offerings at Chichen
Itza are inscriptions of similar bodily practices. Charles Lincoln has suggested that building complexes like the Mercado and its Courtyard of a
Thousand Columns at Chichen Itza were sites of female-gendered ritual
action he compares to the role of the Aztec *cihuacoatl.* While the *tlatoani,*
or speaker, conducted what European observers recognized as the political administration of the Aztec state, the *cihuacoatl* reproduced the state
through other mechanisms and could substitute for the *tlatoani* on ceremonial occasions. Like their counterparts in Mexica royal histories, occupants
of the male/female *tlatoani* and *cihuacoatl* offices operated as alternates in
the spatial and temporal exercise of power. Like Kodi ritual specialists who
could only reinstantiate the duality of the creator deity for short periods,
the *cihuacoatl* was not simply gendered female. His performances were in
fact totalizing, drawing together the split halves of the complementary gender duality of Ometeotl through performances that combined costume elements and actions otherwise distinctive of dichotomous male and female
genders. As an encompassing gender performance, the actions of the *cihuacoatl* invoked the unity of elders within the house, modeled in their turn on
the founding ancestors.[81]

When the midwife addressed the parents of the expectant mother,
she referred to them by the names of ancestral figures lacking well-defined
dichotomous gender: "You who are here, you who are seated here, you who
are our progenitors, who are already the old mothers, the old fathers whom
our lord has set up as gods, who already have become as Oxomoco, who
already have become as Cipactonal." Named among the mythical founding
people who created the institutions of civilized life, Oxomoco and Cipactonal were paired but not securely differentiated by sex:

> And this count of days—so it was claimed—was an invention of the
> two called and named Oxomoco and Cipactonal, who gave it to the

people. Oxomoco they painted as a woman, and Cipactonal a man.
They who were readers of day signs embellished their book of days
with their representations, which they placed in the middle when
they painted them.

They invented the art of medicine. The old ones Oxomoco,
Cipactonal, Tlaltetecui, Xochicaoaca, were Toltecs. They were the
wise ones who discovered, who knew of, medicine; who originated
the medical art. . . . But four remained of the old ones, the wise ones:
one named Oxomoco, one named Cipactonal, one named Tlaltetecui, one named Xochicauaca. . . . Then they devised the book of days,
the book of years, the count of years, the book of dreams.[82]

As patrons of the calendar and of medicine, the successors of Oxomoco and
Cipactonal included both calendar diviners and midwives, the specialists
who initiated the social life of each Aztec child by bestowing on it names,
and who began the gradual process of differentiation between boys and
girls that state authorities and house elders expected would result in the enforcement of the performance of adult heterosexual marriageable genders.

Reinforced by ritual practices on both the intimate scale of the house
compound and the monumental scale of shared calendar festivals; bound
into personal development, social group and state history, and cosmogony
by overlapping narratives; and embedded in competence in everyday labor,
Aztec concepts of gender are far from natural outgrowths of a given biological essence. On both the cosmological and the personal scale, gender is
presented as more complex than the dichotomous male and female pairing
that Spanish observers privileged, including dual-gendered and ambiguous
or neutral-gendered performances.[83] Developed via specific material practices throughout childhood, gender in Aztec society was most strongly differentiated in the physical-appearance cues that reached their peak in the
early teenage years when adult sexuality was under negotiation. Rhetorical
imagery systematically collapsed performance of distinctive gendered labor
together into one category defined primarily in terms of support for the
state. At the same time, resistance to this incorporation of gendered performance of work in official state ideology was maintained, at least for women,
through the continued assertion of individual achievement and pleasure in
weaving.

The media of Aztec gendered performance—personal appearance
and action—are continuous with those established and elaborated in earlier
Mesoamerican societies. But in the Aztec state, the fluidity of gender typi-

cal of Mesoamerican thought was under the greatest pressure in its history to conform to a few tractable forms of personal identity. Along with the historical circumstances that preserved written records of oral texts for analysis, this characteristic of Aztec society makes it a particularly important example for understanding how power, both individual and political, was shaped by and helped shape conceptions of gender. As among the Classic and Postclassic Maya, the labor of individual men and women within their houses provided a potential source of conflict between the assertion of centralized control and local autonomy. In this conflict, particular ideological attention was paid to the contributions of men's and women's gendered labor. Women's production of materials, including cloth and prepared foods, used not only for subsistence but also in political and religious ceremonies, helped maintain house autonomy.

One way to assert control over women's labor, adopted in both Maya and Aztec polities of the Late Postclassic, was the development of public spatial settings for ritual, to which access was denied women in general by using female-gendered specialist males or restricted groups of women to fulfill the requirement of ritual gender complementarity. Males playing female-gendered roles in fact instantiated the primordial gender unity, providing one possible means of legitimating their adoption of this role. Celibate women, lacking investments in the interests of their own offspring, and elderly women who could be selected to avoid possible factions made up of younger adults, could transcend the interests of their own houses. But the restriction of women's participation in this new public sphere did not erase the possibilities for achievement of status presented by the house, where both women and men continued to exercise social and political influence through the socialization of children, the negotiation of alliances in the form of marriage and adoption, and the continued practice of religious rituals whose meaning could not be controlled by distant authorities.

CHAPTER SIX

Performance and Inscription

HUMAN NATURE IN PREHISPANIC MESOAMERICA

Far from simply reiterating a universal story of struggle for dominance between two sexes, male and female, themselves the simple
reflection of natural biological facts—a story that often portrays
women as inevitably losing power, becoming symbolically identified
with the negative poles of all manner of other dichotomies, and finally
coming to represent the undifferentiated mass of nature—the preceding chapters' unraveling of threads connecting concepts and practices
of gender in prehispanic Mesoamerica leads to the shadowy outlines
of a radically different view of human nature and its relations to possibilities of power and authority. In tracing the history of this Mesoamerican way of becoming and being across the three millennia from
the Early Formative to the sixteenth century, a series of practices
repeatedly emerge as sites of the negotiation of gender, never sepa-
rable from other dimensions of Mesoamerican personhood, especially age, work, and social rank. Strain between the relative open-
ness of performative practices and the attempted closure of practices
of inscription created gaps of incongruity, necessitating the repetitive
reinforcement of the stereotyped ways of being that included gender
but always also age, status, and role. And each of the performative
practices through which gender was played out in prehispanic Mesoamerica comes back to the body, not simply as the given determinant
of gender but as the site through which gendering is insistently naturalized by being assumed in the flesh.

To finally attempt to understand what we might make of this exploration, I make use here of Judith Butler's further development of her analyses of gendered performance in *Bodies That Matter.* Far from divorcing gender from the material reality of embodied persons—and their sexuality—examining the social construction of gender ultimately makes it clear that the struggle to delimit the kinds of sex and gender that are legitimate is charged by attempts to discipline individuals, actions central to social control and political power. Gender and power are completely intertwined because the social control of individual experience of the body is the most intimate level of discipline practiced by authorities, whether these are parents training children, elders in a kin group deciding what level of freedom juniors will be allowed, nobles steeped in religious authority claiming unique abilities and privileges denied to commoners, or conquering state bureaucracies demanding that gendered bodies preferentially carry out certain kinds and levels of production.

Human Nature in Prehispanic Mesoamerica

The discussion of Aztec life-cycle rituals and creation traditions in the previous chapter suggests the existence of a concept of gender as a potential that could develop in several different ways. From the neutral potential of the infant's gender, repetitive social action reinforced interdependent polar possibilities of maleness and femaleness. Spatially associated with periphery and center, animated as potentials for activity and stability, and enacted as complementary forms of labor in support of the Aztec state, male and female heterosexual genders reached their peak definition in young adulthood. They were even then marked off against not only the undifferentiated potential of childhood but also the continuing possibility of sexual abstinence to which young men and women were subject if they were attached to temples. Like the need to continually cut and shape the hairstyles that visibly marked their sexual status, the sexualized genders of young men and women were apparently made to persist only through their constant enactment.

The fluidity of gender of supernatural forces reinforces the impression that, for the Aztec, gender was a potential, subject to change and in constant need of stabilization. The duality of the initial creative force, invoked either with the gender-neutral title of Ometeotl or with the masculinized and feminized pairings of Ometecuhtli and Omecihuatl, can be seen as a continuation of the condition of the human child, with its multiple-gender potential, into maturity. Unlike a human's requirement to conform to the great either/or (in its disarming Mesoamerican restatement as the great either/or/or else, that is, sexually active male or female or else abstinent), the Aztec founding deity could maintain potential enactment of male *and* female sexuality. Other deities, notably the maize gods, replayed cycles of change from male to female and from youth to age. Two different temporalities of the same phenomenon, this multiple-gender capacity is one aspect of the ability of Mesoamerican deities to encompass different potentials that in humans had to be separated to maintain order.

While the kinds of documents that show that Aztec children were thought of as undifferentiated, and indeed not even of the same substance as elders, are lacking for other Mesoamerican societies, many of the specific practices associated with the fixing of gender potentials had a long and remarkably stable existence in Mesoamerica. Perhaps most notable are disciplines of bodily appearance, such as the deformation of the skull from childhood, noted among the Classic and Postclassic Maya and in Formative Period populations, or the filing and inlay of teeth, found in many Mesoamerican societies, where it is preferentially a practice of adults and of members of otherwise privileged groups. Body piercing and use of ornaments are two other practices, important in the sixteenth-century accounts of the stabilizing of children in particular adult identities, with long precedents in archaeological remains. Particularly notable here is the exceptional continuity in the use of ear spools by adults, extending back to the Formative Period.

That gender was fluid, and fixed through stereotyped kinds of action, in societies that preceded the Aztecs is further indicated by the inscription of different sexualities in media of inscription. For instance, societies like the Classic Maya city-states provided abundant imagery of dichotomous adult male and female gender statuses, notably marked by specific forms of dress and manners of work, but they also inscribed ambiguous representations of gendered performances that combined aspects of these poles in apparent citation of the encompassment of gender by creators and founding ancestors. Ambiguity of gender and sexuality also marks the central deities depicted at Teotihuacan as sources of water and agricultural fertility. While generally denoted "the Great Goddess" by contemporary scholars, these figures are marked by their total lack of distinguishing bodily features beyond the human commonalities of face and hands. Esther Pasztory has argued forcefully that the generality of images at Teotihuacan is designed to de-emphasize social divisions in this truly metropolitan city.[1]

Understanding the specifically gendered marking of some human representations as a statement of power throws the relative gender ambiguity and explicitness of different Formative Period figurines and monumental images into stark relief. Like later Mesoamerican societies, Formative peoples did not always choose to mark the sexual status of human actors, but often preferred to highlight other dimensions of variation, especially age and ritual status. In Formative Period human imagery, the child gender, merged with the neutral sex of mythological dwarf figures, is itself an object of inscription. The marked sexual statuses most commonly inscribed in different Formative Period societies are those associated with emerging sexual activity and reproduction. Here in Mesoamerica's earliest representational traditions, where even species boundaries seem to be fluid, the flourishing of inscriptions of gender, sex, age, and status-specific forms of human representation as an exercise of control over the development of the potentials implicit in each new child can most clearly be seen.

The Exercise of Power in the Lives of Individuals

In prehispanic Mesoamerica, much of the social and ritual work that inscribed certain performances as recognized genders was directed toward the fixing, however temporary, of potentials out of sets of mutually inconsistent possibilities. Unlike the gods, Aztec children would be required to act as adults in one of a few acceptable sexual styles. The reiteration of the limits required began at birth and continued at the regular intervals marked by ritual transformations of appearance toward that of adult gender performance. More public, formal, larger-scale inscriptions of gender were continually reinforced in the greater intimacy of everyday life as good parents, adult priests, and Masters of Youths trained children for the adult roles already determined in their infancy. The disciplines imposed by these adult monitors were carried over into the most intimate of experiences as youths dressed their hair in distinctive ways, sat, stood, moved, and spoke in prescribed fashions, motivated to compliance by the physical punishments and deprivations detailed in sixteenth-century sources.

Similar overlapping scales and periodicities of discipline of children were recorded in the much more brief account of Postclassic Yucatec Maya society recorded by Bishop Landa. As among the Aztec, rituals of transformation in the life of children, timed by the shared calendars, were carried out in semipublic settings. The formalized physical discipline of children as one aspect of these rituals reiterated the everyday practices through which elders in house compounds attempted to induce conformity with expectations. And, as among the Aztec, discipline was carried to the most intimate level of the shaping of the experience of the body through the manipulation of the infant skull, tattooing, dental modification, hair treatments, and the adoption of specific modes of dress.

Not only are the same kinds of actions evident in the material record of earlier Mesoamerican societies, but so are the different scales of settings that structured the repetition of bodily practices. The most public settings associated with marked gendered performances in sixteenth-century societies were the processional ways and open plazas where wide participation in calendar ceremonies was accommodated. Aztec accounts of such ceremonies describe races, mock battles, games, and especially dances in these most visible shared settings. Landa's account of Yucatec Maya society describes similar events in the open spaces of settlements, and again, dances are prominent. The Aztec accounts associate the maximum beautification of young men and women with these public performances. In both Aztec and Maya accounts, dances include the most sexually charged performances by groups of men and women; in the Maya case, they were apparently so explicit that Landa rejects them as atypical.[2]

Classic Maya settlements include formal processional ways like those of Postclassic cities; in many cases these link outlying house compounds with the great open plazas that were the larger-scale courtyards of ruling house compounds. That performances, including dances by sexually highlighted actors, were among the activities that took place at regular intervals in these spaces is suggested by the interpretation of texts and images inscribed at sites like Yaxchilan as references to dances (Figure 24, for example). Scenes in the Bonampak murals of elaborately costumed males spinning in a dance, accompanied by a band and costumed performers, take place at ground level before stepped terraces like the actual terraces set around the major plaza of the site. Pottery vessels may show mixed groups of men and women performing formal dance movements.[3] Even the women shown holding wrapped cloth bundles tightly in front of them in Classic Maya monuments may be pictured in the act of gendered dance, similar to the dances described in Landa's account of Postclassic Yucatan in which women held bundles of cloth or dishes as they danced (Figure 5).

In the Formative Period settlements that yielded burials of men and women wearing the elaborate costumes inscribed in contemporary small- and large-scale images, the formal equivalent of the open plazas and processional ways are not always as clearly marked. Many villages, like Tlatilco, have no monumental architecture to draw attention to particular open areas as possible sites for more public performances through which gender was incorporated in the bodies of young men and women. Even sites with monumental platforms, like Chalcatzingo or La Venta, lack the more clearly bounded open spaces typical of later Mesoamerican societies. It is thus doubly interesting that the earliest such bounded open space identified in Mesoamerica, from the Archaic Period open-air site of Gheo Shih in the Oaxaca Valley, is simply a formally defined area clear of refuse and outlined by lines of stone, described by the excavators as a possible dance ground. Julia Hendon compares this early form of largely perishable formal public space, and its successors at San José Mogote, to the unusual round platforms that are the first nondomestic structures in Middle Formative Maya sites, interpreted as dance platforms by several authors. David Grove has demonstrated that the placement of representational monumental images at Chalcatzingo, La Venta, and San Lorenzo demarcated not-otherwise-perceptible spatial settings, and it is likely that other sites had, for their inhabitants, locally understood spatial divisions of this sort.[4]

Susan Gillespie, discussing ballcourts, and William Ringle, dealing with ballcourts and processional ways, have emphasized the importance in the Mesoamerican tradition of disciplined movement through space as an expression of transformation, in which temporality combined change with predictability arising from adherence to performance standards.[5] Although the exploration of spatial layouts in Formative Period sites does not always provide clear expressions of the physical location of formalized movement, the artifacts recovered in trash and in burials strongly suggest that rhythmic movement, dance or masked drama, was already part of the repertoire of social disciplines through which gender was enacted.

Throughout Mesoamerican history, however, the marked settings for periodic ritual performances of gender were secondary in abundance and participatory experience to the settings of everyday life. Here there is remarkable commonality across a broad spatial and temporal span. Groups of buildings opening onto small unroofed spaces, or patios, formed house compounds from the Formative Period through the sixteenth century. In some settlements, house compounds were formally demarcated by walls, terraces, or other constructional features. This form of definition reaches a peak in cities like Teotihuacan, where despite dense packing of buildings, entrance and circulation are controlled by passages, stairways, and placement of internal patios, and boundaries between contiguous compounds are strictly defined by walls.[6] Marked off by orientation and boundary features as distinct from other similar units, house compounds are also internally divided into settings for more and less intimate, more and less shared, action.

Physical remains attest to many rituals that took place within house compounds, notably mortuary ceremonies resulting in the interment of members below house compound floors. Sixteenth-century accounts suggest that other events in the life cycle of residents were also played out, at least in part, in these intimate settings. The discipline of the bodies of house members in childhood and young adulthood through forms of body modification, through training in adult labor, and through punishment for transgressions was also practiced within the patios and interior spaces of house compounds. To the extent that control of individual development was a group concern, it was most possible for those people with whom one lived in the most intimate contact. Indeed, Aztec sources make access to the house compound itself the mechanism for the most severe form of discipline: children who would not conform to acceptable standards of decorum and work were threatened with expulsion from their house compounds.

The more and less intimate spatial settings within which gendered performance took place created a contradiction in the control of personhood. While the more public settings of calendar-timed rituals might theoretically be seen as sites of the exercise of state power over individuals, these were also the settings for the display of individual achievement in dance, games, races, and the like; for individual distinction in appearance; and for play and pleasure in the body. It is the more intimate confines of the house compound that provide the setting for physical discipline, admonitions about work, control of sexuality, and enforcement of the power of senior over junior members. Whereas the elder members of houses had interests in controlling their juniors within the house compound, when these same junior members were projected into more public settings, in company with the members of other houses, senior house members had vested interests in their distinction, even when this end was served by the apparent violation of the standards of everyday discipline. What was acceptable and desirable in performing gender in these different settings was variable, and these shifting standards themselves were another part of the exercise of control over individual development in these societies.

Age, Work, and Personhood

Although Euro-American history makes it seem natural to assume that sex/gender will be the single most significant determinant of status or power, in Mesoamerican societies, gender is never independent of age, and age strongly determines relative standing. Richard Lesure's analysis of Formative Period figurines from the Pacific coast of Chiapas emphasizes a major dichotomy in these small-scale inscriptional media, but it is not between male and female: rather, there is a contrast between a group of seated figurines, including both males and females with elaborate masked costumes, with age indicated by wrinkles and (in this agricultural society) prosperity indicated by fleshiness, and a second group of standing figurines depicting nude, armless, apparently youthful females. Anne Cyphers Guillén's argument that Formative figurines from Chalcatzingo depict a series of female life stages also places age, not sex, as central in the figurines' internal marking of differences. Contemporary burials from Tlatilco have no clear marking of sexes as distinct, but complexes of features do demarcate age classes that extend across the sexes. It is through rituals of transformation in age statuses that Postclassic Aztec and Maya peoples reiterated distinctive gendering. The more fragmentary Classic Maya evidence may relate to a similar linking of age-graded ceremony with the differentiation of a youthful male status distinct from both the less differentiated child category and the ultimate status of elder shared by men and women.

The structure of Spanish sources about transformations throughout Aztec life emphasizes the separation of male and female, in accordance with Spanish notions of the essential nature of this dichotomy, but what is fundamental to these transitions in fact is the development of work skills, not sexuality. Work is a crucial commitment of Aztec persons, and one that changes over time. The not-yet-fully-human infant status is tied to the lack of any work discipline, and it is with the introduction of training in labor that children begin to be anchored in their social identities. The long passages in the *Florentine Codex* that comment on the good and bad qualities of various categories of people focus strongly on work, and the degree of skill and dedication shown is what differentiates good from bad.

Like age differences, work differences are also more prominent in the earliest Mesoamerican villages than any simple differentiation by sex. John Clark's analysis of Formative Period Chiapa de Corzo burials identified two groups of burials, internally differentiated by age, with distinctive costume ornaments. He suggests that the symbolism of these two sets of costume ornaments relates to occupational difference between ritual specialists and administrative leaders. The same burials at Tlatilco that demonstrate age-related variation in accompanying costumes exhibit significant variation in items used in different kinds of craft production. In both cases, the labor-based distinctions are shared by groups, not limited to individuals.

Work was also a basis of categorical divisions between Postclassic

Aztec social groups that controlled particular craft specialties, and apparently also between houses of specialists in Postclassic Yucatan, as described by Landa. Classic Maya settlements routinely exhibit associations of craft workshops with individual house compounds, implying a similar house-based organization of specialized labor. At Classic Teotihuacan, such residential-group craft variation reaches an astonishing degree of elaboration that provides some hint of what Teotihuacan might have been like as a settlement. The list of specialized crafts practiced includes the production of several distinct categories of pottery and stone working of both utilitarian and ornamental products. Two enclaves within the limits of Teotihuacan suggest the presence of populations from other regions practicing unique specializations, one of Gulf Coast–affiliated textile specialists, the other of pottery importers and producers with links to Oaxaca.[7]

It is against this apparent Mesoamerican pattern of house-based labor identity that we must reexamine Classic and Postclassic associations of certain kinds of labor with individuals of a particular sex. Repeated images and texts uniquely associate women with spinning and weaving in Maya and Aztec, Classic and Postclassic, sources. Postclassic sources, in particular, assert that all women spun thread and wove, and make of these activities the ground for a stable, enduring differentiation of female gender. Spinning and weaving simultaneously differentiated women from other members of their residential groups and linked them with similar individuals in other groups, apparently overriding the common identity of house members with a dislocated identity as females. But how could such a categorical identification have developed, if we acknowledge that there is in fact no biological basis for assigning these tasks to persons with female sexual organs?

In earlier discussions, I have suggested that the association of these crafts with a class of people (women) could only have taken place through a prior association of distinctive craft production with individuals, a matching of specific craft products with their makers, and the generalization of the characteristics of those individuals onto others, that is, the expectation that other like persons should also be skilled in this area. That projection of expectations might be conceived of as the definition of an arena of competition between members of different houses for simultaneous individual and house aggrandizement. While any craft might be the subject of such competition, the nature of craft products and their social use would define very different kinds of settings for their comparative elaboration and the resulting development of renown for craft workers.

John Clark and Dennis Gosser suggest that pottery serving vessels were the focus of craft elaboration in Early Formative communities of the Pacific coast of Guatemala because of the social significance of patronized feasts in which these vessels could be employed. I have further noted that feasts, as settings, emphasize the creation of face-to-face communities like those involved in daily meals, and that elaboration of pottery vessels thus serves to create small groups of coparticipants. John Clark has also explored the implicit settings that made patronage of obsidian blade production a significant arena of political competition in Formative communities. He points to the significance of the use of blades in ritual action as forging a link between noble patronage, or even control, of ritual practice, and support of craft specialists to produce this item of ritual use. This suggestion could also account for other forms of craft production—that were also directed at creation of regalia and paraphernalia used in ceremony—being supported by noble houses.

The particular characteristics and use made of cloth should provide a basis for understanding why spinning and weaving became distinctive forms of gendered labor in Mesoamerica. Unlike the ritual paraphernalia that included obsidian blades or the pottery vessels of communal feasting, cloth was used first and foremost for individual costume in Mesoamerica. I suggest that it is the intimacy of association between cloth and the body of the individual that allowed the close association of this form of craft production with embodied, sexed, and gendered personhood. By the Postclassic Period, Mesoamerican peoples associated the production of cloth itself with the enactment of heterosexual female sexuality. Aztec riddles established metaphoric links between the actions of the spinner and the young women dancing in public ceremonies wearing the products of their own textile craftworking. The same riddles relate such spinning/dancing to becoming pregnant. Geoffrey and Sharisse McCafferty have explored the extensive linguistic association of weaving with sexual intercourse, implying that the finished cloth is in fact a product of heterosexual collaboration, a metaphoric child of a sexually active couple.

Cloth itself, indeed, can be viewed in Mesoamerica as an additive layer of substance building the body up and out from its core of flesh and bones. Although in Euro-American terms cloth and the body are sharply differentiated as cultural and natural materials, such a division does not seem to apply in Mesoamerican thought. Instead, the person is composed of multiple substances, more and less material, brought together in a specific time and space through the accumulated actions of other social beings:

deities, ancestors, house elders, parents, and women, as spinners and weavers. Classic Maya images showing noble women eliciting the presence of ancestors or spirits through the invocation of visions in the form of serpents may be one end of a continuum of the creation of social beings that also includes the bearing of children and their manifestation through the interventions of midwives; the production and distribution of corn-based foods that formed the substance of bodies; the shaping of the body into social forms through manipulation of the skull, piercing, tattooing, hair-cutting and dressing, and the deliberate crossing of eyes; and the production of exterior layers of elaborate clothing that formed a final social skin—all activities of women wherever information is available on Postclassic Mesoamerican societies.

The women portrayed in monuments in Classic Maya sites swathed in lengths of elaborately embroidered cloth, with underlying layers indicated by overlapping hems, were not simply typical women but exemplary craft workers. The admonitions to noble women recorded in the *Florentine Codex* urge them to excel as weavers not simply, or even primarily, as women but as exemplars of their noble class. The elegant tools made to support spinning and weaving found discarded in the nonruling noble residential quarters of Copan testify to the presence there not just of women, but of noble women with the time and support to develop their skills as textile artists. In this regard, these women were akin to other Mesoamerican women and men we know about from texts who practiced other crafts and distinguished themselves through them: the men and women of the Aztec *amanteca*, the feather workers producing the sumptuary objects used by nobles and rulers to distinguish themselves from others in society; the painters or scribes, male and female, named on Classic Maya polychrome vases and monumental sculptures, whose craft works were used by nobles in daily life and formal ceremonies to demarcate themselves as a class distinct from those they ruled.[8]

Like these and other crafts, textile production most likely drew on the efforts of multiple kinds of people, men and women, young and old, who planted and cared for cotton and maguey plants, processed them to extract the fibers, secured and processed dyes and applied them to the spun threads, and helped in the warping of backstrap looms.[9] All of these other participants are anonymous and unrecorded in the inscriptional media of societies like the Classic Maya and Postclassic Aztec and Maya that preferentially present spinning and weaving as exclusively female activities. The representation of women as a class of weavers should be seen as artificial and as an artifice serving particular political interests.

For the Aztec state, this form of symbolic naming placed all women in a direct relationship to the state unmediated by their membership in individual, distinctive houses. Women's labor was directly accountable to the state, as women were disciplined through the demands for cloth tribute. As the Mexica informants for the *Florentine Codex* themselves suggested, the creation of a class of women was directly parallel to the creation of a class of men equally responsible to the state, through the provision of service in warfare demanded of all young men. And just as women's participation in the defining activities of spinning and weaving was projected onto their bodies through their adoption of the elaborately woven textiles they wore as costume, men's participation in warfare was inscribed on their bodies through ornaments and costumes marking distinctive accomplishment in warfare, directly granted by the Aztec government. Far from being a long-term, stable aspect of individual gender identity, the highlighting of these particular forms of work should be seen as a further discipline of individuals by an intrusive state. The correspondence between Aztec concepts of women as spinners and weavers and contemporary Yucatec Maya practices, and those of other Postclassic states, may reflect practices shared by states linked together through a common set of concepts of value, in which cloth circulated as a material marker of political hierarchy, the materialization of control over the labor of individuals at the smallest-scale level of the household and of control over the materialization of the body through the most intimate media of costume.

Naturalizing the Inscriptional, Performing the Body

The many routes to understanding Mesoamerican genders and their complex relations with age and status lead repeatedly to a concern with the ways that the body served as a site through which individuals were made to experience particular disciplines of their personhood as natural. Judith Butler argues in *Bodies That Matter* that the kinds of socially recognized performances that constitute gender, race, and class in Euro-American society take form through just this kind of embodied performance of intelligible ways of being. She returns to the concept of gender as performance that she proposed in *Gender Trouble* in order to make clear that she was not suggesting a theatrical model for gender, but something I argue is closer to the concept of *habitus* proposed by Pierre Bourdieu. Rephrasing performance as a form of repeated *citation* of a disciplinary norm moves the focus from individual agency alone to individual action within culturally delimited frameworks that make certain kinds of action intelligible as the performance of gender, which is simultaneously the performance of other recognized dimensions of social being. Performance in this sense corresponds to what Paul Connerton calls "practices of bodily incorporation," which are more open and potentially generative of new meanings than their transcription into more permanent media, accomplished by what he calls "practices of inscription." The latter, Connerton suggests, foreclose, or attempt to foreclose, variation, divergence from what Butler would call disciplinary norms, which provide the limits of intelligibility of performance, the expectations through which a viewer in the past or in the present is able to identify a social actor as male or female, adult, elderly, or child.[10]

The absorption of disciplinary norms into bodily practices conveys these into the most intimate aspects of individual being. To the extent that individuals experience their own bodies through their enactment of such reiterated bodily practices, social prescription is naturalized as simply the way things are. The effects of distinguishing clothing, body ornaments, and labor practices along lines of sex include the production of distinctive ways of moving, resting, and acting that cease to be seen as products of specific social practices and instead come to be understood as outcomes of essential biological difference. That this sense of essential, natural difference is a product of specific social circumstances requires repetition, since this fact continues to be ignored or misconstrued in contemporary responses to gender theory.

Clarifying her concept of performative gender is one major objective of Butler's *Bodies That Matter;* another is to confront the materiality of sex. She notes that her exploration of this topic was spurred on by critiques of constructionist approaches to gender and their central claim that genders are socially determined, not innate, biological essentials. Such critiques present the physical existence of bodies with distinct sexual parts, prior to and independent of social interpretations, as inescapably anchoring gender in dichotomous sex. But as Butler notes, these critiques ignore the specific histories by which the apparently "natural" male/female bodily sexual dichotomy is differentially recognized and conceived in different social traditions.

Ruth Hubbard, in *The Politics of Women's Biology,* has offered a concise account of ways that contemporary medicine, in the treatment of anomalously sexed individuals, rationalizes divergence in real bodies from an expectation of clear dichotomies and parallelism from the molecular scale on up. Thomas Laqueur has demonstrated that the contemporary medical model of dichotomous oppositional difference developed from a

quite different understanding of biological sex, based on the European tradition, as the greater and lesser expression of a single, shared human poten-
tiality, including the construal of sexual organs as two versions of a single
form. Page DuBois, in *Sowing the Body,* examines a series of Classical Greek
literary texts in which physical images for femininity—field, furrow, stone,
oven, and tablet—shift over time toward a rhetoric of the female as a "de-
fective" male that is the beginning point of the tradition Laqueur examines.
DuBois demonstrates that what is taken in contemporary psychoanalytic
literature as an ahistorical view of bodily sex is a historically situated set of
representations inscribed in specific Greek literary texts, part of the appa-
ratus for citational performance of gender that Butler's theoretical perspective demands. While bodies have a material reality that is crucial to understanding the relationships of sex and gender, there is no simple physical
priority in which maleness and femaleness are givens.[11]

Connerton stresses the shift that occurs between practices of bodily
incorporation and practices of inscription, which he sees as facilitating the
control of social meaning and attempts to limit—in Butler's terms, "discipline"—social action. He identifies as key features of inscription the use of
more permanent media whose temporal and physical scales are more extensive than those achieved by individualized practices of bodily incorporation. Unlike bodily practices, inscriptional practices persist over longer
spans of time and may be known, seen, and responded to by larger numbers of people. These characteristics—of persistence and greater temporal
and social scale—are shared by a series of practices related to the discipline
of the body initiated in the Formative Period in Mesoamerica. From Central Mexico to Honduras, burials began to incorporate body ornaments in
durable materials, with both forms and materials becoming highly standardized through time. Concurrently, a series of styles of hand-modeled
ceramic figurines present permanent inscriptions of ornamented bodies.
During the same critical interval at a few sites, larger-scale human representations were carved in stone or painted on natural rock surfaces outside
and inside caves. I argue that these three developments are linked inscriptions of practices of bodily incorporation that, among other things, served
as media for the creation of precedents for the citational performance of
gender within emerging centralized polities with interests in the control of
the subjectivity of their population. However else they served, these media
together inscribed certain forms of bodily existence as normative.

Contradiction in the Performative and the Inscriptional

As Butler demonstrates for textual media in the European tradition, the normative presentation of certain bodily ways of being, sexed positions, not only provides the basis for the citational performance of gender, it also creates an arena of abjection, where individual subjectivity is neither recognized nor produced. In this sense, she argues, the materiality of the body is itself a product of the discursive rendering of sex as gender; some bodies, by failing to conform, become the residue, or bodies that literally do not matter. The contemporary Western medical practices described by Hubbard are in part attempts to change such abject bodies into bodies that matter, whose material form is intelligible. The inscription of bodily appearance in Mesoamerica, in both small- and large-scale permanent media, provided a mirror for everyday practices of bodily incorporation, a mirror against which individual performance could be evaluated as better or worse citations of inscribed practices. But Butler argues that all citational performances are guaranteed to fail in their attempts to match the disciplinary norm, a failure that opens the way for transformative potentials.

Inscriptional media like the monuments of the Classic Maya and the narratives of Mexica noble men recorded by the Spanish friar Bernardino de Sahagún in the *Florentine Codex* can be seen as citations of and for particular materializations of the sexed body that assert what Butler calls the heterosexual imperative as ahistorical, permanent, timeless, and natural. But the hegemony of these materializations of sexed bodies rests on the repetitive actions of individuals who enacted them in the residential and performative spaces of Mesoamerican settlements. Within house compounds, infants and children were subjected to the constant presentation of citational performances of adult genders and to periodic demands for disciplined performances on their own part, serving both to incorporate gender in their own bodies and inscribe gendered performance as the repetition of historical precedent.

Practices of bodily incorporation, while not absolutely free of normative constraint, never completely foreclose the difference between a norm and its citation in action. Butler argues that the failure to match the norm in its performative citation leads to repetition of the practice, marking such repetition as a signal of sites of tension. All of the inscriptional sources considered in the previous chapters are characterized by stylization and repetition, by their concern with stereotyping individual performance, and all should be seen as media for the attempted erasure of the actual lapse between citational norms and lived reality. Contradictions between different media have proven a particularly useful point of entry into the arenas where real performances may have diverged most from attempts to discipline them. For example, variation between the imagery of monumental inscriptions in Classic Maya settlements, with their presentation of a unified noble class acting in concert, and the small-scale medium of figurines, highlighting actors marked as explicitly female or male engaged in distinctive activities, pointed to the intersection of ruling-class interests and the assertion of particular gendered ways of being.

The overflow of performance beyond the bounds of the disciplinary norm is also evident in other aspects of Mesoamerican inscriptional media. As Butler suggests, disciplinary materializations of the body simultaneously create a domain of bodily abjection that is specific to the context of their creation. Whereas in Butler's analysis of the Euro-American tradition the domain of the abject is provided by same-sex desire, Mesoamerican histories of the body provide different others: the hermaphrodite, the dwarf, and beings incompletely human, inter-species hybrids. The anxiety of the Euro-American tradition is engaged with sexuality; that of Mesoamerica, with humanity. The construction of Mesoamerican subjectivities is drenched in the instability of species boundaries, as when newborn Aztec infants are described as mineral or vegetal materials needing to be worked into adult human substance. These forms of unintelligibility were given narrative expression in Mesoamerican accounts of cosmogonic action in mythological time.

As Eva Hunt noted, several conquest-era Mesoamerican deities were described as sexually ambiguous, sometimes male, sometimes female. She drew particular attention to the association of such ambiguity with cyclic phenomena, such as the growth of maize (leading to characterizations of maize as male or female at different stages of growth) and the phases of the moon. Several Mesoamerican mythologies place a dual-gendered being at the beginning of creation as the singular parent or creator of subsequent fixed, dichotomously gendered supernaturals. The figure Ometecuhtli of Aztec belief is the most fully described example. Other Aztec deities exhibit gender ambiguity. Cecelia Klein has examined the gender-ambiguous earth deity, Tlaltecuhtli, and the rain and fertility deity, Tlaloc. Other categories of originary beings also tend to display gender duality, as for example the Aztec human founders Oxomoco and Cipactonal or actors in royal histories of the Mexica. These concepts are not limited to the Aztec. Modern ethnographies record the use by specific Maya groups (in this case, the Zinacantec Tzotzil speakers studied by Evon Vogt) of terms like *mothers/fathers (totilme'il)* for the corporate ancestors. Leslie Devereaux argues that dual gender is necessary for the active role of Maya ancestors in founding lines of descent, but it is not separated analytically as a First Mother and First Father.[12]

A direct analogue of the dual-gendered ancestors of contemporary Maya ethnography may be provided by two monuments from Yaxchilan, one naming "Penis Jaguar" as the (presumably male) founder of the line of rulers, the other naming as "founder" a figure shown swathed in the typical robe of Classic Maya women, in this case uniquely tied at the waist by a strip of cloth indistinguishable from a loincloth (Figure 12). The main text of this lintel attributes the actions shown to the contemporary male ruler of the site. Together, these texts from Yaxchilan suggest that the Classic Maya considered lineages to have been founded by a male/female duality, which may have been represented in ritual action by specially costumed males. I have argued that Classic Maya depictions of actors dressed in variations of a beaded net skirt represent similar reenactments of gender-encompassing primordial creativity by Maya rulers. Other scholars have identified these costumes as "male" accoutrements because they are worn by temporally early supernatural beings, the maize god, the moon god, and a fishlike character named in mythological texts at Palenque, GI of the Palenque Triad of gods, presumed to be male. It is notable that these are precisely the same categories of deities whose gender Eva Hunt identified as cyclical.[13] Support for actual gender-ambiguous performances by nobles comes from sixteenth-century descriptions of the Mexica *cihuacoatl*, a male who wore a mixed-gender costume and played a leading role in certain ceremonies.

The dwarf is a second rhetorical figure of the instability of attempts to discipline bodily subjectivity in Mesoamerica, and like dual-gendered beings, was relegated through narratives to ancient times of creation, before the imposition of orderly organization that was required for daily life. Posthispanic texts from the highlands of Guatemala that record the specific creation traditions of different political factions of Quiché and Cakquichel Maya provide examples of these narratives. The best-known of these texts, that of the dominant Quiché lineage, translated as the *Popol Vuh*, features actions of Hero Twins through which cosmological order is enjoined. Among the feats performed by the Hero Twins is an episode related to the construction of a house, perhaps the first house in creation, by a group called the four hundred boys. The word translated as "boys" is in fact ambiguous in the original Quiché: used in modern and colonial Quiché to refer to either male or female youths, it is also cognate with terms for un-ripe fruit. These unripe youths in fact fail to construct their house. Like other dwarfs, they have no descendants.[14]

Folk traditions from contemporary Maya in highland Guatemala, Chiapas, and lowland Yucatan reflect similar conceptions of the dwarf as an immature form of human from early creation times, sometimes of am-biguous sexual status, that fails to have descendants to continue its heri-tage. Modern Quiché tell tales of a dwarf who lives in one of the major volcanoes and operates as a trickster. The traditions of the Chamula and Zinacantec Tzotzil Maya of Chiapas include tales of dwarf people from previous creations who continue to exist in the interior of the earth, envi-ous of contemporary humanity. Yucatecan stories of creation also assign the dwarf people to an early stage of creation and attribute their inability to persist to their failures in specific social arenas: they cannibalized their own offspring and thus were condemned to the earth's interior.[15]

The figure of the dwarf appears in the visual imagery of prehispanic Mesoamerican societies in ways that suggest it was a materialization of primordial being, outside the disciplinary norms of performative subjec-tivity that these societies sought to enforce.[16] In Classic Maya artworks, dwarf figures are a constant element of a composition known as the "Hol-mul dancer," after the site where a group of these images were executed on pottery. This composition depicts an ambiguously gendered deity, usually identified as the maize god, dancing in company with a dwarf in a watery setting marked by the presence of long-necked cormorants. Monumen-tal sculptures attributed to the site of Calakmul show a pair of histori-cal nobles dressed in costumes related to this scene engaged in a similar masked dance. On one stela, a figure named in text as the male ruler is pre-sented wearing a jewel-encrusted mask and feather panaches, with water lilies in his headdress at which fish are shown nibbling. Facing this sculp-ture, a second stela shows a person named in the text as a noble woman dressed in the netted skirt of the deity in the Holmul dancer scene. In front of her stands a dwarf, engaged (as are the man and woman) in the motions of the dance. At Yaxchilan, another sculpture associates a living ruler with the figure of the dwarf in a context marked as taking place in the ancient past by the use of calendrical notation. Inscribed on the riser of an exterior stairway leading to a temple perched on a hill, this monument presents an anthropomorphic figure, dressed in the beaded skirt and bearing an entire crocodilian on its back, standing at the base of a set of stairs along with two dwarf figures (Figure 26). Here the movement of the dance is replaced by

Figure 26. A figure dressed in a net-skirt kilt plays ball accompanied by two dwarf figures. The text cites an ancient ballgame linked to a historic game played by the ruler of the site. Yaxchilan Structure 33, Hieroglyphic Stairway 2, Step VII. Ian Graham, *Corpus of Maya Hieroglyphic Inscriptions, Volume 3, Part 3, Yaxchilan.* Peabody Museum of Archaeology and Ethnology. Courtesy of Ian Graham. Copyright 1982 by the President and Fellows of Harvard College.

Figure 27. Altar from San Lorenzo with ledge held up by dwarf figures. Potrero Nuevo, Monument 2. Figure 496 from *In the Land of the Olmec*, Volume 1: *The Archaeology of San Lorenzo Tenochtitlan*, by Michael Coe and Richard Diehl, copyright 1980. Courtesy of the University of Texas Press.

the formalized movement of the ballgame, as the anthropomorphic figure bends a knee to receive a ball that rolls down the stairs. The text on this monument places the action millennia before the Classic Maya Period, but names the actor with the names and titles of the eighth-century Maya ruler. The spatiotemporal setting of the scene, in a primordial ballcourt, places the action before the institution of orderly discipline, which, among other effects, relegated dwarfs to a realm of bodily abjection.

The inscribed figure of the dwarf had already been in use in Mesoamerica for over one thousand years when the Classic Maya employed it in their creation narratives. Three-dimensional Formative Period Gulf Coast Olmec monuments, the stone seats of power originally labeled "altars," include a number depicting figures holding small-scale anthropomorphic figures, sometimes described as "were-jaguar babies." [17] These figures present a hybrid of human and nonhuman features: fangs and non-natural eyes, cleft heads, and the proportions of dwarf figures. In addition to their promi-

Figure 28. Drainstone from San Lorenzo in shape of dwarf figure. San Lorenzo, Monument 52. Figure 494 from *In the Land of the Olmec*, Volume 1: *The Archaeology of San Lorenzo Tenochtitlan*, by Michael Coe and Richard Diehl, copyright 1980. Courtesy of the University of Texas Press.

nence in compositions where they are held loosely or struggle in the arms of human actors, such dwarf figures are depicted in both monumental and small-scale media as independent subjects. In monumental art, dwarf figures are shown holding up the ledge on a monumental stone throne (Figure 27), a location otherwise marked as the earth interior. One dwarf figure was pierced to serve as a drainstone in the formal water channeling system of San Lorenzo (Figure 28). Smaller-scale dwarf figures made as hollow clay effigies, most without excavation provenience, are typical of a variety of Highland Central Mexican village sites of the Early Formative Period. These "baby" figures are notable for their depiction as nude and sexless, forming a counterpoint to contemporary solid hand-modeled figurines from the same region that represent explicit female anatomy and gendered male dress in the form of loincloths.[18]

The narrative setting of dwarf figures on Gulf Coast monuments associates them with the earth interior to which caves provided access, and from which Olmec rulers showed themselves emerging. The sides of one Olmec altar show a series of anthropomorphic figures struggling to control animated dwarf figures, but failing to approximate the serenity and control exhibited by the central person on the front of the same monument, in whose arms lies a relaxed dwarf figure (Figure 29). The collapse of the segregation of the cave from the settlement in these monuments, and the active threat to order provided by the dwarf, serve to emphasize the control exercised over this domain of abjection by the ruler portrayed. The manipulation of figurines of the dwarf in ceremonial performance reiterated the same control. The lack of the bodily signs of adult gender on Formative Period dwarf figures, a sign of their sexed position as one of abjection, makes of them media for the assertion of discipline by authorities, of power over individual subjectivity. The dwarf figures shown at rest in the arms of rulers, holding up the throne or channeling rainwater in controlled fashion, are provided with the trappings of sexed adult positions: loincloths, shaped hair, ear and body ornaments. As a statement of power, such Formative monuments asserted an ability to discipline even the overflow of intelligibility.

Gender, Discipline, Power, and Resistance

Judith Butler's analyses take the societal imperative of heterosexuality as a driving force behind constructions of normative gender in Euro-American cultures. Mesoamerican systems of thought made the political circumscrip-

Figure 29. Side of altar showing seated adult male figure struggling to control dwarf figure. La Venta Altar 5. Drawing courtesy of David C. Grove.

tion of gender challenging for authorities seeking to discipline gendered performance into the narrow confines of acceptable citational practices. That such attempts were an issue would be evident from the stereotyping of Mesoamerican human representations alone, even without abundant sixteenth-century documentation of this desire. The admonitions of Aztec parents to their children, the discipline of Aztec children in gendered labor, dress, and action, and the denunciations of deviation from these norms of decorum found in the *Florentine Codex* amply testify to the concerns of one of Mesoamerica's most centralized polities with the production of dichotomous heterosexual adult genders. Although the material is more terse and native voices are absent, the descriptions of Postclassic Yucatec Maya society provided by the sixteenth-century *Relación de las cosas de Yucatán* of Bishop Diego de Landa express a parallel concern with the production of disciplined, heterosexual adult men and women in these smaller-scale states. Far from reflecting a reification of an essential gender dichotomy, these late Mesoamerican disciplinary practices were carried out against a philosophical background of original gender fluidity and were themselves an activity through which stable genders emerged.

Unlike the modern European solution to the imposition of disciplinary norms of gender and the production of sexed positions, the citational norms of Mesoamerica were based on the conception of human subjectivity as fluid. The emergence of heterosexually reproductive male and female sexed positions in early adulthood, brought about through social action, was not only undermined by the simultaneous production of the sexed position of abstinence shared by boys and girls dedicated to the temples, but was also by no means permanent. Like the cyclical phenomena of nature embodied in the deity personalities of maize and the moon, human beings continued to shift their sexed positions, and in older age, adults again formed more of a common category than a parallel dichotomy. In keeping with the somewhat different disciplinary concerns of Mesoamerican authorities, the realm of abjection that served to demarcate citational intelligibility was marked by species instability, the absence or overabundance of genitalia, and not primarily—or perhaps at all—by the figure of same-sex desire. Without that figure as an image of abjection, we simply are not in a position to know how alternative sexualities were received in Mesoamerican societies. We are in no position to foreclose, as Mesoamerican inscriptions did not, the possibility of elective sexual abstinence, or of sexual activity without reproduction, both heterosexual and homosexual.

The admonitions recorded in sixteenth-century sources emanated from state governments actively involved in extending their control of, and power over, individuals and houses. There can be no doubt that these states did desire to limit and control the expression of human possibilities. But the continued persistence of houses as the primary context of socialization, even in the most centralized states of the immediate preconquest period, clearly counterbalanced the intrusion of the state into daily life. While specific rhetoric and practices in the Aztec state served to extract all young men and present them as an abstract class of warriors, some proportion, probably quite large, of these same young men left the Houses of Youths to take up a place in their house of birth and follow a craft or occupation there. And even those men who were distinguished as career warriors continued to be subject to reappropriation by other house members, as when the warrior's house celebrated a particularly illustrious capture. Although women were in theory abstracted as a category (exemplified by noble women) by being given a single common defining experience as spinners and weavers serving the state economy, in practice many women were not primarily engaged in these activities. And those that were, subverted the official state ideology through their own association of pleasure, including sexual pleasure, with weaving.

As house societies, Mesoamerican states were subject to the possibility of a contest of control between political authorities and house elders. As it was in Tokugawa Japan, this possibility was largely resolved by the unique institutions of the Aztec state, although the accounts of *pochteca* consumption and concerns with claiming due status without overstepping allowable boundaries show that it was not completely absent. State and house control formed a more evident site of tension in contemporary Postclassic Yucatec states, where government was limited in the level of demands that it could make on the production of individual houses. In Classic Maya cities, houses reclaimed credit for the productive actions of their women, excised or reinterpreted in official imagery through the creation of divergent images in different media.

Political competition that took place between ruling and other noble houses opened up specific kinds of space for individuals to resist control of imposed sexed positions. To the extent that houses sought to maintain their own independent pools of labor by retaining all offspring as residents, alternatives to compulsory heterosexual marriage might have been possible. In her ethnographic account of the noble houses of Tanimbar, in Indonesia, Susan McKinnon demonstrates that the restriction of formal marriage to a very few individuals in great houses actually increased the possibility of alternative arrangements for others. We need to populate our Mesoamerican landscapes with single women and men engaged in consensual sexual relations without jural sanctions to match such ethnographic realities, instead of imagining a landscape of idealized heterosexually reproductive marital couples. We need to allow for the presence in Mesoamerican settlements of young men's houses, establishments of ritual specialists, and other settings within which individuals could choose not to follow the single routine that late states attempted to represent as the only reality.

The media of inscription that we have recovered from prehispanic Mesoamcrican societies are not simply reflections of reality; they are means through which certain contended territories were anxiously subjected to attempts at control, of both practice and interpretation, by authorities at multiple scales. We must consider such media as suggestive hints at the lack of uniformity, rather than the reverse. We need to allow for the openings made, when the interests in control of different authorities clashed, for individuals to create some freedom of action. And we must allow the possibility that the people living these realities entertained different understandings of their place in the world than the construals made by central authorities, or we will simply project the political claims of certain groups on reality and deliver for them a result they could never have effected in the world they actually inhabited.

Notes

1. GENDER, PERFORMANCE, POWER, AND REPRESENTATION

1. Rosaldo and Lamphere (1974); compare Moore (1988), di Leonardo (1991).

2. "The 'facts of life' with which man [*sic*] has had to come to terms in the process of adaptation, and which are immediately relevant to the study of kinship and marriage, can perhaps be reduced to four basic 'principles': . . . Principle 3 The men usually exercise control. . . . Gestation, impregnation, domination, and the avoidance of incest lie at the root of all social organization. The first two are unremarkable but unavoidable. . . . The third is no doubt contentious, but I feel that objections to it are somehow unreal. By and large it is overwhelmingly true and for very good reasons. One does not need to recapitulate the evolutionary history of man to see why. For the greater part of human history, women were getting on with their highly specialized task of bearing and rearing the children. It was the men who hunted the game, fought the enemies, and made the decisions. This is, I am convinced, rooted in primate nature, and while social conditions in the very recent past of some advanced societies have given women the opportunity to have more say in things, I still think that most women would agree with the contention. This is not to say that from her hearth the woman does not exercise enormous influence—that is why I have qualified it by saying 'usually'; but the sheer physiological facts of existence make her role secondary to that of the male in the decision-making process at any level higher than the purely domestic. . . . Given a few 'by and large' and 'other things being equal' clauses, I feel that Principle 3 holds good" (R. Fox 1967:31–32).

3. See Ortner (1974), Ortner and Whitehead (1981).

4. See di Leonardo (1991:26–27), Conkey and Tringham (1995).

5. See essays collected in MacCormack and Strathern (1980), Ortner and Whitehead (1981), Strathern (1987), and Sanday and Goodenough (1990). Visweswaran (1997) reviews the development of feminist ethnography and the challenges to essentialism. For examination of the intersections of class, race, age, and gender, see

Silverblatt (1987), Yanagisako and Collier (1987), and Zavella (1991). In archaeology, see especially Gilchrist (1994, 1999) and Meskell (1999).

6. Conkey and Williams (1991:122), citing Elshtain (1986).

7. Seler (1923), Tozzer (1957), Proskouriakoff (1961), Schele (1979), Taube (1985), A. Stone (1991); see R. Joyce (1994, 1996a), and Chapter 3 below.

8. See Hubbard (1990) and Laqueur (1990).

9. See Butler (1990, 1993).

10. Niederberger (1976).

11. See, for example, Agurcia (1977, 1978), Grove and Gillespie (1984), Gillespie (1987), R. Joyce (1992d, 1993b), Cyphers Guillén (1993), Clark (1994), Lesure (1997b), J. Marcus (1999); see also Chapter 2 below.

12. Such as for Postclassic Yucatan (Landa 1941:128-129, 151-160) and Postclassic Tenochtitlan (Sahagún 1954, 1961); also see Chapters 4 and 5 below.

13. Connerton (1989:72-104); compare Davis (1993). See R. Joyce (1998).

14. Herzfeld (1991).

15. Parmentier (1987:1-15, 107-126, 305-309).

16. Compare R. Joyce (1992c, 1993b, 1996a).

17. Munn (1986:96-97, 101-102).

18. Kensinger (1991:43, 47-48), Howard (1991:62).

19. Weiner (1976), Kensinger (1991), Munn (1986).

20. O'Neale (1932, 1945), Friedrich (1970), Hardin (1977, 1979, 1983); compare Whitten (1985:105-214).

21. Compare Coggins (1975:184-186), J. Marcus (1987).

22. See Weiner (1976, 1992), Kan (1989), McKinnon (1991).

23. Gillespie and Joyce (1997).

24. Morley and Morley (1938), Proskouriakoff (1974), Freidel and Sabloff (1984), Andrews (1986), Matos Moctezuma (1996).

25. Tate (1992).

26. M. Coe (1966), Schele and Miller (1986:119).

27. Houston and Taube (1987); see also Mathews (1979), Justeson (1983), and R. Joyce and Shumaker (1995:46).

28. Proskouriakoff (1944, 1974), Mathews (1979, 1985:44), Mathews and Pendergast (1979), Stuart (1985), Schele and Miller (1986:118, 120-121).

29. Sperber (1992:60-64); quotation from p. 63, emphasis added.

30. Herzfeld (1992:68-69); original emphasis.

31. Barthes (1977a:73).

32. Barthes (1977c:38-39).

33. Herzfeld (1992:79); original emphasis.

34. Barthes (1977b:92-101; 1977c:48-51).

35. Barthes (1977b:101, 120-122).

36. Barthes (1977c:45-46); see also (1977b:116).

2. NEGOTIATING SEX AND GENDER IN FORMATIVE
MESOAMERICA

1. See Grove (1981a), Stark (1981), Clark and Gosser (1995).

2. Flannery and Winter (1976), Winter (1976); see also Prindiville and Grove (1987), Tolstoy (1989), Wilk and Wilhite (1991), Rust (1992), Hendon (1999).

3. Blake (1991), Clark (1991, 1994), Clark and Blake (1993), and Lesure (1997a, 1997b).

4. Lévi-Strauss (1983, especially pp. 172-174; 1987), Errington (1987), Boon (1990:213-218); compare J. J. Fox (1980:10-11) and essays in Joyce and Gillespie (2000).

5. For example, McKinnon (1991:84-106); compare Weiner (1976), Munn (1986).

6. Cunningham (1964), Waterson (1990).

7. Lévi-Strauss (1983:174); compare Weiner (1992).

8. Schneider (1984), Kan (1989).

9. McKinnon (1991:134-162, 199-226).

10. Boon (1990:215).

11. McKinnon (1991:259-276).

12. D. Chase and A. Chase (1992), J. Marcus (1992); compare Hirth (1992), G. Marcus (1992).

13. Gillespie and Joyce (1997).

14. Grove (1993, 1999); compare Baudez and Becquelin (1973), Flannery and Marcus (1976), Sharer (1978), M. Coe and Diehl (1980), Lowe (1981), Grove and Angulo (1987), Gerhardt and Hammond (1991), González Lauck (1994), Cyphers Guillén (1999).

15. R. Joyce (1992d, 1992e, 1999), Love (1992, 1999).

16. Flannery and Winter (1976), J. Marcus (1989); compare Grove (1987a, 1987b, 1987c), Prindiville and Grove (1987), Love (1991, 1999), Rust (1992), Cyphers Guillén (1999).

17. Pires-Ferreira (1976), Clark and Lee (1984), Clark (1987, 1991), R. Joyce (1999).

18. Drennan (1976), Flannery (1976), R. Joyce (1999).

19. Grove (1989, 1993); compare Demarest (1989), Clark (1990), R. Joyce (1992d).

20. P. Friedrich (1991:34), Herzfeld (1992:83-84).

21. Clark and Blake (1993), Clark and Gosser (1995, especially p. 216), Hoopes (1995:192), Lesure (1998).

22. Longacre (1995:279).

23. Compare Munn (1986:20).

24. Tolstoy (1989), R. Joyce (1999).

25. Pyne (1976), J. Marcus (1989), Flannery and Marcus (1994).

26. Compare R. Joyce, Edging, Lorenz, and Gillespie (1991), R. Joyce (1992e, 1996c, 1999), Flannery and Marcus (1994), J. Marcus (1999); see also Gordon (1898a), Popenoe (1934), Baudez and Becquelin (1973), Healy (1974), Viel and Cheek (1983), Fash (1985), Rue, Freter, and Ballinger (1989), R. Joyce and Henderson (1996).

27. Clark and Blake (1993:23–28).

28. Compare M. Friedrich (1970), Hardin (1979, 1983).

29. R. Joyce (1999); see, for example, Baudez and Becquelin (1973), Lowe (1981), Clark (1983), R. Joyce (1987), Merry de Morales (1987).

30. Porter (1953), Piña Chan (1958), and García Moll et al. (1991); compare Serra and Sugiura (1987), Tolstoy (1989), and R. Joyce (1999).

31. Findley (1990); compare Anawalt (1981).

32. D1 figurines; George Vaillant (1930).

33. Anawalt (1981).

34. Unless otherwise noted, all comments on Tlatilco burials are from the analysis reported in R. Joyce (1999), based on García Moll et al. (1991).

35. Carlsen (1988); Museo de San Pedro Sula, Honduras (personal observation).

36. Serra and Sugiura (1987), Tolstoy (1989).

37. Ochoa (1996c:189); compare Niederberger (1996:87).

38. Lesure (1997b).

39. Gordon (1898b), Popenoe (1930, 1934), Strong, Kidder, and Paul (1938), D. Stone (1941:70–71, 73–75, fig. 68, 74), Kennedy (1981), Pope (1985), Hendon and Joyce (1993), R. Joyce and Henderson (1996).

40. Agurcia (1977, 1978).

41. Agurcia (1977:23), Kennedy (1981:278), Healy (1992:94–96).

42. R. Joyce (1997); compare R. Joyce (1993b). All percentages refer to the Peabody Museum collection.

43. Peabody Museum catalogue numbers 20/2474, 2476.

44. Peabody Museum catalogue number 33-57-20/2523.

45. For example, Peabody Museum catalogue number 36-46-20/C11019.

46. For example, Peabody Museum catalogue numbers 33-57-20/2770, 96-35-20/C1144, 33-57-20/2471, 2478, 2486, 36-97-20/4626.

47. Canby (1951:81), Baudez and Becquelin (1973:21–23, 47–51, 393–396), Joesink-Mandeville (1987:203), R. Joyce (1992d, 1992e, 1999).

48. Popenoe (1934); compare R. Joyce (1992d, 1996c, 1999).

49. See Sheets (1978:45–47).

50. Baudez and Becquelin (1973:49, 91–93); compare Clark (1983), R. Joyce (1987, 1999), Merry de Morales (1987).

51. Grove and Angulo (1987), Prindiville and Grove (1987: 63), Grove (1999).

52. Grove and Gillespie (1984), Gillespie (1987), Grove (1987a:423–426), Cyphers Guillén (1993).

53. Prindiville and Grove (1987:65, 66); compare Blake (1991), Lesure (1997a).

54. Grove and Cyphers Guillén (1987:34, 37–41, 46–48).

55. Merry de Morales (1987), Thomson (1987).

56. Pohorilenko (1996:121–124).

57. Grove (1981b:60), Cyphers Guillén (1984), Grove and Angulo (1987).

58. Grove (1981b); compare J. Porter (1989).

59. De la Fuente (1973, especially p. 33), M. Coe and Diehl (1980, especially pp. 307, 309, 320), Grove (1981b:66), Grove and Angulo (1987).

60. The following discussion is summarized from R. Joyce (1987), based on data in Drucker (1952) and Drucker, Heizer, and Squier (1959); compare González Lauck (1994, 1996).

61. Grove (1981a, 1984).
62. De la Fuente (1996).
63. Merry de Morales (1987), Grove and Gillespie (1992).
64. Compare Schele and Miller (1986:68).
65. R. Joyce, Edging, Lorenz, and Gillespie (1991); compare M. Coe (1977).
66. Andrews (1987).
67. See Castro-Leal (1996).
68. Serra and Sugiura (1987), Tolstoy (1989), García Moll et al. (1991), R. Joyce (1999).
69. Carlson (1981).
70. Serra and Sugiura (1987), Tolstoy (1989).
71. J. Marcus (1989:169, 195-196; 1999).
72. Merry de Morales (1987), Grove and Gillespie (1992).
73. Cyphers Guillén (1984), Grove (1989:142-145).
74. Compare Lesure (1997b).
75. Grove and Angulo (1987), Grove (1999).
76. Clark and Lee (1984), Clark (1987, 1991).
77. Clark and Parry (1990), Clark (1996).
78. Clark and Blake (1993), Clark and Gosser (1995).
79. Arnold (1985), R. Wright (1991); compare Reents (1985), Reents-Budet (1994).
80. M. Friedrich (1970), Lathrap (1976, 1983), Hardin (1977, 1983), Lathrap and DeBoer (1979), Whitten (1985).
81. Whitehead (1981:88, 102, 104).
82. Flannery and Winter (1976), Carlson (1981), Grove (1987a, 1987b), Thomson (1987), Love (1991, 1992, 1999), R. Joyce (1992d, 1999), Rust (1992), Garber, Grove, Hirth, and Hoopes (1993), Hendon (1999), J. Marcus (1999). See Pohl (1991) for a proposal that Formative Period Maya women specialized in the same economic activities later noted for them in the Postclassic Period.
83. J. Porter (1989), Gillespie (1994), Cyphers Guillén (1999).

3. NARRATIVES OF GENDER AMONG THE CLASSIC MAYA

1. In using the term "Maya world," I am specifically indebted to John S. Henderson. See essays in Sabloff and Henderson (1993).
2. Almazán St. Hill (1994).
3. See essays in Macri and Ford (1997); compare essays in Justeson and Campbell (1984) and MacLeod (1987).
4. See especially Schele and Miller (1986), Schele and Freidel (1990), Freidel, Schele, and Parker (1993).
5. See Hammond (1992, 1999), Sharer (1992), Valdés (1992), Hendon (1999), Ringle (1999).
6. Aveni (1980), Justeson (1988).
7. Sharer and Sedat (1973), J. Marcus (1975), M. Coe (1976), Justeson (1986), Sedat (1992).
8. Freidel and Schele (1988a, 1988b); compare Freidel (1988, 1993).
9. Sanders and Webster (1988); see also J. Marcus (1983), D. Chase, A. Chase, and Haviland (1990).

10. Gillespie and Joyce (1997); compare Willey (1981), Tourtellot (1983), Hendon (1991, 1992c, 1997, 1999), Sharer (1993), McAnany (1995).

11. Kurjack and Andrews (1976), Kurjack (1979), Ringle (1999); compare Folan (1991).

12. For example, Pohl (1985), Lentz (1991), Ball (1993), Gerry (1997); compare Chase and Chase (1992).

13. See Hammond (1991), Mathews (1991), J. Marcus (1992), Stuart (1997); compare A. Chase (1992).

14. Tourtellot (1983), Webster and Gonlin (1988), Haviland and Moholy-Nagy (1992), Hendon (1992a), McAnany (1995).

15. Harrison (1970), W. Coe (1990).

16. Jones and Satterthwaite (1982), Haviland (1997).

17. A. Stone (1988, 1995).

18. By Proskouriakoff (1961), J. Miller (1974), J. Marcus (1976:157–179; 1987), Schele (1979), and Bruhns (1988); compare R. Joyce (1992a, 1996a).

19. Taube (1985), A. Stone (1991:201–202).

20. See R. Joyce (1994); compare Gillespie and Joyce (1998).

21. Clancy (1983, 1986); see Barthes (1977b, 1977c).

22. Justeson (1984).

23. Closs (1992).

24. See R. Joyce (1992a, 1992c, 1993b, 1996a).

25. R. Joyce (1992a); see also W. Morris (1985a, 1985b). J. E. S. Thompson (1962:361–362), Justeson (1984:356), Schele and Miller (1986:83, 124, 151, 326–327), and Lounsbury (1989) document the "sky penis" title.

26. Hendon (1991:902; 1992b; 1997).

27. For example, Willey (1972:7–8; 1978:7–9), Hammond (1975:371–374), Hendon (1991:909–910); compare Beaudry (1984).

28. See Rands and Rands (1965); compare T. Joyce (1933:plate IV, 8), Willey (1972:figs. 34b, 34f), Clancy, Coggins, and Culbert (1985:65, 159), Schele and Miller (1986:plate 51), Hammond (1988:fig. 6.2).

29. Pohl and Feldman (1982), Pohl (1991).

30. Conides (1984).

31. Clarkson (1978), Foncerrada de Molina and Lombardo de Ruiz (1979); compare Hammond (1975:320, fig. 116c; 1988:figs. 5.3 and 6.3), Clancy, Coggins, and Culbert (1985:163, 179), Reents-Budet (1994:253–275).

32. Clancy, Coggins, and Culbert (1985:141; fig. 8); compare Schele and Freidel (1990, opposite page 255), Eggebrecht, Eggebrecht, and Grube (1992:149).

33. Reents-Budet (1994:328).

34. Eggebrecht, Eggebrecht, and Grube (1992:476).

35. Stuart (1988b), Houston, Stuart, and Taube (1989), Hall, Tarka, Hurst, Stuart, and Adams (1990), Reents-Budet (1994).

36. See R. Joyce (1996a); compare A. Stone (1988).

37. Proskouriakoff (1960).

38. W. Morris (1985a:253).

39. Bruhns (1988); compare Carlson and Landis (1985).

40. Taube (1985).

41. J. Marcus (1987:149).

42. R. Joyce (1992a); compare Taube (1985), Schele and Miller (1986:53, 77).

43. Robertson (1974), Schele and Miller (1986:45).

44. A. Stone (1995:143-146).

45. J. E. S. Thompson (1961), Joralemon (1973), Stuart (1984, 1988a), Schele and Miller (1986, especially 180-181, 192, 193, plates 68, 72).

46. J. E. S. Thompson (1962:361-362), Justeson (1984:356), Schele and Miller (1986:83, 151), Lounsbury (1989).

47. Hunt (1977), Taube (1985).

48. J. Marcus (1976), Proskouriakoff (1993:92-93, 127-128); compare Schele and Freidel (1990:315-316, 486), Fash (1991).

49. Berlin (1963), Kelley (1965), Lounsbury (1976, 1980, 1985), Schele (1976, 1990), Clancy (1986), Schele and Freidel (1990:237-261), Josserand (1991), R. Joyce (1992b), Houston (1996), Schele and Villela (1996).

50. Schele and Mathews (1991), Gillespie and Joyce (1997).

51. J. Marcus (1976:150-182; 1987), Closs (1984, 1985), Houston and Mathews (1985), Houston (1993); compare Gossen and Leventhal (1993).

52. Schele (1979), Schele and Freidel (1990:216-261); compare Bassie-Sweet (1991).

53. Proskouriakoff (1960), J. A. Fox and Justeson (1986); see also P. Thompson (1982).

54. Proskouriakoff (1963, 1964), R. Carrasco (1985), Schele and Miller (1986:186-190), Schele and Freidel (1990:262-305), Tate (1991, 1992).

55. See R. Joyce (1992a, 1996a, 1996b); compare Schele (1991a:74-75), Schele and Mathews (1991:234-239), Tate (1992:89, 204, 276).

56. Gailey (1987a, 1987b).

57. For example, Muller (1987), Kan (1989).

58. Weiner (1976, 1989).

59. Compare Gailey (1987b) with Silverblatt (1987; 1988:439-444); see also Murra (1989).

4. TRANSFORMING GENDER: CLASSIC TO POSTCLASSIC MAYA

1. After Wonderley (1981, 1985).

2. See Culbert (1973a).

3. Culbert (1973b).

4. A. Chase (1985b, 1990), Freidel (1985), D. Rice (1986), P. Rice (1986), D. Rice and P. Rice (1990), Proskouriakoff (1993:185-187).

5. Bullard (1973), Willey (1973); see also Leventhal, Ashmore, LeCount, Hetrick, and Jamison (1992), Leventhal, Zeleznik, Jamison, LeCount, McGovern, Sanchez, and Keller (1993), Leventhal (1996).

6. D. Chase and A. Chase (1982), E. Graham (1985), Pendergast (1986), D. Chase (1990), Pyburn (1990); compare Fields (1994).

7. R. Joyce (1986, 1991a); compare E. Graham (1985), Pendergast (1986), E. Graham and Pendergast (1989), Guderjan, Garber, Smith, Stross, Michel, and Asaro (1989).

8. Fash and Lane (1983), Sharer (1985), R. Joyce (1986, 1991b), Webster and

Freter (1990), Freter (1992), Webster, Rue, and Freter (1993), Paine and Freter (1996), Paine, Freter, and Webster (1996); but contrast Fash and Sharer (1991), Braswell (1992).

9. Sabloff and Willey (1967), Adams (1973), J. Graham (1973), Rands (1973), Sabloff (1973).

10. Shimkin (1973).

11. Abrams and Rue (1988).

12. Saul (1973); compare Storey (1992), L. Wright and White (1996), L. Wright (1997).

13. See essays in Culbert (1991).

14. A. Chase (1985b)

15. A. Chase, N. Grube, and D. Chase (1991), Schele (1991b), B. Fash, W. Fash, Lane, Larios, Schele, Stomper, and Stuart (1992).

16. Cowgill (1979).

17. Houston and Mathews (1985), Houston (1993), Demarest (1997), Demarest, O'Mansky, Wolley, van Tuerenhout, Inomata, Palka, and Escobedo (1997), Escobedo (1997), Inomata (1997), Valdés (1997).

18. Compare J. Marcus (1992).

19. Wonderley (1981, 1985); compare Fox (1994), Pohl and Pohl (1994).

20. Miller (1993). See Tozzer (1957) and Lincoln (1990) for syntheses of the archaeology of Chichen Itza, and Ruppert (1952) for an overview of architectural plans. Coggins and Shane (1984) and Coggins (1992) provide reviews of the history of research at the site.

21. See Bolles (1977) for a description of the largest of these palace complexes, the Monjas, and Ruscheinsky (1995) for a discussion of gender hierarchy implicit in the features of this palace.

22. Cohodas (1978), Ball (1979), Lincoln (1986, 1990).

23. Ruppert (1931), Ashmore (1991).

24. E. Morris (1925), E. Thompson (1938), Ruppert (1952).

25. For details of the investigation of the Caracol and the Temple of the Warriors, see E. Morris, Charlot, and A. Morris (1931) and Ruppert (1935).

26. Cohodas (1978) and Wren (1991, 1994) discuss the Great Ballcourt complex.

27. Ruppert (1943); compare Ruppert (1950), Ruppert and Smith (1955).

28. Tozzer (1957:110, 173-175, 268); compare Schele and Freidel (1990:346-376).

29. The following discussion is based on R. Joyce (1990). Compare A. Stone (1999) for a very different examination of the same images.

30. Tozzer (1957), J. E. S. Thompson (1970).

31. Seler (1923); compare Tozzer (1957:90, 119, 175-176).

32. A. Miller (1977), Coggins (1984).

33. Tozzer (1957:175).

34. For example, Cohodas (1978), Coggins (1984).

35. Tozzer (1957:110, 175, 268).

36. See E. Morris, Charlot, and A. Morris (1931), Wren and Schmidt (1991), and Wren (1994).

37. Freidel (1981); see also Stromsvik (1937), Ruppert (1943, 1950).

38. Lincoln (1990:625), following Klein (1987:298-317).
39. Wren and Schmidt (1991:215-222), Wren (1994).
40. Kelley (1968, 1982), Kowalski (1989), Ringle (1990), Schele and Freidel (1990:349-352, 355-367, 370-374), Wren and Schmidt (1991).
41. A. Miller (1977), Coggins (1984).
42. Wren, Schmidt, and Krochock (1989), Wren (1991).
43. Ball and Ladd (1992), Coggins and Ladd (1992).
44. Moholy-Nagy, Ladd, and Trembour (1992).
45. Krochock (1998).
46. Kelley (1968, 1982), Proskouriakoff (1970), Grube and Stuart (1987:8-10), Kowalski (1989), Ringle (1990), Schele and Freidel (1990:356-364), Krochock (1991), J. A. Fox (1997).
47. Freidel (1992a:112); compare Schele and Miller (1986), Mathews and Willey (1991:65), Schele and Mathews (1991:245-248).
48. Webster (1993); compare Wren and Schmidt (1991:209-210), Freidel (1992a).
49. Landa (1941); compare J. Marcus (1976), Clendinnen (1982), A. Stone (1988, 1991).
50. Compare Landa (1941:114) and Codex Tro-Cortesianus (1967:95).
51. Landa (1941:128-129; compare 143-147); emphasis added.
52. For the sections cited, see Landa (1941:128-129, 143, 145, 147).
53. For the sections cited, see Landa (1941:143, 145, 92, 128).
54. Landa (1941:154, 155)
55. Landa (1941:125-129, 159); compare Clark and Houston (1995) on weaving.
56. Landa (1941:159).
57. For the sections cited, see Landa (1941:88, 125, 126).
58. Landa (1941:125, 88, 129, 102).
59. Landa (1941:102-106, 125, 129); compare Schneider (1984).
60. Landa (1941:159).
61. Landa (1941:102, 124, 100, 129); see also Gillespie and Joyce (1997); compare Kan (1989).
62. A. Stone (1999).
63. Rands and Rands (1965:545, fig. 24), Eggebrecht, Eggebrecht, and Grube (1992: catalogue number 164).
64. For example, Kelemen (1956:plate 134c).
65. Ruppert, Thompson, and Proskouriakoff (1955), M. Miller (1986); see also Mathews (1980), Houston (1984), M. Miller (1985, 1988).
66. Schele and Freidel (1990:235-237, 239-240, 470-471), Schele and Miller (1986:114).
67. Compare Closs (1984, 1985), R. Joyce (in press).
68. In the J. E. S. Thompson (1962) system, this is glyph compound T294:670; compare Schele (1982:351) for T294.
69. Schele (1990), Schele and Freidel (1990:246-247, 252-261, 472 n. 33, n. 34).
70. Schele and Miller (1986:53), Freidel (1990, 1992b, 1993), Fields (1991).
71. Schele and Miller (1986:49).
72. Cardós de Méndez (1987:122-123).

73. Pohl (1981, 1983, 1985); compare Reents-Budet (1994:fig. 6:35, cat. no. 79).
74. Ortiz (1969:37-41, 82, 86-89, 106, 112-114).
75. Lowie (1963:106-113, 163, plate 17); compare Almstedt (1968).
76. The "Palace Tablet"; compare Schele (1990).
77. Schele and Miller (1986:136-137, 148-150).
78. Tate (1985, 1992).
79. Schele (1976), Schele and Freidel (1990:470-471); compare Lounsbury (cited in Schele and Freidel 1990:470), Bassie-Sweet (1991:203-204).

5. BECOMING HUMAN: BODY AND PERSON IN AZTEC TENOCHTITLAN

1. See Smith and Berdan (1992), Hodge and Smith (1994), Parsons, Brumfiel, and Hodge (1996).
2. See Kellogg (1995:71-72) on the importance of Mexica concepts of order in early colonial legal disputes.
3. Calnek (1972; 1974, especially pp. 200-204; 1976; 1992), Lockhart (1992: 141-163); compare J. Marcus (1992).
4. Matos Moctezuma (1984, 1992), Berdan and Anawalt (1997:222-225, 229).
5. Calnek (1976:296; 1988:171), Lockhart (1992:16-19, 43-44, 59-93), Brumfiel (1994, 1998), Kellogg (1995:181-183).
6. Monzón (1983); compare Kirchhoff (1955), P. Carrasco (1971, 1976), Calnek (1974, 1976), Hicks (1982), van Zantwijk (1985), Kellogg (1986; 1993; 1995:172-186).
7. Especially Sahagún (1951, 1953a, 1953b, 1954, 1959, 1961, 1969); compare Edmonson (1974), Brown (1983), Klor de Alva, Nicholson, and Quiñones Keber (1988) for critical approaches to these texts.
8. Van Zantwijk (1985), Rojas (1986), Lockhart (1992:142); compare Charlton, Charlton, and Nichols (1993).
9. Sahagún (1959); see also Brumfiel (1980), P. Carrasco (1980), Isaac (1986), Smith (1990), Berdan (1993).
10. Van Zantwijk (1985), Rojas (1986), Calnek (1988:171-173).
11. Calnek (1988:171-173), Kellogg (1995:169-186).
12. Waterson (1995:63-66), Chance (1998), Sandstrom (2000); compare Monaghan (1996).
13. Calnek (1988:175-177).
14. Calnek (1972, 1976), Brumfiel (1992, 1994); compare Nichols and Frederick (1993).
15. Compare Clendinnen (1991), Kellogg (1995:169-186).
16. See Smith (1979, 1980), Brumfiel (1980), P. Carrasco (1980).
17. See Parry and Bloch (1989), and especially Sallnow (1989:221-228) and Toren (1989:144-154).
18. Molina (1970).
19. Sahagún (1954, 1961).
20. Smith and Hirth (1988), Brumfiel (1991, 1996b, 1997), S. McCafferty and G. McCafferty (1991, 1994), Hicks (1994); compare J. Marcus (1992), Gillespie and Joyce (1997).

21. Sahagún (1951), Brown (1983), Broda (1991), J. Furst (1992), Graulich (1992), Grigsby and Cook de Leonard (1992).

22. Matos Moctezuma (1984, 1988, 1992), Boone (1987), Aveni, Calnek, and Hartung (1988), Broda (1991).

23. Sahagún (compare 1953a, chap. 1; 1951, chap. 34). In this and succeeding citations, I refer to chapters rather than pages because the individual volumes in this series were reissued and sometimes have different pagination.

24. S. McCafferty and G. McCafferty (1988, 1991), G. McCafferty and S. McCafferty (1990); compare León-Portilla (1963:99-111), Hoskins (1990:275).

25. Sahagún (1951, 1953a, 1954, 1961, 1969); compare Clendinnen (1991:153-167, 184-193) for a somewhat different set of conclusions drawn from the same data.

26. Hoskins (1990:295).

27. Sahagún (1969, chaps. 25, 27, 33), Brumfiel (1998:145-152); compare Sullivan (1980), Clendinnen (1991:223-228, 244-248, 250-253).

28. Sahagún (1969, chaps. 28, 30, 33; 1951, chap. 21).

29. Sahagún (1969, chaps. 30, 31, 37).

30. Sahagún (1969, chap. 36).

31. Sahagún (1969, chap. 37).

32. Codex Mendoza (1978), Calnek (1992), Berdan and Anawalt (1997:145-152); compare Sahagún (1953a, appendix 4; 1954, chap. 16; 1969, chap. 18).

33. Calnek (1988), Berdan and Anawalt (1997:146, 150).

34. Sahagún (1969, chap. 39).

35. Codex Mendoza (1978:58-60), Berdan and Anawalt (1997:153-165, 166-171).

36. Ortiz (1969:29-59).

37. Sahagún (1951, chap. 33; 1969, chap. 39).

38. Sahagún (1951, chaps. 37-38); compare Clendinnen (1991:189-192) for a somewhat different reading of the same passages.

39. Codex Mendoza (1978:61, 68).

40. Sahagún (1953b, chap. 3, appendix).

41. Sahagún (1969, chap. 37).

42. Borrowing Terry Turner's (1980) term.

43. Sahagún (1954, chap. 21); compare Codex Mendoza (1978:61), Berdan and Anawalt (1997:166-171, 174-175, 183-202).

44. Sahagún (1954, chap. 15); compare Codex Mendoza (1978:61, 68).

45. Sahagún (1961:29).

46. Dozier (1954), Sherzer (1983), van de Guchte (1992).

47. Compare Codex Mendoza (1978:60-62).

48. Sahagún (1951, chap. 24).

49. Sahagún (1969, chap. 23); compare Codex Mendoza (1978:61).

50. Compare Arvey (1988:182-184).

51. Sahagún (1951, chap. 38); see Klein (1990-1991; 1993b:21-25).

52. Berdan and Anawalt (1997:167). All songs quoted from Sahagún (1951, appendix), with word choice and line breaks altered to present more poetic renderings.

53. Sahagún (1951, chaps. 21, 28).

54. Sahagún (1951, chap. 27).

55. Sahagún (1951, chap. 23).
56. Sahagún (1969, chap. 42), Sullivan (1982), S. McCafferty and G. McCafferty (1991).
57. Sahagún (1961, chap. 13).
58. Sahagún (1961, chap. 14; compare chap. 11).
59. Sahagún (1961, chaps. 11, 15); compare G. McCafferty and S. McCafferty (1999).
60. Sahagún (1961, chap. 15; compare 1954, chap. 18); compare Arvey (1988), G. McCafferty and S. McCafferty (1999).
61. Sahagún (1969, chap. 43).
62. Sahagún (1969, chap. 18).
63. Sahagún (1969, chap. 23).
64. S. McCafferty and G. McCafferty (1988, 1991), G. McCafferty and S. McCafferty (1999).
65. Whitehead (1981), Weiner (1989); compare Anawalt (1984, 1990), Brumfiel (1991, 1996b, 1997), Hicks (1991, 1994), Berdan (1993), Aguilera (1997).
66. Brumfiel (1991, 1996a).
67. Nash (1978, 1980), Klein (1988), Clendinnen (1991:164–173), Brumfiel (1996a:155–160); compare León-Portilla (1978), Matos Moctezuma (1988:fig. 14). See Milbrath (1997) for a discussion of images of Coyolxauhqui.
68. Sahagún (1951, chaps. 24, 37; 1953a, chap. 1).
69. Sahagún (1951, chaps. 26, 27, 30, appendix); see Sullivan (1982) for a discussion of the iconography and identity of the various goddesses.
70. Sahagún (1951, chaps. 32, 33, 36, appendix).
71. Klein (1988, 1993a, 1994).
72. Sahagún (1951, chaps. 24, 21, 32, 33, appendix).
73. León-Portilla (1978).
74. For example, Nicholson (1971), Sullivan (1982).
75. Sahagún (1961, chap. 1; 1970, chaps. 6, 7, 8); see Sahagún (1951, chaps. 26, 27, 30) for details of the ceremonies. Compare S. McCafferty and G. McCafferty (1988), Gillespie (1989).
76. Sahagún (1951, chaps. 24, 32; 1970).
77. Sahagún (1969, chap. 29).
78. Sahagún (1969, chaps. 28, 30, 33).
79. Sahagún (1969, chap. 29).
80. Gillespie (1989).
81. Gillespie (1989:62–63, 133, 224–225), Lincoln (1990:145, 629–630, 639–642); compare Kellogg (1995:99–100).
82. Sahagún (1957; 1961, chap. 29; 1969, chap. 27); compare López Austin (1988:238).
83. For example, Klein (1976; 1980:157–165), J. Furst (1982:209–210); compare Hunt (1977:95–109, 139), Taggart (1983:60–66).

6. PERFORMANCE AND INSCRIPTION: HUMAN NATURE
IN PREHISPANIC MESOAMERICA

1. Pasztory (1988, 1992); compare P. Furst (1974), Taube (1983), C. Millon (1988), Berlo (1992).

2. Landa (1941:128; compare 93–94, 129, 142–143, 145, 147, 152, 154).

3. M. Miller (1985, 1986, 1988), Grube (1992).

4. Flannery and Marcus (1976), Drennan (1983a, 1983b), Grove (1999), Hendon (1999).

5. Gillespie (1991), Ringle (1999).

6. R. Millon (1981).

7. R. Millon (1981), McClung and Rattray (1987).

8. Sahagún (1959, chaps. 18–21), Closs (1992), Reents-Budet (1994).

9. Evans (1995); compare R. Wright (1991).

10. Bourdieu (1973, 1977), Connerton (1989), Butler (1990; 1993:1–16, 22–23, 93–119, 137–140). For another archaeological application of Butler's work, see Meskell (1996, 1998, 1999).

11. DuBois (1988), Hubbard (1990), Laqueur (1990).

12. Klein (1976; 1980:157–165), Hunt (1977:95–109, 139), Devereaux (1987).

13. R. Joyce (1992a, 1994, 1996a, 1996b); compare Taube (1985), A. Stone (1991:201–202).

14. See D. Tedlock (1985). This observation is based on collaborative work, in progress, with Susan D. Gillespie.

15. Laughlin (1977), Burns (1983), B. Tedlock (1986).

16. J. Miller (1974), Reents (1985), Schele and Freidel (1991:290–295, 302–308), Reents-Budet (1994).

17. M. Coe (1965a, 1965b), Grove (1973:135; 1981b:64; 1999), M. Coe and Diehl (1980:294), J. Porter (1989).

18. Cyphers Guillén (1996), Ochoa (1996a, 1996b), Pohorilenko (1996:121–123).

References Cited

Abrams, Elliot, and David Rue

1988   Causes and Consequences of Deforestation among the Prehistoric Maya. *Human Ecology* 16(4):377-395.

Adams, Richard E. W.

1973   Maya Collapse: Transformation and Termination in the Ceramic Sequence at Altar de Sacrificios. In *The Classic Maya Collapse*, edited by T. Patrick Culbert, pp. 133-163. Albuquerque: University of New Mexico Press.

Aguilera, Carmen

1997   Of Royal Mantles and Blue Turquoise: The Meaning of the Mexica Emperor's Mantle. *Latin American Antiquity* 8(1):3-19.

Agurcia, Ricardo

1977   The Playa de los Muertos Figurines. Master's thesis, Department of Anthropology, Tulane University, New Orleans.

1978   Las figurillas de Playa de los Muertos, Honduras. *Yaxkin* 2(4):221-240.

Almazán St. Hill, Marco Aurelio

1994   The Northern Mesoamerican States-System, 1350-1524 A.D.: Structure and Dynamics: A Thesis. Ph.D. diss., Department of Political Science, Harvard University.

Almstedt, Ruth

1968   *Diegueno Deer Toe Rattles*. Ethnic Technology Notes, no. 2. San Diego: San Diego Museum of Man.

Anawalt, Patricia

1981   *Indian Clothing before Cortez: Mesoamerican Costumes from the Codices*. Norman: University of Oklahoma Press.

1984   Memory Clothing: Costumes Associated with Aztec Human Sacrifice. In *Ritual Human Sacrifice in Mesoamerica*, edited by Elizabeth H. Boone, pp. 165-193. Washington, D.C.: Dumbarton Oaks.

1990   The Emperor's Cloak: Aztec Pomp, Toltec Circumstances. *American Antiquity* 55(2):291-307.

Andrews, E. Wyllys, V

1986   Olmec Jades from Chacsinkin, Yucatan, and Maya Ceramics from La Venta, Tabasco. In *Research and Reflections in Archaeology and History: Essays in Honor of Doris Stone*, edited by E. Wyllys Andrews V, pp. 11-49. Middle American Research Institute Publication 57. New Orleans: Tulane University.

1987   Spoons and Knuckledusters in Formative Mesoamerica. Revised version of paper presented at the Third Texas Symposium, "Olmec, Izapa, and the Development of Maya Civilization." University of Texas, Institute for Latin American Studies, Austin.

Arnold, Dean E.

1985   *Ceramic Theory and Cultural Process*. Cambridge: Cambridge University Press.

Arvey, Margaret

1988   Women of Ill Repute in the Florentine Codex. In *The Role of Gender in Precolumbian Art and Architecture*, edited by Virginia E. Miller, pp. 179-204. Lanham, Md.: University Press of America.

Ashmore, Wendy

1991   Site-planning Principles and Concepts of Directionality among the Ancient Maya. *Latin American Antiquity* 2(3):199-226.

Aveni, Anthony F.

1980   *Skywatchers of Ancient Mexico*. Austin: University of Texas Press.

Aveni, Anthony F., Edward E. Calnek, and Horst Hartung

1988   Myth, Environment, and the Orientation of the Templo Mayor of Tenochtitlan. *American Antiquity* 53(2):287-309.

Ball, Joseph W.

1979   Ceramics, Culture History, and the Puuc Tradition: Some Alternative Possibilities. In *The Puuc: New Perspectives; Papers Presented at the Puuc Symposium, Central College, May 1977*, edited by Lawrence Mills, pp. 18-35. Scholarly Studies in the Liberal Arts, Publication no. 1. Pella, Iowa: Central College.

1993   Pottery, Potters, Palaces, and Polities: Some Socioeconomic and Political Implications of Late Classic Maya Ceramic Industries. In *Lowland Maya Civilization in the Eighth Century A.D.*, edited by Jeremy Sabloff and John Henderson, pp. 243-272. Washington, D.C.: Dumbarton Oaks.

Ball, Joseph W., and John M. Ladd

1992   Ceramics. In *Artifacts from the Cenote of Sacrifice, Chichen Itza, Yucatan: Textiles, Basketry, Stone, Bone, Shell, Ceramics, Wood, Copal, Rubber, Other Organic Materials, and Mammalian Remains*, edited by Clemency C. Coggins, pp. 191-233. Peabody Museum of Archaeology and Ethnology Memoirs 10(3). Harvard University, Cambridge, Mass.

Barthes, Roland

1977a   Diderot, Brecht, Eisenstein. In *Image-Music-Text*, translated by Stephen Heath, pp. 69-78. New York: Noonday Press.

1977b Introduction to the Structural Analysis of Narratives. In *Image-Music-Text*, translated by Stephen Heath, pp. 79–124. New York: Noonday Press.

1977c Rhetoric of the Image. In *Image-Music-Text*, translated by Stephen Heath, pp. 32–51. New York: Noonday Press.

Bassie-Sweet, Karen

1991 *From the Mouth of the Dark Cave: Commemorative Sculpture of the Late Classic Maya.* Norman: University of Oklahoma Press.

Baudez, Claude, and Pierre Becquelin

1973 *Archéologie de los Naranjos, Honduras.* Etudes mesoaméricaines 2. Mexico City: Mission Archéologique et Ethnologique Française au Mexique.

Beaudry, Marilyn P.

1984 *Ceramic Production and Distribution in the Southeastern Maya Periphery: Late Classic Painted Serving Vessels.* BAR International Series 203. Oxford.

Berdan, Frances F.

1993 Trade and Tribute in the Aztec Empire. In *Current Topics in Aztec Studies: Essays in Honor of Dr. H. B. Nicholson*, edited by Alana Cordy-Collins and Douglas Sharon, pp. 71–84. San Diego Museum Papers, vol. 30. San Diego: San Diego Museum of Man.

Berdan, Frances F., and Patricia Anawalt

1997 *The Essential Codex Mendoza.* Berkeley: University of California Press.

Berlin, Heinrich

1963 The Palenque Triad. *Journal de la Société des Américanistes* (Paris), n.s., 52: 91–99.

Berlo, Janet Catherine

1992 Icons and Ideologies at Teotihuacan: The Great Goddess Reconsidered. In *Art, Ideology, and the City of Teotihuacan*, edited by Janet Catherine Berlo, pp. 129–168. Washington, D.C.: Dumbarton Oaks.

Blake, Michael

1991 An Emerging Early Formative Chiefdom at Paso de la Amada, Chiapas, Mexico. In *The Formation of Complex Society in Southeastern Mesoamerica*, edited by William R. Fowler, pp. 27–46. Boca Raton: CRC Press.

Bolles, John S.

1977 *Las Monjas: A Major Pre-Mexican Architectural Complex at Chichen Itza.* Norman: University of Oklahoma Press.

Boon, James A.

1990 Balinese Twins Times Two: Gender, Birth Order, and "Household" in Indonesia/Indo-Europe. In *Power and Difference: Gender in Island Southeast Asia*, edited by Jane Monnig Atkinson and Shelly Errington, pp. 209–233. Stanford: Stanford University Press.

Boone, Elizabeth H., ed.

1987 *The Aztec Templo Mayor.* Washington, D.C.: Dumbarton Oaks.

Bourdieu, Pierre

1973 The Berber House. In *Rules and Meanings: The Anthropology of Everyday Knowledge*, edited by Mary Douglas, pp. 98–110. Harmondsworth: Penguin Books.

1977 *Outline of a Theory of Practice.* Cambridge: Cambridge University Press.

Braswell, Geoffrey E.

1992   Obsidian Hydration Dating, the Coner Phase, and Revisionist Chronology at Copan, Honduras. *Latin American Antiquity* 3(2):130-147.

Broda, Johanna

1991   Sacred Landscape of Aztec Calendar Festivals: Myth, Nature, and Society. In *To Change Place: Aztec Ceremonial Landscapes,* edited by David Carrasco, pp. 74-120. Niwot: University Press of Colorado.

Brown, Betty Ann

1983   Seen But Not Heard: Women in Aztec Ritual—the Sahagún Texts. In *Text and Image in Pre-Columbian Art,* edited by Janet C. Berlo, pp. 119-154. BAR International Series 180. Oxford.

Bruhns, Karen

1988   Yesterday the Queen Wore . . . An Analysis of Women and Costume in Public Art of the Late Classic Maya. In *The Role of Gender in Precolumbian Art and Architecture,* edited by Virginia Miller, pp. 105-134. Lanham, Md.: University Press of America.

Brumfiel, Elizabeth M.

1980   Specialization, Market Exchange, and the Aztec State: A View from Huexotla. *Current Anthropology* 21(4):459-478.

1991   Weaving and Cooking: Women's Production in Aztec Mexico. In *Engendering Archaeology: Women and Prehistory,* edited by Joan Gero and Margaret Conkey, pp. 224-251. Oxford: Basil Blackwell.

1992   Distinguished Lecture in Archeology: Breaking and Entering the Ecosystem: Gender, Class, and Faction Steal the Show. *American Anthropologist* 94(3):551-567.

1994   Ethnic Groups and Political Development in Ancient Mexico. In *Factional Competition and Political Development in the New World,* edited by Elizabeth M. Brumfiel and John W. Fox, pp. 89-102. Cambridge: Cambridge University Press.

1996a   Figurines and the Aztec State: Testing the Effectiveness of Ideological Domination. In *Gender and Archaeology,* edited by Rita Wright, pp. 143-166. Philadelphia: University of Pennsylvania Press.

1996b   Quality of Tribute Cloth: The Place of Evidence in Archaeological Argument. *American Antiquity* 61(3):453-462.

1997   Tribute Cloth Production and Compliance in Aztec and Colonial Mexico. *Museum Anthropology* 21(2):55-71.

1998   The Multiple Identities of Aztec Craft Specialists. In *Craft and Social Identity,* edited by Cathy Lynne Costin and Rita P. Wright, pp. 145-152. Archeological Papers of the American Anthropological Association, no. 8. Washington, D.C.

Bullard, William R., Jr.

1973   Postclassic Culture in Central Peten and Adjacent British Honduras. In *The Classic Maya Collapse,* edited by T. Patrick Culbert, pp. 221-241. Albuquerque: University of New Mexico Press.

Burns, Allan

1983   *An Epoch of Miracles: Oral Literature of the Yucatec Maya.* Austin: University of Texas Press.

Butler, Judith
1990   *Gender Trouble: Feminism and the Subversion of Identity.* New York: Rout-
        ledge.
1993   *Bodies That Matter: On the Discursive Limits of "Sex."* New York: Rout-
        ledge.

Calnek, Edward E.
1972   Settlement Pattern and *Chinampa* Agriculture at Tenochtitlan. *American An-
        tiquity* 37(1):104-155.
1974   The Sahagún Texts as a Source of Sociological Information. In *Sixteenth-
        Century Mexico: The Work of Sahagún,* edited by Munro Edmonson, pp.
        189-204. Albuquerque: University of New Mexico Press.
1976   The Internal Structure of Tenochtitlan. In *The Valley of Mexico: Studies in
        Pre-Hispanic Ecology and Society,* edited by Eric Wolf, pp. 287-302. Albu-
        querque: University of New Mexico Press.
1988   The Calmecac and the Telpochcalli in Pre-Conquest Tenochtitlan. In *The
        Work of Bernardino de Sahagún: Pioneer Ethnographer of Sixteenth-Century
        Aztec Mexico,* edited by J. Jorge Klor de Alva, Henry B. Nicholson, and
        Eloise Quiñones Keber, pp. 169-178. Albany: Institute for Mesoamerican
        Studies, State University of New York at Albany.
1992   The Ethnographic Context of the Third Part of the *Codex Mendoza.* In *The
        Codex Mendoza,* Vol. 1, *Interpretation,* edited by Frances Berdan and Patricia
        Anawalt, pp. 81-91. Berkeley: University of California Press.

Canby, Joel
1951   Possible Chronological Implications of the Long Ceramic Sequence Re-
        covered at Yarumela, Spanish Honduras. In *The Civilizations of Ancient
        America, Selected Papers of the 29th International Congress of Americanists,
        Volume 1,* edited by Sol Tax, pp. 79-92. New York: Cooper Square Pub-
        lishers.

Cardós de Méndez, Amalia
1987   *Estudio de la colección de escultura maya del Museo Nacional de Antropología.*
        Mexico City: Instituto Nacional de Antropología e Historia.

Carlsen, Robert
1988   Preliminary Investigations into the Ceramic Seals and Roller Stamps of
        Costa Rica. In *Costa Rican Art and Archaeology,* edited by Frederick W.
        Lange, pp. 189-200. Boulder: University of Colorado.

Carlson, John B.
1981   Olmec Concave Iron-Ore Mirrors: The Aesthetics of a Lithic Technology
        and the Lord of the Mirror (with an Illustrated Catalogue of Mirrors). In
        The Olmec and Their Neighbors, edited by Elizabeth Benson, pp. 117-148.
        Washington, D.C.: Dumbarton Oaks.

Carlson, John B., and Linda C. Landis
1985   Bands, Bicephalic Dragons, and Other Beasts: The Skyband in Maya Art
        and Iconography. In *Fourth Palenque Round Table, 1980,* edited by Eliza-
        beth P. Benson, pp. 115-140. San Francisco: Pre-Columbian Art Research
        Institute.

Carrasco, Pedro
1971   Social Organization of Ancient Mexico. In *Handbook of Middle American*

Indians 10:349–375. Edited by Robert Wauchope, Gordon Ekholm, and Ignacio Bernal. Austin: University of Texas Press.

1976   Los linajes nobles del México antiguo. In *Estratificación social en la Mesoamérica prehispánica,* edited by Pedro Carrasco and Johanna Broda, pp. 19–36. Mexico City: Instituto Nacional de Antropología e Historia.

1980   Markets and Merchants in the Aztec Economy. *Journal of the Steward Anthropological Society* (Urbana, Ill.) 11(2):249–272.

Carrasco V., Ramón

1985   Señora Cimi, señora de la familia de la luna en las inscripciones tardías de Yaxchilan y Bonampak. In *Fifth Palenque Round Table, 1983,* edited by Virginia M. Fields, pp. 85–95. San Francisco: Pre-Columbian Art Research Institute.

Castro-Leal, Marcia

1996   Catalogue Entry 51: Seated Female Figurine with Polished Hematite Disk. In *Olmec Art of Ancient Mexico,* edited by Elizabeth P. Benson and Beatriz de la Fuente, p. 216. Washington, D.C.: National Gallery of Art.

Chance, John

1998   Descent and the Nahua Noble House. A paper presented in the session "Bloodlines: Lineages and Genealogies in Mesoamerican Societies" at the annual meeting of the American Anthropological Association, Philadelphia, Pa.

Charlton, Cynthia Otis, Thomas H. Charlton, and Deborah L. Nichols

1993   Aztec Household-Based Craft Production: Archaeological Evidence from the City-State of Otumba, Mexico. In *Prehispanic Domestic Units in Western Mesoamerica: Studies of the Household, Compound, and Residence,* edited by Robert Santley and Kenneth Hirth, pp. 147–171. Boca Raton: CRC Press.

Chase, Arlen F.

1985a   Troubled Times: The Archaeology and Iconography of the Terminal Classic Southern Lowland Maya. In *Fifth Palenque Round Table, 1983,* edited by Virginia Fields, pp. 103–114. San Francisco: Pre-Columbian Art Research Institute.

1985b   Postclassic Peten Interaction Spheres: The View from Tayasal. In *The Lowland Maya Postclassic,* edited by Arlen F. Chase and Prudence Rice, pp. 184–205. Austin: University of Texas Press.

1990   Maya Archaeology and Population Estimates in the Tayasal-Paxcaman Zone, Peten, Guatemala. In *Precolumbian Population History in the Maya Lowlands,* edited by T. Patrick Culbert and Don Rice, pp. 149–165. Albuquerque: University of New Mexico Press.

1992   Elites and the Changing Organization of Classic Maya Society. In *Mesoamerican Elites: An Archaeological Assessment,* edited by Diane Z. Chase and Arlen F. Chase, pp. 30–49. Norman: University of Oklahoma Press.

Chase, Arlen F., Nikolai Grube, and Diane Z. Chase

1991   Three Terminal Classic Monuments from Caracol, Belize. *Research Reports on Ancient Maya Writing,* no. 36. Washington, D.C.: Center for Maya Research.

Chase, Diane Z.
1990   Invisible Maya: Population History and Archaeology at Santa Rita Coro-
        zal. In *Precolumbian Population History in the Maya Lowlands*, edited by
        T. Patrick Culbert and Don Rice, pp. 199–213. Albuquerque: University of
        New Mexico Press.
Chase, Diane Z., and Arlen F. Chase
1982   Yucatec Influence in Terminal Classic Northern Belize. *American Antiquity*
        47(3):596–614.
1992   An Archaeological Assessment of Mesoamerican Elites. In *Mesoamerican
        Elites: An Archaeological Assessment*, edited by Diane Z. Chase and Arlen F.
        Chase, pp. 303–317. Norman: University of Oklahoma Press.
Chase, Diane Z., Arlen F. Chase, and William A. Haviland
1990   The Classic Maya City: Reconsidering the "Mesoamerican Urban Tradi-
        tion." *American Anthropologist* 92(2):499–506.
Clancy, Flora S.
1983   Comparison of Highland Zapotec and Lowland Maya Graphic Styles. In
        Highland-Lowland Interaction in Mesoamerica, edited by Arthur Miller, pp.
        223–240. Washington, D.C.: Dumbarton Oaks.
1986   Text and Image in the Tablets of the Cross Group at Palenque. *Res: Anthro-
        pology and Aesthetics* 11:17–32.
Clancy, Flora, Clemency C. Coggins, and T. Patrick Culbert
1985   Catalogue. In *Maya: Treasures of an Ancient Civilization*, edited by Charles
        Gallenkamp and Regina Johnson, pp. 97–231. New York: Harry N. Abrams
        and the Albuquerque Museum.
Clark, John E.
1983   A Preclassic Mesoamerican Society: Analysis of Francesca-Phase Burials
        from Chiapa de Corzo, Mexico. Unpublished paper provided courtesy of
        the author.
1987   Politics, Prismatic Blades, and Mesoamerican Civilization. In *The Organi-
        zation of Core Technology*, edited by Jay K. Johnson and Carol A. Morrow,
        pp. 259–284. Boulder and London: Westview Press.
1990   Olmecas, olmequismo y olmequización en Mesoamérica. *Arqueología* (Se-
        gunda Epoca) 3:49–56.
1991   The Beginnings of Mesoamerica: Apologia for the Soconusco Early For-
        mative. In *The Formation of Complex Society in Southeastern Mesoamerica*,
        edited by William R. Fowler, pp. 13–26. Boca Raton: CRC Press.
1994   The Development of Early Formative Rank Societies in the Soconusco,
        Chiapas, Mexico. Ph.D. diss., Department of Anthropology, University of
        Michigan, Ann Arbor.
1996   Craft Specialization and Olmec Civilization. In *Craft Specialization and
        Social Evolution: In Memory of V. Gordon Childe*, edited by Bernard Wailes,
        pp. 187–199. University Museum Symposium Series, vol. 6. University Mu-
        seum Monograph 93. Philadelphia: The University Museum of Archae-
        ology and Anthropology, University of Pennsylvania.
Clark, John E., and Michael Blake
1993   The Power of Prestige: Competitive Generosity and the Emergence of Rank

Societies in Lowland Mesoamerica. In *Factional Competition and Political Development in the New World*, edited by Elizabeth M. Brumfiel and John W. Fox, pp. 17–30. Cambridge: Cambridge University Press.

Clark, John, and Dennis Gosser
1995   Reinventing Mesoamerica's First Pottery. In *The Emergence of Pottery: Technology and Innovation in Ancient Societies*, edited by William Barnett and John Hoopes, pp. 209–222. Washington, D.C.: Smithsonian Institution Press.

Clark, John, and Stephen Houston
1995   An Ethnohistoric Survey of Maya Artisans: Issues of Production, Consumption, and Social Identity. Paper presented at the annual meeting of the American Anthropological Association, Washington, D.C.

Clark, John, and Thomas A. Lee
1984   Formative Obsidian Exchange and the Emergence of Public Economies in Chiapas, Mexico. In *Trade and Exchange in Early Mesoamerica*, edited by Kenneth Hirth, pp. 235–274. Albuquerque: University of New Mexico Press.

Clark, John, and William Parry
1990   Craft Specialization and Cultural Complexity. *Research in Economic Anthropology* 12:289–346.

Clarkson, Persis
1978   Classic Maya Pictorial Ceramics: A Survey of Content and Theme. In *Papers on the Economy and Architecture of the Ancient Maya*, edited by Raymond Sidrys, pp. 86–141. University of California at Los Angeles, Institute of Archaeology Monograph 8.

Clendinnen, Inga
1982   Yucatec Maya Women and the Spanish Conquest: Role and Ritual in Historical Reconstruction. *Journal of Social History* 15:427–442.
1991   *Aztecs: An Interpretation*. Cambridge: Cambridge University Press.

Closs, Michael P.
1984   Dynastic History of Naranjo: The Early Period. *Estudios de Cultura Maya* 15:77–96.
1985   Dynastic History of Naranjo: The Middle Period. In *Fifth Palenque Round Table, 1983*, edited by Virginia M. Fields, pp. 65–77. San Francisco: Pre-Columbian Art Research Institute.
1992   "I Am a Kahal; My Parents Were Scribes"/Soy un Kahal; mis padres fueron escribas. *Research Reports on Ancient Maya Writing*, no. 39. Washington, D.C., and Mexico City: Center for Maya Research and Instituto Nacional de Antropología e Historia.

Codex Mendoza
1978   *Codex Mendoza*. Fribourg: Productions Liber S.A.

Codex Tro-Cortesianus
1967   *Codex Tro-Cortesianus (Codex Madrid). Museo de América, Madrid*. Graz: Akademisches Druck u Verlagsanstalt.

Coe, Michael
1965a   *The Jaguar's Children: Pre-Classic Central Mexico*. New York: The Museum of Primitive Art.

1965b The Olmec Style and Its Distributions. In *Handbook of Middle American Indians* 3:739–775. Edited by Robert Wauchope and Gordon R. Willey. Austin: University of Texas Press.

1966 *An Early Stone Pectoral from Southeastern Mexico.* Studies in Pre-Columbian Art and Archaeology, no. 1. Washington, D.C.: Dumbarton Oaks.

1976 Early Steps in the Evolution of Maya Writing. In *Origins of Religious Art and Iconography in Preclassic Mesoamerica,* edited by Henry B. Nicholson, pp. 107–122. Publication 31. Los Angeles: UCLA Latin American Studies Center.

1977 Olmec and Maya: A Study in Relationships. In *The Origins of Maya Civilization,* edited by Richard E. W. Adams, pp. 183–195. School of American Research Advanced Seminar Series. Albuquerque: University of New Mexico Press.

Coe, Michael D., and Richard A. Diehl

1980 *In the Land of the Olmec.* Vol. 1, *The Archaeology of San Lorenzo Tenochtitlan.* Austin: University of Texas Press.

Coe, William R.

1990 *Excavations in the Great Plaza, North Terrace, and North Acropolis of Tikal.* Tikal Reports no. 14. University Museum Monograph no. 61. Philadelphia: University Museum of Archaeology and Anthropology, University of Pennsylvania.

Coggins, Clemency C.

1975 Painting and Drawing Styles at Tikal: An Historical and Iconographic Reconstruction. Ph.D. diss., Department of Art History, Harvard University. Ann Arbor: University Microfilms.

1984 Murals in the Upper Temple of the Jaguars, Chichen Itza. In *Cenote of Sacrifice: Maya Treasures from the Sacred Well at Chichen Itza,* edited by Clemency C. Coggins and Orrin C. Shane III, pp. 157–166. Austin: University of Texas Press.

1992 Dredging the Cenote. In *Artifacts from the Cenote of Sacrifice, Chichen Itza, Yucatan: Textiles, Basketry, Stone, Bone, Shell, Ceramics, Wood, Copal, Rubber, Other Organic Materials, and Mammalian Remains,* edited by Clemency C. Coggins, pp. 9–31. Peabody Museum of Archaeology and Ethnology Memoirs 10(3). Harvard University, Cambridge, Mass.

Coggins, Clemency C., and John M. Ladd

1992 Copal and Rubber Offerings. In *Artifacts from the Cenote of Sacrifice, Chichen Itza, Yucatan: Textiles, Basketry, Stone, Bone, Shell, Ceramics, Wood, Copal, Rubber, Other Organic Materials, and Mammalian Remains,* edited by Clemency C. Coggins, pp. 345–357. Peabody Museum of Archaeology and Ethnology Memoirs 10(3). Harvard University, Cambridge, Mass.

Coggins, Clemency C., and Orrin C. Shane III, eds.

1984 *Cenote of Sacrifice: Maya Treasures from the Sacred Well at Chichen Itza.* Austin: University of Texas Press.

Cohodas, Marvin

1978 *The Great Ball Court at Chichen Itza, Yucatan, Mexico.* New York: Garland Press.

Conides, Cynthia
1984   The Iconography of Female Figurines from Campeche: A Conceptual Ap-
        proach to the Study of Maya Symbolism. Master's thesis, Department of
        Art History, Columbia University, New York.
Conkey, Margaret, and Ruth Tringham
1995   Archaeology and the Goddess: Exploring the Contours of Feminist Archae-
        ology. In *Feminisms in the Academy: Rethinking the Disciplines,* edited by
        Abigail Stewart and Domna Stanton, pp. 199–247. Ann Arbor: University
        of Michigan Press.
Conkey, Margaret, and Sarah Williams
1991   Original Narratives: The Political Economy of Gender in Archaeology. In
        *Gender at the Crossroads of Knowledge: Feminist Anthropology in the Post-
        modern Era,* edited by Micaela di Leonardo, pp. 102–139. Berkeley: Univer-
        sity of California Press.
Connerton, Paul
1989   *How Societies Remember.* Cambridge: Cambridge University Press.
Cowgill, George
1979   Teotihuacan, Internal Militaristic Competition, and the Fall of the Classic
        Maya. In *Maya Archaeology and Ethnohistory,* edited by Norman Hammond
        and Gordon Willey, pp. 51–62. Austin: University of Texas Press.
Culbert, T. Patrick
1973a   (editor) *The Classic Maya Collapse.* Albuquerque: University of New Mexico
        Press.
1973b   The Maya Downfall at Tikal. In *The Classic Maya Collapse,* edited by
        T. Patrick Culbert, pp. 63–92. Albuquerque: University of New Mexico
        Press.
1991   (editor) *Classic Maya Political History: Hieroglyphic and Archaeological Evi-
        dence.* Cambridge: Cambridge University Press.
Cunningham, Clark
1964   Order in the Atoni House. *Bijdragen tot de Taal-, Land- en Volkenkunde* 120:
        34–68.
Cyphers Guillén, Ann
1984   The Possible Role of a Woman in Formative Exchange. In *Trade and Ex-
        change in Early Mesoamerica,* edited by Kenneth G. Hirth, pp. 115–123.
        Albuquerque: University of New Mexico Press.
1993   Women, Rituals, and Social Dynamics at Ancient Chalcatzingo. *Latin
        American Antiquity* 4(3):209–224.
1996   Catalogue Entry 3: Potrero Nuevo Monument 2. In *Olmec Art of Ancient
        Mexico,* edited by Elizabeth P. Benson and Beatriz de la Fuente, pp. 158–159.
        Washington, D.C.: National Gallery of Art.
1999   From Stone to Symbols: Olmec Art in Social Context at San Lorenzo
        Tenochtitlan. In *Social Patterns in Pre-Classic Mesoamerica,* edited by David
        C. Grove and Rosemary A. Joyce, pp. 155–181. Washington, D.C.: Dum-
        barton Oaks.
Davis, Whitney
1993   Writing Culture in Prehistoric Central America. In *Reinterpreting Prehistory*

of Central America, edited by Mark Miller Graham, pp. 253-276. Boulder: University of Colorado Press.

De la Fuente, Beatriz

1973 *Escultura monumental olmeca: Catálogo.* Cuadernos de Historia del Arte 1. Mexico City: Instituto de Investigaciones Estéticas, Universidad Nacional Autónoma de México.

1996 Catalogue Entry 5: San Martín Pajapan Monument 1—Crouching Figure with Headdress and Ceremonial Bar. In *Olmec Art of Ancient Mexico*, edited by Elizabeth P. Benson and Beatriz de la Fuente, pp. 162-163. Washington, D.C.: National Gallery of Art.

Demarest, Arthur

1989 The Olmec and the Rise of Civilization in Eastern Mesoamerica. In *Regional Perspectives on the Olmec*, edited by Robert J. Sharer and David C. Grove, pp. 148-197. Cambridge: Cambridge University Press.

1992 Ideology in Ancient Maya Cultural Evolution: The Dynamics of Galactic Polities. In *Ideology and Pre-Columbian Civilizations*, edited by Arthur A. Demarest and Geoffrey Conrad, pp. 135-157. Santa Fe: School of American Research Press.

1997 The Vanderbilt Petexbatun Regional Archaeological Project 1989-1994. *Ancient Mesoamerica* 8(2):209-228.

Demarest, Arthur, Matt O'Mansky, Claudia Wolley, Dirk van Tuerenhout, Takeshi Inomata, Joel Palka, and Héctor Escobedo

1997 Classic Maya Defensive Systems and Warfare in the Petexbatun Region: Archaeological Evidence and Interpretations. *Ancient Mesoamerica* 8(2): 229-254.

Devereaux, Leslie

1987 Gender Difference and Relations of Inequality in Zinacantan. In *Dealing with Inequality: Analysing Gender Relations in Melanesia and Beyond*, edited by Marilyn Strathern, pp. 89-111. Cambridge: Cambridge University Press.

di Leonardo, Micaela

1991 Introduction: Gender, Culture, and Political Economy: Feminist Anthropology in Historical Perspective. In *Gender at the Crossroads of Knowledge: Feminist Anthropology in the Postmodern Era*, edited by Micaela di Leonardo, pp. 1-48. Berkeley: University of California Press.

Dozier, Edward P.

1954 *The Hopi-Tewa of Arizona.* University of California Publications in American Archaeology and Ethnology, vol. 44, no. 3. Berkeley, Calif.

Drennan, Robert D.

1976 Religion and Social Evolution in Formative Mesoamerica. In *The Early Mesoamerican Village*, edited by Kent V. Flannery, pp. 345-368. New York: Academic Press.

1983a Ritual and Ceremonial Development at the Early Village Level. In *The Cloud People: Divergent Evolution of the Zapotec and Mixtec Civilizations*, edited by Kent V. Flannery and Joyce Marcus, pp. 46-50. New York: Academic Press.

1983b Ritual and Ceremonial Development at the Hunter-Gatherer Level. In *The Cloud People: Divergent Evolution of the Zapotec and Mixtec Civilizations*, edited by Kent V. Flannery and Joyce Marcus, pp. 30–32. New York: Academic Press.

Drucker, Philip
1952   *La Venta, Tabasco: A Study of Olmec Ceramics and Art.* Bureau of American Ethnology Bulletin 153. Washington, D.C.: Smithsonian Institution.

Drucker, Philip, Robert F. Heizer, and Robert Squier
1959   *Excavations at La Venta, Tabasco, 1955.* Bureau of American Ethnology Bulletin 170. Washington, D.C.: Smithsonian Institution.

DuBois, Page
1988   *Sowing the Body: Psychoanalysis and Ancient Representations of Women.* Chicago: University of Chicago Press.

Edmonson, Munro, ed.
1974   *Sixteenth-Century Mexico: The Work of Sahagún.* Albuquerque: University of New Mexico Press.

Eggebrecht, Eva, Arne Eggebrecht, and Nikolai Grube, eds.
1992   *Die Welt der Maya: Archaologische Schatze aus drei Jahrtausenden.* Mainz am Rhine: Philipp von Zabern.

Elshtain, Jean
1986   The New Feminist Scholarship. *Salmagundi* 70–71:3–26.

Errington, Shelly
1987   Incestuous Twins and the House Societies of Insular Southeast Asia. *Cultural Anthropology* 2:403–444.

Escobedo, Hector L.
1997   Arroyo de Piedra: Sociopolitical Dynamics of a Secondary Center in the Petexbatun Region. *Ancient Mesoamerica* 8:307–320.

Evans, Susan Toby
1995   The Household Division of Labor among Aztec Farmers: Men, Women, and Maguey. Prepared for inclusion in the volume *Agave, Mescal, Maguey: Prehistoric Cultivation in North America,* edited by Suzanne Fish and Jeffrey Parsons. Manuscript provided courtesy of the author.

Fash, Barbara, William Fash, Sheree Lane, Rudy Larios, Linda Schele, Jeffrey Stomper, and David Stuart
1992   Investigations of a Classic Maya Council House at Copan, Honduras. *Journal of Field Archaeology* 19(4):419–442.

Fash, William
1985   La secuencia de ocupación del grupo 9N-8, Las Sepulturas, Copán, y sus implicaciones teóricas. *Yaxkin* 8(1–2):135–150.
1991   *Scribes, Warriors, and Kings: The City of Copan and the Ancient Maya.* London: Thames and Hudson.

Fash, William, and Sheree Lane
1983   El juego de pelota B. In *Introducción a la arqueología de Copán, Honduras,* vol. 2, edited by Claude Baudez, pp. 501–562. Tegucigalpa: SECTUR.

Fash, William, and Robert J. Sharer
1991   Sociopolitical Developments and Methodological Issues at Copan, Honduras: A Conjunctive Perspective. *Latin American Antiquity* 2(2):166–187.

Fields, Virginia
1991   Iconographic Heritage of the Maya Jester God. In *Sixth Palenque Round*

Table, 1986, edited by Virginia Fields, pp. 167–174. Norman: University of Oklahoma Press.

1994   The Royal Charter at Xunantunich. In *Xunantunich Archaeological Project: 1994 Field Season*, pp. 65–74. Los Angeles: UCLA Institute of Archaeology.

Findley, Sheila

1990   The Iconographic Theme of Travel in Maya Classic Period Ceramics. Undergraduate honors thesis, Department of Anthropology, Harvard University.

Flannery, Kent V.

1976   Contextual Analysis of Ritual Paraphernalia from Formative Oaxaca. In *The Early Mesoamerican Village*, edited by Kent V. Flannery, pp. 333–345. New York: Academic Press.

Flannery, Kent V., and Joyce Marcus

1976   Evolution of the Public Building in Formative Oaxaca. In *Cultural Change and Continuity: Essays in Honor of James Bennett Griffin*, edited by Charles E. Cleland, pp. 205–221. New York: Academic Press.

1994   *Early Formative Pottery of the Valley of Oaxaca*. Prehistory and Human Ecology of the Valley of Oaxaca, vol. 10. Museum of Anthropology Memoirs no. 27. Ann Arbor: University of Michigan.

Flannery, Kent V., and Marcus Winter

1976   Analyzing Household Activities. In *The Early Mesoamerican Village*, edited by Kent V. Flannery, pp. 34–47. New York: Academic Press.

Folan, William

1991   Sacbes of the Northern Maya. In *Ancient Road Networks and Settlement Hierarchies in the New World*, edited by Charles D. Trombold, pp. 222–229. Cambridge: Cambridge University Press.

Foncerrada de Molina, Marta, and Sonia Lombardo de Ruiz

1979   *Vasijas pintadas mayas en contexto arqueológico (Catálogo)*. Instituto de Investigaciones Estéticas, Estudios y Fuentes del Arte en México, no. 39. Mexico City: Universidad Nacional Autónoma de México.

Fox, James A.

1997   Phoneticism, Dates, and Astronomy at Chichen Itza. In *The Language of Maya Hieroglyphs*, edited by Martha Macri and Anabel Ford, pp. 13–32. San Francisco: Pre-Columbian Art Research Institute.

Fox, James A., and John S. Justeson

1986   Classic Maya Dynastic Alliance and Succession. In *Handbook of Middle American Indians, Supplement* 4:7–34. Edited by Victoria Bricker and Ronald Spores. Austin: University of Texas Press.

Fox, James J.

1980   Introduction. In *The Flow of Life: Essays on Eastern Indonesia*, edited by James J. Fox, pp. 1–18. Cambridge: Harvard University Press.

Fox, John W.

1994   Political Cosmology among the Quiche Maya. In *Factional Competition and Political Development in the New World*, edited by Elizabeth M. Brumfiel and John W. Fox, pp. 158–170. Cambridge: Cambridge University Press.

Fox, Robin

1967   *Kinship and Marriage: An Anthropological Perspective*. Baltimore, Md.: Penguin Books.

Freidel, David A.

1981   Continuity and Disjunction: Late Postclassic Settlement Patterns in North-
        ern Yucatan. In *Lowland Maya Settlement Patterns,* edited by Wendy Ash-
        more, pp. 311–332. Albuquerque: University of New Mexico Press.

1985   New Light on the Dark Age: A Summary of Major Themes. In *The Lowland
        Maya Postclassic,* edited by Arlen F. Chase and Prudence Rice, pp. 285–309.
        Austin: University of Texas Press.

1988   Discourse Patterns in Maya Art and Architecture of the Late Preclassic
        Lowlands: Antecedents for Classic Period Texts and Images. *Journal of
        Mayan Linguistics* 6:23–46.

1990   Jester God: The Beginning and End of a Maya Royal Symbol. In *Vision and
        Revision in Maya Studies,* edited by Flora S. Clancy and Peter D. Harrison,
        pp. 67–78. Albuquerque: University of New Mexico Press.

1992a   Children of the First Father's Skull: Terminal Classic Warfare in the North-
        ern Maya Lowlands and the Transformation of Kingship and Elite Hier-
        archies. In *Mesoamerican Elites: An Archaeological Assessment,* edited by
        Arlen F. Chase and Diane Z. Chase, pp. 99–117. Norman: University of
        Oklahoma Press.

1992b   Trees of Life: Ahau as Idea and Artifact in Classic Lowland Maya Civiliza-
        tion. In *Ideology and Pre-Columbian Civilizations,* edited by Arthur Demarest
        and Geoffrey Conrad, pp. 115–133. Santa Fe: School of American Research
        Press.

1993   Jade Ahau: Toward a Theory of Commodity Value in Maya Civilization. In
        Precolumbian Jade: New Geological and Cultural Interpretations, edited by
        Frederick W. Lange, pp. 149–165. Salt Lake City: University of Utah Press.

Freidel, David, and Jeremy Sabloff

1984   *Cozumel: Late Maya Settlement Patterns.* New York: Academic Press.

Freidel, David, and Linda Schele

1988a   Kingship in the Late Preclassic Maya Lowlands: The Instruments and Places
        of Ritual Power. *American Anthropologist* 90(3):547–567.

1988b   Symbol and Power: A History of the Lowland Maya Cosmogram. In *Maya
        Iconography,* edited by Elizabeth P. Benson and Gillett G. Griffin, pp. 44–93.
        Princeton: Princeton University Press.

Freidel, David, Linda Schele, and Joy Parker

1993   *Maya Cosmos: Three Thousand Years on the Shaman's Path.* New York: Quill/
        William Morrow.

Freter, AnnCorrine

1992   Chronological Research at Copan: Methods and Implications. *Ancient
        Mesoamerica* 3(1):117–133.

Friedrich, Margaret Hardin

1970   Design Structure and Social Interaction: Archaeological Implications of an
        Ethnographic Analysis. *American Antiquity* 35(3):332–343.

Friedrich, Paul

1991   Polytropy. In *Beyond Metaphor: The Theory of Tropes in Anthropology,* edited
        by James W. Fernandez, pp. 17–55. Stanford: Stanford University Press.

Furst, Jill

1982   Skeletonization in Mixtec Art: A Re-evaluation. In *The Art and Iconography of Late Post-Classic Central Mexico*, edited by Elizabeth Boone, pp. 207–226. Washington D.C.: Dumbarton Oaks.

1992   Aztec New Fire Ritual: A World Renewal Rite. *Journal of Latin American Lore* 18(1-2):29–36.

Furst, Peter

1974   Morning Glory and Mother Goddess at Tepantitla, Teotihuacan: Iconography and Analogy in Pre-Columbian Art. In *Mesoamerican Archaeology: New Approaches*, edited by Norman Hammond, pp. 187–215. Austin: University of Texas Press.

Gailey, Christine Ward

1987a   Culture Wars: Resistance to State Formation. In *Power Relations and State Formation*, edited by Thomas C. Patterson and Christine Ward Gailey, pp. 35–56. Washington, D.C.: Archaeology Section, American Anthropological Association.

1987b   *Kinship to Kingship: Gender Hierarchy and State Formation in the Tongan Islands.* Austin: University of Texas Press.

Garber, James, David C. Grove, Kenneth Hirth, and John Hoopes

1993   Jade Use in Portions of Mexico and Central America. In *Pre-Columbian Jade*, edited by Frederick W. Lange, pp. 211–231. Salt Lake City: University of Utah Press.

García Moll, Roberto, Daniel Juárez Cossio, Carmen Pijoan Aguade, María Elena Salas Cuesta, and Marcela Salas Cuesta

1991   *Catálogo de Entierros de San Luis Tlatilco, México, Temporada IV.* Serie Antropología Física-Arqueología. Mexico City: Instituto Nacional de Antropología e Historia.

Gerhardt, Juliette C., and Norman Hammond

1991   The Community of Cuello: The Ceremonial Core. In *Cuello: An Early Maya Community in Belize*, edited by Norman Hammond, pp. 98–117. Cambridge: Cambridge University Press.

Gero, Joan M.

1992   Feasts and Females: Gender Ideology and Political Meals in the Andes. *Norwegian Archaeological Review* 25(1):15–30.

Gerry, John P.

1997   Bone Isotope Ratios and Their Bearing on Elite Privilege among the Classic Maya. *Geoarchaeology* 12(1):41–69.

Gilchrist, Roberta

1994   *Gender and Material Culture: The Archaeology of Religious Women.* London: Routledge.

1999   *Gender and Archaeology: Contesting the Past.* London: Routledge.

Gillespie, Susan D.

1987   Distributional Analysis of Chalcatzingo Figurines. In *Ancient Chalcatzingo*, edited by David C. Grove, pp. 264–270. Austin: University of Texas Press.

1989   *The Aztec Kings: The Construction of Rulership in Mexica History.* Tucson: University of Arizona Press.

1991   Ballgames and Boundaries. In *The Mesoamerican Ballgame*, edited by Vernon L. Scarborough and David R. Wilcox, pp. 317–346. Tucson: University of Arizona Press.

1994   Llano del Jícaro: An Olmec Monument Workshop. *Ancient Mesoamerica* 5: 231–242.

Gillespie, Susan D., and Rosemary A. Joyce

1997   Gendered Goods: The Symbolism of Maya Hierarchical Exchange Relations. In *Women in Prehistory: North America and Mesoamerica*, edited by Cheryl Claassen and Rosemary A. Joyce, pp. 189–207. Philadelphia: University of Pennsylvania Press.

1998   Deity Relationships in Mesoamerican Cosmologies: The Case of the Maya God L. *Ancient Mesoamerica* 9:1–18.

González Lauck, Rebecca

1994   La antigua ciudad olmeca en La Venta, Tabasco. In *Los olmecas en Mesoamérica*, edited by John E. Clark, pp. 93–111. Mexico City: Citibank.

1996   La Venta: An Olmec Capital. In *Olmec Art of Ancient Mexico*, edited by Elizabeth P. Benson and Beatriz de la Fuente, pp. 73–82. Washington, D.C.: National Gallery of Art.

Gordon, George Byron

1898a   *Caverns of Copan, Honduras.* Peabody Museum of Archaeology and Ethnology Memoirs 1(5). Harvard University, Cambridge, Mass.

1898b   *Researches in the Uloa Valley, Honduras.* Peabody Museum of Archaeology and Ethnology Memoirs 1(4). Harvard University, Cambridge, Mass.

Gossen, Gary H., and Richard M. Leventhal

1993   Topography of Ancient Maya Religious Pluralism: A Dialogue with the Present. In *Lowland Maya Civilization in the Eighth Century A.D.,* edited by Jeremy Sabloff and John S. Henderson, pp. 185–217. Washington, D.C.: Dumbarton Oaks.

Graham, Elizabeth

1985   Facets of Terminal to Postclassic Activity in the Stann Creek District, Belize. In *The Lowland Maya Postclassic,* edited by Arlen F. Chase and Prudence Rice, pp. 215–229. Austin: University of Texas Press.

Graham, Elizabeth, and David Pendergast

1989   Excavations at the Marco Gonzalez Site, Ambergris Cay, Belize, 1986. *Journal of Field Archaeology* 16(1):1–16.

Graham, John

1973   Aspects of Non-Classic Presences in the Inscriptions and Sculptural Art of Seibal. In *The Classic Maya Collapse,* edited by T. Patrick Culbert, pp. 207–219. Albuquerque: University of New Mexico Press.

Graulich, Michael

1992   Aztec Festivals of the Rain Gods. *Indiana* (Berlin) 12:21–54.

Grigsby, Thomas L., and Carmen Cook de Leonard

1992   Xilonen in Tepoztlan: A Comparison of Tepoztecan and Aztec Agrarian Ritual Schedules. *Ethnohistory* (Durham) 39(2):108–147.

Grove, David C.

1973   Olmec Altars and Myths. *Archaeology* 26:128–135.

1981a   The Formative Period and the Evolution of Complex Cultures. In *Handbook of Middle American Indians, Supplement* 1:373–391. Edited by Victoria Bricker and Jeremy Sabloff. Austin: University of Texas Press.

1981b   Olmec Monuments: Mutilation as a Clue to Meaning. In *The Olmec and Their Neighbors,* edited by Elizabeth P. Benson, pp. 49–68. Washington, D.C.: Dumbarton Oaks.

1984   *Chalcatzingo: Excavations on the Olmec Frontier.* London and New York: Thames and Hudson.

1987a   Comments on the Site and Its Organization. In *Ancient Chalcatzingo,* edited by David C. Grove, pp. 420–433. Austin: University of Texas Press.

1987b   Other Ceramic and Miscellaneous Artifacts. In *Ancient Chalcatzingo,* edited by David C. Grove, pp. 271–294. Austin: University of Texas Press.

1987c   Raw Materials and Sources. In *Ancient Chalcatzingo,* edited by David C. Grove, pp. 376–386. Austin: University of Texas Press.

1989   Olmec: What's in a Name? In *Regional Perspectives on the Olmec,* edited by Robert J. Sharer and David C. Grove, pp. 8–14. Cambridge: Cambridge University Press.

1993   "Olmec" Horizons in Formative Mesoamerica: Diffusion or Social Evolution? In *Latin American Horizons,* edited by Don Rice, pp. 83–111. Washington, D.C.: Dumbarton Oaks.

1999   Public Monuments and Sacred Mountains: Observations on Three Formative Period Sacred Landscapes. In *Social Patterns in Pre-Classic Mesoamerica,* edited by David C. Grove and Rosemary A. Joyce, pp. 255–299. Washington, D.C.: Dumbarton Oaks.

Grove, David C., and Jorge Angulo V.

1987   A Catalog and Description of Chalcatzingo's Monuments. In *Ancient Chalcatzingo,* edited by David C. Grove, pp. 114–131. Austin: University of Texas Press.

Grove, David C., and Ann Cyphers Guillén

1987   The Excavations. In *Ancient Chalcatzingo,* edited by David C. Grove, pp. 21–55. Austin: University of Texas Press.

Grove, David C., and Susan D. Gillespie

1984   Chalcatzingo's Portrait Figurines and the Cult of the Ruler. *Archaeology* 37(4):27–33.

1992   Archaeological Indicators of Formative Period Elite: A Perspective from Central Mexico. In *Mesoamerican Elites: An Archaeological Assessment,* edited by Diane Z. Chase and Arlen F. Chase, pp. 191–205. Norman: University of Oklahoma Press.

Grube, Nikolai

1992   Classic Maya Dance: Evidence from Hieroglyphs and Iconography. *Ancient Mesoamerica* 3(2):201–218.

Grube, Nikolai, and David Stuart

1987   Observations on T110 as the Syllable *ko. Research Reports on Ancient Maya Writing,* no. 8. Washington, D.C.: Center for Maya Research.

Guderjan, Thomas, James F. Garber, Herman A. Smith, Fred H. Stross, Helen V. Michel, and Frank Asaro

1989   Maya Maritime Trade and Sources of Obsidian at San Juan, Ambergris Cay, Belize. *Journal of Field Archaeology* 16(3):363–369.

Hall, Grant D., Stanley M. Tarka, Jr., W. Jeffrey Hurst, David Stuart, and Richard E. W. Adams
1990   Cacao Residues in Ancient Maya Vessels from Rio Azul, Guatemala. *American Antiquity* 55(1):138–143.
Hammond, Norman
1975   *Lubaantun: A Classic Maya Realm*. Peabody Museum of Archaeology and Ethnology Monograph no. 2. Harvard University, Cambridge, Mass.
1988   *Ancient Maya Civilization*. New Brunswick, N.J.: Rutgers University Press.
1991   Inside the Black Box: Defining Maya Polity. In *Classic Maya Political History: Hieroglyphic and Archaeological Evidence*, edited by T. Patrick Culbert, pp. 253–284. Cambridge: Cambridge University Press.
1992   Preclassic Maya Civilization. In *New Theories on the Ancient Maya*, edited by Elin Danien and Robert J. Sharer, pp. 137–144. University Museum Monograph no. 77. Philadelphia: University Museum of Archaeology and Anthropology, University of Pennsylvania.
1999   The Genesis of Hierarchy: Mortuary and Offertory Ritual in the Preclassic at Cuello, Belize. In *Social Patterns in Pre-Classic Mesoamerica*, edited by David C. Grove and Rosemary A. Joyce, pp. 49–66. Washington, D.C.: Dumbarton Oaks.
Hardin, Margaret
1977   Individual Style in San José Pottery Painting: The Role of Deliberate Choice. In *The Individual in Prehistory: Studies of Variability in Style in Prehistoric Technologies*, edited by James N. Hill and Joel Gunn, pp. 109–136. New York: Academic Press.
1979   The Cognitive Basis of Productivity in a Decorative Art Style: Implications of an Ethnographic Study for Archaeologists' Taxonomies. In *Ethnoarchaeology: Implications of Ethnography for Archaeology*, edited by Carol Kramer, pp. 75–101. New York: Columbia University Press.
1983   The Structure of Tarascan Pottery Painting. In *Structure and Cognition in Art*, edited by Dorothy K. Washburn, pp. 8–24. Cambridge: Cambridge University Press.
Harrison, Peter
1970   The Central Acropolis, Tikal, Guatemala: A Preliminary Study of the Functions of Its Structural Components during the Late Classic Period. Ph.D. diss., University of Pennsylvania. Ann Arbor: University Microfilms.
Haviland, William A.
1997   The Rise and Fall of Sexual Inequality: Death and Gender at Tikal, Guatemala. *Ancient Mesoamerica* 8(1):1–12.
Haviland, William A., and Hattula Moholy-Nagy
1992   Distinguishing the High and Mighty from the Hoi Polloi at Tikal, Guatemala. In *Mesoamerican Elites: An Archaeological Assessment*, edited by Diane Z. Chase and Arlen F. Chase, pp. 50–60. Norman: University of Oklahoma Press.
Healy, Paul
1974   The Cuyamel Saves: Preclassic Sites in Northeast Honduras. *American Antiquity* 39:433–437.

1992   Ancient Honduras: Power, Wealth, and Rank in Early Chiefdoms. In *Wealth and Hierarchy in the Intermediate Area,* edited by Frederick W. Lange, pp. 85–108. Washington, D.C.: Dumbarton Oaks.

Hendon, Julia

1991   Status and Power in Classic Maya Society: An Archeological Study. *American Anthropologist* 93(4):894–918.

1992a   Architectural Symbols of the Maya Social Order: Residential Construction and Decoration in the Copan Valley, Honduras. In *Ancient Images, Ancient Thought: the Archaeology of Ideology,* edited by A. Sean Goldsmith, Sandra Garvie, David Selin, and Jeannette Smith, pp. 481–495. Proceedings of the 23rd Annual Chacmool Conference. Calgary: Archaeological Association, University of Calgary.

1992b   Hilado y tejido en la época prehispánica: Tecnología y relaciones sociales de la producción textil. In *La indumentaria y el tejido mayas a través del tiempo,* edited by Linda Asturias de Barrios and Dina Fernández García, pp. 7–16. Guatemala City: Museo Ixchel del Traje Indígena de Guatemala.

1992c   Variation in Classic Maya Sociopolitical Organization. *American Anthropologist* 94(4):940–941.

1997   Women's Work, Women's Space, and Women's Status among the Classic-Period Maya Elite of the Copan Valley, Honduras. In *Women in Prehistory: North America and Mesoamerica,* edited by Cheryl Claassen and Rosemary A. Joyce, pp. 33–46. Philadelphia: University of Pennsylvania Press.

1999   The Preclassic Maya Compound as the Focus of Social Identity. In *Social Patterns in Pre-Classic Mesoamerica,* edited by David C. Grove and Rosemary A. Joyce, pp. 97–125. Washington, D.C.: Dumbarton Oaks.

Hendon, Julia, and Rosemary A. Joyce

1993   Questioning "Complexity" and "Periphery": Archaeology in Yoro, Honduras. A paper presented at the annual meeting of the Society for American Archaeology, St. Louis.

Herzfeld, Michael

1991   *A Place in History: Social and Monumental Time in a Cretan Town.* Princeton: Princeton University Press.

1992   Metapatterns: Archaeology and the Uses of Evidential Scarcity. In *Representations in Archaeology,* edited by Jean Gardin and Christopher Peebles, pp. 66–86. Bloomington: Indiana University Press.

Hicks, Frederick

1982   Texcoco in the Early Sixteenth Century: The State, the City, and the *Calpolli. American Ethnologist* 9:320–349.

1991   Gift and Tribute: Relations of Dependency in Aztec Mexico. In *Early State Economics,* edited by Henri J. M. Claessen and Pieter van de Velde, pp. 199–213. Political and Legal Anthropology Series, vol. 8. New Brunswick, N.J.: Transaction Publishers.

1994   Cloth in the Political Economy of the Aztec State. In *Economies and Polities in the Aztec Realm,* edited by Mary Hodge and Michael Smith, pp. 89–111. Albany: Institute of Mesoamerican Studies, University at Albany, State University of New York.

Hirth, Kenneth
1992   Interregional Exchange as Elite Behavior: An Evolutionary Perspective. In *Mesoamerican Elites: An Archaeological Assessment,* edited by Diane Z. Chase and Arlen F. Chase, pp. 18–29. Norman: University of Oklahoma Press.

Hodge, Mary G., and Michael E. Smith, eds.
1994   *Economies and Polities in the Aztec Realm.* Albany: Institute for Mesoamerican Studies, University at Albany, State University of New York.

Hoopes, John
1995   Interaction in Hunting and Gathering Societies as a Context for the Emergence of Pottery in the Central American Isthmus. In *The Emergence of Pottery: Technology and Innovation in Ancient Societies,* edited by W. Barnett and J. Hoopes, pp. 185–198. Washington, D.C.: Smithsonian Institution Press.

Hoskins, Janet
1990   Doubling Deities, Descent and Personhood: An Exploration of Kodi Gender Categories. In *Power and Difference: Gender in Island Southeast Asia,* edited by Jane Monnig Atkinson and Shelly Errington, pp. 273–306. Stanford: Stanford University Press.

Houston, Stephen D.
1984   Quetzal Feather Dance at Bonampak, Chiapas, Mexico. *Journal de la Société des Américanistes* (Paris), n.s., 70:127–137.
1993   *Hieroglyphs and History at Dos Pilas: Dynastic Politics of the Classic Maya.* Austin: University of Texas Press.
1996   Symbolic Sweatbaths of the Maya: Architectural Meaning in the Cross Group at Palenque, Mexico. *Latin American Antiquity* 7(2):132–151.

Houston, Stephen D., and Peter Mathews
1985   *The Dynastic Sequence of Dos Pilas, Guatemala.* Monograph 1. San Francisco: Pre-Columbian Art Research Institute.

Houston, Stephen D., David Stuart, and Karl A. Taube
1989   Folk Classification of Classic Maya Pottery. *American Anthropologist* 91(3): 720–726.

Houston, Stephen, and Karl Taube
1987   Name-Tagging in Classic Mayan Script. *Mexikon* 9(2):38–41.

Howard, Catherine
1991   Fragments of the Heavens: Feathers as Ornaments among the Waiwai. In *Gift of Birds,* edited by Ruben Reina and Ken Kensinger, pp. 50–69. Philadelphia: University of Pennsylvania Museum.

Hubbard, Ruth
1990   *The Politics of Women's Biology.* New Brunswick, N.J.: Rutgers University Press.

Hunt, Eva
1977   *The Transformation of the Hummingbird: Cultural Roots of a Zinacantecan Mythical Poem.* Ithaca, N.Y.: Cornell University Press.

Inomata, Takeshi
1997   The Last Day of a Fortified Classic Maya Center: Archaeological Investigations at Aguateca, Guatemala. *Ancient Mesoamerica* 8(2):337–352.

Isaac, Barry L.
1986   Notes on Obsidian, the Pochteca, and the Position of Tlatelolco in the Aztec Empire. In *Economic Aspects of Prehistoric Highland Mexico*, edited by Barry L. Isaac, pp. 319–343. Research in Economic Anthropology, Supplement 2. Greenwich, Conn.: JAI Press.

Joesink-Mandeville, Leroy
1987   Yarumela, Honduras: Formative Period Cultural Conservatism and Diffusion. In *Interaction on the Southeast Mesoamerican Frontier: Prehistoric and Historic Honduras and El Salvador*, edited by Eugenia J. Robinson, pp. 196–214. BAR International Series 327(i). Oxford.

Jones, Christopher, and Linton Satterthwaite
1982   *The Monuments and Inscriptions of Tikal*. Tikal Reports no. 33. University Museum Monograph vol. 44. Philadelphia: University of Pennsylvania Museum.

Joralemon, David
1973   Ritual Blood-Sacrifice among the Ancient Maya, Part 1. In *Primera Mesa Redonda de Palenque, Part 2*, edited by Merle Greene Robertson, pp. 59–75. Pebble Beach, Calif.: Robert Louis Stevenson School.

Josserand, J. Kathryn
1991   Narrative Structure of Hieroglyphic Texts at Palenque. In *Sixth Palenque Round Table, 1986*, edited by Virginia M. Fields, pp. 12–31. Norman: University of Oklahoma Press.

Joyce, Rosemary A.
1986   Terminal Classic Interaction on the Southeastern Maya Periphery. *American Antiquity* 51:313–329.
1987   Gender, Role, and Status in Middle Formative Mesoamerica: Implications of Burials from La Venta, Tabasco, Mexico. A paper presented at the Third Texas Symposium, "Olmec, Izapa, and the Development of Maya Civilization." University of Texas, Institute for Latin American Studies, Austin.
1990   The Construction of Gender in Classic Maya Sculpture. A paper presented in the session "The Engendered Subject: Practice and Representation in Mesoamerica" (Veronica Kann and Geoffrey McCafferty, organizers). American Anthropological Association, New Orleans.
1991a   *Cerro Palenque: Power and Identity on the Maya Periphery*. Austin: University of Texas Press.
1991b   Review of "Introducción a la Arqueología de Copán, Honduras," edited by Claude Baudez. *American Antiquity* 56(1):170–171.
1992a   Dimensiones simbólicas del traje en monumentos clásicos mayas: La construcción del género a través del vestido. In *La indumentaria y el tejido mayas a través del tiempo*, edited by Linda Asturias de Barrios and Dina Fernández García, pp. 29–38. Guatemala City: Museo Ixchel del Traje Indígena de Guatemala.
1992b   Ideology in Action: Classic Maya Ritual Practice. In *Ancient Images, Ancient Thought: The Archaeology of Ideology*, edited by A. Sean Goldsmith, Sandra Garvie, David Selin, and Jeannette Smith, pp. 497–505. Proceedings of the 23rd Annual Chacmool Conference. Calgary: Archaeological Association, University of Calgary.

1992c Images of Gender and Labor Organization in Classic Maya Society. In *Exploring Gender through Archaeology: Selected Papers from the 1991 Boone Conference*, edited by Cheryl Claassen, pp. 63–70. Monographs in World Archaeology, no. 11. Madison, Wis.: Prehistory Press.

1992d Innovation, Communication, and the Archaeological Record: A Reassessment of Middle Formative Honduras. *Journal of the Steward Anthropological Society* (Urbana, Ill.) 20(1–2):235–256.

1992e The Social Construction of Power in Formative Period Honduras. Paper presented at the annual meeting of the American Anthropological Association, San Francisco.

1993a *Embodying Personhood in Prehispanic Costa Rica*. Wellesley, Mass.: Davis Museum and Cultural Center.

1993b Women's Work: Images of Production and Reproduction in Prehispanic Southern Central America. *Current Anthropology* 34(3):255–274.

1994 On Engendering Monte Alban Tomb 7. *Current Anthropology* 35(3):284.

1996a The Construction of Gender in Classic Maya Monuments. In *Gender and Archaeology*, edited by Rita Wright, pp. 167–195. Philadelphia: University of Pennsylvania Press.

1996b Performance and Inscription: Negotiating Sex and Gender in Classic Maya Society. A paper presented in the Precolumbian Studies Symposium "Recovering Gender in Precolumbian America," organized by Cecelia Klein. Dumbarton Oaks, Washington, D.C.

1996c Social Dynamics of Exchange: Changing Patterns in the Honduran Archaeological Record. In *Chieftains, Power, and Trade: Regional Interaction in the Intermediate Area of the Americas*, edited by Carl Henrik Langebaek and Felipe Cárdenas-Arroyo, pp. 31–45. Bogotá, Colombia: Departamento de Antropología, Universidad de los Andes.

1997 Playa de los Muertos Figurines and Their Predecessors. Manuscript in possession of the author.

1998 Performing the Body in Prehispanic Central America. *Res: Anthropology and Aesthetics* 33 (spring):147–165.

1999 Social Dimensions of Pre-Classic Burials. In *Social Patterns in Pre-Classic Mesoamerica*, edited by David C. Grove and Rosemary A. Joyce, pp. 15–47. Washington, D.C.: Dumbarton Oaks.

In press Tikal Stela 31: Some comments on Chronology, Text, and Image. *Research Reports on Ancient Maya Writing*. Washington, D.C.: Center for Maya Research.

Joyce, Rosemary A., Richard Edging, Karl Lorenz, and Susan D. Gillespie

1991 Olmec Bloodletting: An Iconographic Study. In *Sixth Palenque Round Table, 1986*, edited by Virginia M. Fields, pp. 143–150. Norman: University of Oklahoma Press.

Joyce, Rosemary A., and Susan D. Gillespie, eds.

2000 *Beyond Kinship: Social and Material Reproduction in House Societies*. Philadelphia: University of Pennsylvania Press.

Joyce, Rosemary A., and John S. Henderson

1996 Before Playa de los Muertos: The Early Formative Archaeology of the

Lower Ulua River Valley. Paper presented at the annual meeting of the Society for American Archaeology, New Orleans.

Joyce, Rosemary A., and Susan A. M. Shumaker
1995   *Encounters with the Americas.* Cambridge, Mass.: Peabody Museum of Archaeology and Ethnology, Harvard University.

Joyce, Thomas A.
1933   The Pottery Whistle Figurines of Lubaantun. *Journal of the Royal Anthropological Institute* 63:15–25.

Justeson, John S.
1983   Mayan Hieroglyphic "Name-Tagging" of a Pair of Rectangular Jade Plaques from Xcalumkin. In *Recent Contributions to Maya Hieroglyphic Decipherment, Number 1,* edited by Stephen D. Houston, pp. 40–43. New Haven: Human Relations Area Files.
1984   Appendix B: Interpretations of Mayan Hieroglyphs. In *Phoneticism in Mayan Hieroglyphic Writing,* edited by John S. Justeson and Lyle Campbell, pp. 315–362. Publication no. 9. Albany: Institute for Mesoamerican Studies, State University of New York at Albany.
1986   Origin of Writing Systems: Preclassic Mesoamerica. *World Archaeology* 17(3):437–458.
1988   Non-Maya Calendars of Southern Veracruz-Tabasco and the Antiquity of the Civil and Agricultural Years. *Journal of Mayan Linguistics* 6:1–21.

Justeson, John S., and Lyle Campbell, eds.
1984   *Phoneticism in Mayan Hieroglyphic Writing.* Publication no. 9. Albany: Institute for Mesoamerican Studies, State University of New York at Albany.

Kan, Sergei
1989   *Symbolic Immortality: The Tlingit Potlatch of the Nineteenth Century.* Washington, D.C.: Smithsonian Institution Press.

Kelemen, Pal
1956   *Medieval American Art: Masterpieces of the New World before Columbus.* New York: Macmillan.

Kelley, David
1965   The Birth of the Gods at Palenque. *Estudios de Cultura Maya* 5:93–134.
1968   Kakupacal and the Itzas. *Estudios de Cultura Maya* 7:255–268.
1982   Notes on Puuc Inscriptions and History. Supplement to *The Puuc: New Perspectives,* edited by Lawrence W. Mills. Scholarly Studies in the Liberal Arts, Publication no. 1. Pella, Iowa: Central College.

Kellogg, Susan
1986   Aztec Inheritance in Sixteenth-Century Mexico City: Colonial Patterns, Prehispanic Influences. *Ethnohistory* (Durham) 33(3):313–330.
1993   The Social Organization of Households among the Mexica before and after Conquest. In *Prehispanic Domestic Units in Western Mesoamerica: Studies of the Household, Compound, and Residence,* edited by Robert Santley and Kenneth Hirth, pp. 207–224. Boca Raton: CRC Press.
1995   *Law and the Transformation of Aztec Culture, 1500–1700.* Norman: University of Oklahoma Press.

Kennedy, Nedenia
1981   The Formative Period Ceramic Sequence from Playa de los Muertos, Hon-

duras. Ph.D. diss., Department of Anthropology, University of Illinois, Urbana-Champaign. Ann Arbor: University Microfilms.

Kensinger, Kenneth
1991   Feathers Make Us Beautiful: The Meaning of Cashinahua Feather Headdresses. In *Gift of Birds,* edited by Ruben Reina and Ken Kensinger, pp. 40-49. Philadelphia: University of Pennsylvania Museum.

Kirchhoff, Paul
1955   The Principles of Clanship in Human Society. *Davidson Journal of Anthropology* 1:1-10.

Klein, Cecelia F.
1976   *The Face of the Earth: Frontality in Two-Dimensional Mesoamerican Art.* New York: Garland.
1980   Who Was Tlaloc? *Journal of Latin American Lore* 6(2):155-204.
1987   The Ideology of Autosacrifice at the Templo Mayor. In *The Aztec Templo Mayor,* edited by Elizabeth H. Boone, pp. 293-370. Washington, D.C.: Dumbarton Oaks.
1988   Rethinking Cihuacoatl: Aztec Political Imagery of the Conquered Woman. In *Smoke and Mist: Mesoamerican Studies in Memory of Thelma D. Sullivan,* edited by J. Kathryn Josserand and K. Dakin, pp. 237-277. BAR International Series 402. Oxford.
1990-1991   Snares and Entrails: Mesoamerican Symbols of Sin and Punishment. *Res: Anthropology and Aesthetics* 19-20:81-103.
1993a   Shield Women: Resolution of an Aztec Gender Paradox. In *Current Topics in Aztec Studies: Essays in Honor of Dr. H. B. Nicholson,* edited by Alana Cordy-Collins and Douglas Sharon, pp. 39-64. San Diego Museum Papers, vol. 30. San Diego: San Diego Museum of Man.
1993b   Teocuitlatl, "Divine Excrement": The Significance of "Holy Shit" in Ancient Mexico. *Art Journal* 52(3):20-27.
1994   Fighting with Femininity: Gender and War in Aztec Mexico. *Estudios de Cultura Nahuatl* 24:219-253.

Klor de Alva, J. Jorge, Henry B. Nicholson, and Eloise Quiñones Keber, eds.
1988   *The Work of Bernardino de Sahagún: Pioneer Ethnographer of Sixteenth-Century Aztec Mexico.* Albany: Institute for Mesoamerican Studies, State University of New York at Albany.

Kowalski, Jeff Karl
1989   Who Am I among the Itza? Links between Northern Yucatan and the Western Maya Lowlands and Highlands. In *Mesoamerica after the Decline of Teotihuacan: A.D. 700-900,* edited by Richard Diehl and Janet Catherine Berlo, pp. 173-186. Washington, D.C.: Dumbarton Oaks.

Krochock, Ruth
1991   Dedication Ceremonies at Chichen Itza: The Glyphic Evidence. In *Sixth Palenque Round Table, 1986,* edited by Virginia M. Fields, pp. 43-50. Norman: University of Oklahoma Press.
1998   The Development of Political Rhetoric at Chichen Itza, Yucatan, Mexico. Ph.D. diss., Department of Anthropology, Southern Methodist University.

Kurjack, Edward B.
1979   *Sacbeob:* Parentesco y desarrollo del estado maya. In *Los procesos de cambio*

en Mesoamérica y áreas circunvecinas 1:217–230. XV Mesa Redonda, Sociedad Mexicana de Antropología. Guanajuato.

Kurjack, Edward B., and E. Wyllys Andrews V
1976   Early Boundary Maintenance in Northwest Yucatan, Mexico. *American Antiquity* 41:318–325.

Landa, Diego de
1941   *Landa's "Relación de las cosas de Yucatan."* Translated by Alfred M. Tozzer. Peabody Museum of Archaeology and Ethnology Papers, vol. 18. Harvard University, Cambridge, Mass.

Laqueur, Thomas
1990   *Making Sex: Body and Gender from the Greeks to Freud.* Cambridge, Mass.: Harvard University Press.

Lathrap, Donald W.
1976   Shipibo Tourist Art. In *Ethnic and Tourist Arts,* edited by Nelson Graburn, pp. 197–207. Berkeley: University of California Press.
1983   Recent Shipibo-Conibo Ceramics and Their Implications for Archaeological Interpretation. In *Structure and Cognition in Art,* edited by Dorothy K. Washburn, pp. 25–39. Cambridge: Cambridge University Press.

Lathrap, Donald W., and Warren R. DeBoer
1979   The Making and Breaking of Shipibo-Conibo Ceramics. In *Ethnoarchaeology: Implications of Ethnography for Archaeology,* edited by Carol Kramer, pp. 102–138. New York: Columbia University Press.

Laughlin, Robert, comp.
1977   *Of Cabbages and Kings: Tales from Zinacantan.* Smithsonian Contributions to Anthropology, no. 23. Washington, D.C.: Smithsonian Institution Press.

Lentz, David L.
1991   Maya Diets of the Rich and Poor: Paleoethnobotanical Evidence from Copan. *Latin American Antiquity* 2(3):269–287.

León-Portilla, Miguel
1963   *Aztec Thought and Culture.* Norman: University of Oklahoma Press.
1978   *México-Tenochtitlan, su espacio y tiempo sagrados.* Mexico City: Instituto Nacional de Antropología e Historia.

Lesure, Richard
1997a Early Formative Platforms at Paso de la Amada, Chiapas, Mexico. *Latin American Antiquity* 8(3):217–235.
1997b Figurines and Social Identities in Early Sedentary Societies of Coastal Chiapas, Mexico. In *Women in Prehistory: North America and Mesoamerica,* edited by Cheryl Claassen and Rosemary Joyce, pp. 227–248. Philadelphia: University of Pennsylvania Press.
1998   Vessel Form and Function in an Early Formative Ceramic Assemblage from Coastal Mexico. *Journal of Field Archaeology* 25(1):19–36

Leventhal, Richard
1996   The End at Xunantunich: The Architecture and Setting in the Terminal Classic. In *Xunantunich Archaeological Project: 1996 Field Season,* pp. 9–16. Los Angeles: UCLA Institute of Archaeology.

Leventhal, Richard, Wendy Ashmore, Lisa LeCount, Virginia Hetrick, and Thomas Jamison

1992   Xunantunich Archaeological Project: 1992 Research [a paper presented at the 91st Annual Meeting of the American Anthropological Association, San Francisco, Calif., December 1992 (revised version)]. In *Xunantunich Archaeological Project: 1992 Field Season*, pp. 8–21. Los Angeles: UCLA Institute of Archaeology.

Leventhal, Richard, Scott Zeleznik, Thomas Jamison, Lisa LeCount, James O. McGovern, Julia Sanchez, and Angela Keller

1993   Xunantunich: A Late and Terminal Classic Center in the Belize River Valley [a paper presented at the Palenque Mesa Redonda, Aniversario Katun, 1973–1993, June 1993, Palenque, Mexico]. In *Xunantunich Archaeological Project: 1993 Field Season*, pp. 7–15. Los Angeles: UCLA Institute of Archaeology.

Lévi-Strauss, Claude

1983   *The Way of the Masks*. Translated by Sylvia Modelski. Seattle: University of Washington Press.

1987   *Anthropology and Myth: Lectures, 1951–1982*. Oxford: Basil Blackwell.

Lincoln, Charles E.

1986   The Chronology of Chichen Itza: A Review of the Literature. In *Late Lowland Maya Civilization: Classic to Postclassic*, edited by Jeremy A. Sabloff and E. Wyllys Andrews V, pp. 141–196. Albuquerque: University of New Mexico Press.

1990   Ethnicity and Social Organization at Chichen Itza, Yucatan, Mexico. Ph.D. diss., Department of Anthropology, Harvard University. Ann Arbor: University Microfilms International.

Lockhart, James

1992   *The Nahuas after the Conquest*. Stanford: Stanford University Press.

Longacre, William

1995   Why Did They Invent Pottery Anyway? In *The Emergence of Pottery: Technology and Innovation in Ancient Societies*, edited by W. Barnett and J. Hoopes, pp. 277–280. Washington, D.C.: Smithsonian Institution Press.

López Austin, Alfredo

1988   *The Human Body and Ideology: Concepts of the Ancient Nahuas*. Translated by Thelma Ortiz de Montellano and Bernard Ortiz de Montellano. Salt Lake City: University of Utah Press.

Lounsbury, Floyd

1976   A Rationale for the Initial Date of the Temple of the Cross at Palenque. In *Art, Iconography, and Dynastic History of Palenque, Part III: Proceedings of the Segunda Mesa Redonda de Palenque, Palenque, Chiapas, Mexico, December 14–21, 1974*, edited by Merle Greene Robertson, pp. 211–224. Pebble Beach, Calif.: Robert Louis Stevenson School, Pre-Columbian Art Research.

1980   Some Problems in the Interpretation of the Mythological Portion of the Hieroglyphic Text of the Temple of the Cross at Palenque. In *Third Palenque Round Table, 1978 — Part 2: Proceedings of the Tercera Mesa Redonda de*

Palenque, June 11-18, 1978, edited by Merle Greene Robertson, pp. 99-115. Austin: University of Texas Press.

1985   Identities of the Mythological Figures in the Cross Group Inscriptions of Palenque. In *Fourth Palenque Round Table, 1980,* edited by Elizabeth P. Benson, pp. 45-58. San Francisco: Pre-Columbian Art Research Institute.

1989   The Names of a King: Hieroglyphic Variants as a Key to Decipherment. In *Word and Image in Maya Culture,* edited by William Hanks and Don Rice, pp. 73-91. Salt Lake City: University of Utah Press.

Love, Michael W.

1991   Style and Social Complexity in Formative Mesoamerica. In *The Formation of Complex Society in Southeastern Mesoamerica,* edited by William R. Fowler, pp. 47-76. Boca Raton: CRC Press.

1992   Material Culture and Social Practice in Preclassic Pacific Guatemala. A paper presented at the annual meeting of the American Anthropological Association, San Francisco.

1999   Ideology, Material Culture, and Daily Practice in Pre-Classic Mesoamerica: A Pacific Coast Perspective. In *Social Patterns in Pre-Classic Mesoamerica,* edited by David C. Grove and Rosemary A. Joyce, pp. 127-153. Washington, D.C.: Dumbarton Oaks.

Lowe, Gareth

1981   Olmec Horizons Defined in Mound 20, San Isidro, Chiapas. In *The Olmec and Their Neighbors,* edited by Elizabeth P. Benson, pp. 231-256. Washington, D.C.: Dumbarton Oaks.

Lowie, Robert H.

1963   *Indians of the Plains.* American Museum of Natural History Science Books. Garden City, N.Y.: Natural History Press.

MacCormack, Carol, and Marilyn Strathern, eds.

1980   *Nature, Culture, and Gender.* Cambridge: Cambridge University Press.

MacLeod, Barbara

1987   *An Epigrapher's Annotated Index to Cholan and Yucatecan Verb Morphology.* Museum of Anthropology, University of Missouri–Columbia, Monographs in Anthropology, no. 9. Columbia, Mo.

Macri, Martha J., and Anabel Ford, eds.

1997   *The Language of Maya Hieroglyphs.* San Francisco: Pre-Columbian Art Research Institute.

Marcus, George

1992   The Concern with Elites in Archaeological Reconstructions: Mesoamerican Materials. In *Mesoamerican Elites: An Archaeological Assessment,* edited by Diane Z. Chase and Arlen F. Chase, pp. 292-302. Norman: University of Oklahoma Press.

Marcus, Joyce

1975   The Origins of Mesoamerican Writing. *Annual Review of Anthropology* 5: 35-67.

1976   *Emblem and State in the Classic Maya Lowlands.* Washington, D.C.: Dumbarton Oaks.

1983   On the Nature of the Mesoamerican City. In *Prehistoric Settlement Patterns:*

Essays in Honor of Gordon R. Willey, edited by Evon Z. Vogt and Richard Leventhal, pp. 195–242. Albuquerque: University of New Mexico Press.

1987   *The Inscriptions of Calakmul: Royal Marriage at a Maya City in Campeche, Mexico.* Technical Report 21. Ann Arbor: University of Michigan, Museum of Anthropology.

1989   Zapotec Chiefdoms and the Nature of Formative Religions. In *Regional Perspectives on the Olmec,* edited by Robert J. Sharer and David C. Grove, pp. 148–197. Cambridge: Cambridge University Press.

1992   Royal Families, Royal Texts: Examples from the Zapotec and Maya. In *Mesoamerican Elites: An Archaeological Assessment,* edited by Diane Z. Chase and Arlen F. Chase, pp. 221–241. Norman: University of Oklahoma Press.

1999   Men's and Women's Ritual in Formative Oaxaca. In *Social Patterns in Pre-Classic Mesoamerica,* edited by David C. Grove and Rosemary A. Joyce, pp. 67–96. Washington, D.C.: Dumbarton Oaks.

Mathews, Peter

1979   The Glyphs from the Ear Ornament from Tomb A 1/1. In *Excavations at Altun Ha, Belize, 1964-1970, Volume 1,* edited by David Pendergast, pp. 79–80. Toronto: Royal Ontario Museum.

1980   Notes on the Dynastic Sequence of Bonampak, Part I. In *Third Palenque Round Table, 1978—Part 2: Proceedings of the Tercera Mesa Redonda de Palenque, June 11-18, 1978,* edited by Merle Greene Robertson, pp. 60–73. Austin: University of Texas Press.

1985   Maya Early Classic Monuments and Inscriptions. In *Considerations of the Early Classic Period in the Maya Lowlands,* edited by Gordon R. Willey and Peter Mathews, pp. 5–54. Albany: Institute for Mesoamerican Studies, State University of New York at Albany.

1991   Classic Maya Emblem Glyphs. In *Classic Maya Political History: Hieroglyphic and Archaeological Evidence,* edited by T. Patrick Culbert, pp. 19–29. Cambridge: Cambridge University Press.

Mathews, Peter, and David Pendergast

1979   The Altun Ha Jade Plaque: Deciphering the Inscription. In *Studies in Ancient Mesoamerica, IV,* edited by John Graham, pp. 197–214. Contributions of the University of California Archaeological Research Facility, no. 41. Berkeley, Calif.

Mathews, Peter, and Gordon R. Willey

1991   Prehistoric Polities of the Pasión Region: Hieroglyphic Texts and Their Archaeological Settings. In *Classic Maya Political History: Hieroglyphic and Archaeological Evidence,* edited by T. Patrick Culbert, pp. 30–71. Cambridge: Cambridge University Press.

Matos Moctezuma, Eduardo

1984   The Templo Mayor of Tenochtitlan: Economics and Ideology. In *Ritual Human Sacrifice in Mesoamerica,* edited by Elizabeth H. Boone, pp. 133–164. Washington, D.C.: Dumbarton Oaks.

1988   *The Great Temple of the Aztecs: Treasures of Tenochtitlan.* Translated by Doris Heyden. New York: Thames and Hudson.

1992 The Aztec Main Pyramid: Ritual Architecture at Tenochtitlan. In *Ancient Americas: Art from Sacred Landscapes*, edited by Richard Townsend, pp. 186-195. Chicago and Munich: Art Institute of Chicago.

1996 Catalogue Entry 94: Deity Mask. In *Olmec Art of Ancient Mexico*, edited by Elizabeth P. Benson and Beatriz de la Fuente, p. 252. Washington, D.C.: National Gallery of Art.

McAnany, Patricia A.

1995 *Living with the Ancestors: Kinship and Kingship in Ancient Maya Society*. Austin: University of Texas Press.

McCafferty, Geoffrey G., and Sharisse D. McCafferty

1990 Gender Ideologies and Practice in Postclassic Mexico. A paper presented in the session "The Engendered Subject: Practice and Representation in Mesoamerica" (Veronica Kann and Geoffrey McCafferty, organizers). American Anthropological Association, New Orleans.

1999 The Metamorphosis of Xochiquetzal: A Window on Womanhood in Pre- and Post-Conquest Mexico. In *Manifesting Power: Gender and the Interpretation of Power in Archaeology*, edited by Tracy Sweely, pp. 103-125. London: Routledge.

McCafferty, Sharisse D., and Geoffrey G. McCafferty

1988 Powerful Women and the Myth of Male Dominance in Aztec Society. *Archaeological Review from Cambridge* 7(1):45-59.

1991 Spinning and Weaving as Female Gender Identity in Post-Classic Mexico. In *Textile Traditions of Mesoamerica and the Andes: An Anthology*, edited by Janet Catherine Berlo, Margot Schevill, and Edward B. Dwyer, pp. 19-44. New York: Garland.

1994 Engendering Tomb 7 at Monte Alban: Respinning an Old Yarn. *Current Anthropology* 35(2):143-166.

McClung de Tapia, Emily, and Evelyn Rattray, eds.

1987 *Teotihuacan: Nuevos datos, nuevas síntesis, nuevos problemas*. Serie Antropológica, no. 72. Mexico City: Instituto de Investigaciones Antropológicas, Universidad Nacional Autónoma de México.

McKinnon, Susan

1991 *From a Shattered Sun: Hierarchy, Gender, and Alliance in the Tanimbar Islands*. Madison: University of Wisconsin Press.

Merry de Morales, Marcia

1987 Chalcatzingo's Burials as Indicators of Social Ranking. In *Ancient Chalcatzingo*, edited by David C. Grove, pp. 95-113. Austin: University of Texas Press.

Meskell, Lynn

1996 The Somatisation of Archaeology: Institutions, Discourses, Corporeality. *Norwegian Archaeological Review* 29(1):1-16.

1998 The Irresistible Body and the Seduction of Archaeology. In *Changing Bodies, Changing Meanings: Studies on the Human Body in Antiquity*, edited by Dominique Montserrat, pp. 139-161. London: Routledge.

1999 *Archaeologies of Social Life: Age, Sex, Class, etc., in Ancient Egypt*. Oxford: Blackwell.

Milbrath, Susan
1997   Decapitated Lunar Goddesses in Aztec Art, Myth, and Ritual. *Ancient Mesoamerica* 8(2):197-225.
Miller, Arthur G.
1977   "Captains of the Itza": Unpublished Mural Evidence from Chichen Itza. In *Social Process in Maya Prehistory*, edited by Norman Hammond, pp. 197-225. New York: Academic Press.
Miller, Jeffrey
1974   Notes on a Stela Pair Probably from Calakmul, Campeche, Mexico. In *Primera Mesa Redonda de Palenque, Part 1*, edited by Merle Greene Robertson, pp. 149-161. Pebble Beach, Calif.: The Robert Louis Stevenson School.
Miller, Mary Ellen
1985   Architectural Backdrops of the Murals of Structure 1, Bonampak. In *Fourth Palenque Round Table, 1980*, edited by Elizabeth P. Benson, pp. 185-191. San Francisco: Pre-Columbian Art Research Institute.
1986   *The Murals of Bonampak*. Princeton: Princeton University Press.
1988   The Boys in the Bonampak Band. In *Maya Iconography*, edited by Elizabeth P. Benson and Gillett G. Griffin, pp. 318-330. Princeton: Princeton University Press.
1993   On the Eve of the Collapse: Maya Art of the Eighth Century. In *Lowland Maya Civilization in the Eighth Century A.D.*, edited by Jeremy Sabloff and John S. Henderson, pp. 355-413. Washington, D.C.: Dumbarton Oaks.
Millon, Clara
1988   Great Goddess Fragment. In *Feathered Serpents and Flowering Trees: Reconstructing the Murals of Teotihuacan*, edited by Kathleen Berrin, pp. 226-228. San Francisco: The Fine Arts Museums of San Francisco.
Millon, René
1981   Teotihuacan: City, State, and Civilization. In *Handbook of Middle American Indians, Supplement* 1:198-243. Edited by Victoria Bricker and Jeremy Sabloff. Austin: University of Texas Press.
Moholy-Nagy, Hattula, John M. Ladd, and Fred Trembour
1992   Objects of Stone, Shell, and Bone. In *Artifacts from the Cenote of Sacrifice, Chichen Itza, Yucatan: Textiles, Basketry, Stone, Bone, Shell, Ceramics, Wood, Copal, Rubber, Other Organic Materials, and Mammalian Remains*, edited by Clemency C. Coggins, pp. 99-152. Peabody Museum of Archaeology and Ethnology Memoirs 10(3). Harvard University, Cambridge, Mass.
Molina, Fray Alonso de
1970   [orig. 1571] *Vocabulario en lengua castellana y mexicana, y mexicana u castellana*. Mexico City: Editorial Porrúa.
Monaghan, John
1996   The Mesoamerican Community as a "Great House." In *Mesoamerican Community Organization: Barrios and Other Customary Social Units, Part II*, edited by E. M. Mulhare. Special issue of *Ethnology* 35(3):181-194.
Monzón, Arturo
1983   *El calpulli en la organización social de los tenochca*. Clásicos de la Antropología, Colección no. 15. Mexico City: Instituto Nacional Indigenista.

Moore, Henrietta
1988   *Feminism and Anthropology*. Minneapolis: University of Minnesota Press.
Morley, Frances, and Sylvanus G. Morley
1938   The Age and Provenance of the Leyden Plate. In *Contributions to American Anthropology and History* 24:1–17. Carnegie Institution of Washington Publication 509. Washington, D.C.
Morris, Earl H.
1925   Report of E. H. Morris on the Temple on the Northeast Bank of the Xtoloc Cenote (Station 3). Carnegie Institution of Washington, *Year Book* 24:263–265. Washington, D.C.
Morris, Earl H., Jean Charlot, and Ann Axtell Morris
1931   *Temple of the Warriors at Chichen Itza, Yucatan*. Carnegie Institution of Washington Publication 406. Washington, D.C.
Morris, Walter F.
1985a   Fall Fashions: Lagartero Figurine Costumes at the End of the Classic Period. In *Fifth Palenque Round Table, 1983*, edited by Virginia M. Fields, pp. 245–254. San Francisco: Pre-Columbian Art Research Institute.
1985b   Warped Glyphs: A Reading of Maya Textiles. In *Fourth Palenque Round Table, 1980,* edited by Elizabeth P. Benson, pp. 317–323. San Francisco: Pre-Columbian Art Research Institute.
Muller, Viana
1987   Kin Reproduction and Elite Accumulation in the Archaic States of Northwest Europe. In *Power Relations and State Formation,* edited by Thomas C. Patterson and Christine Ward Gailey, pp. 81–97. Washington, D.C.: Archaeology Section, American Anthropological Association.
Munn, Nancy
1986   *The Fame of Gawa*. Durham: Duke University Press.
Murra, John V.
1989   Cloth and Its Function in the Inca State. In *Cloth and Human Experience,* edited by Annette Weiner and Jane Schneider, pp. 275–302. Washington, D.C.: Smithsonian Institution Press.
Nash, June
1978   The Aztecs and the Ideology of Male Dominance. *Signs* 4(2):349–362.
1980   Aztec Women: The Transition from Status to Class in Empire and Colony. In *Women and Colonization,* edited by Mona Etienne and Eleanor Leacock, pp. 134–148. New York: Praeger.
Nichols, Deborah L., and Charles D. Frederick
1993   Irrigation Canals and Chinampas: Recent Research in the Northern Basin of Mexico. In *Economic Aspects of Water Management in the Prehispanic New World,* edited by Vernon L. Scarborough and Barry L. Isaac, pp. 123–150. Research in Economic Anthropology, Supplement 7. Greenwich, Conn.: JAI Press.
Nicholson, Henry B.
1971   Religion in Pre-Hispanic Central Mexico. In *Handbook of Middle American Indians* 10:395–446. Edited by Robert Wauchope, Gordon Ekholm, and Ignacio Bernal. Austin: University of Texas Press.

Niederberger, Christine

1976   Zohapilco: Cinco milenios de ocupación humana en sitio lacustre de la cuenca de México. Colección Científica no. 30. Mexico City: Instituto Nacional de Antropología e Historia.

1996   The Basin of Mexico: A Multimillenial Development toward Cultural Complexity. In Olmec Art of Ancient Mexico, edited by Elizabeth P. Benson and Beatriz de la Fuente, pp. 83–94. Washington, D.C.: National Gallery of Art.

Ochoa, Patricia

1996a   Catalogue Entry 21: Hollow Seated Figure with Upraised Arm. In Olmec Art of Ancient Mexico, edited by Elizabeth P. Benson and Beatriz de la Fuente, p. 185. Washington, D.C.: National Gallery of Art.

1996b   Catalogue Entry 23: Personage of Atlihuayan. In Olmec Art of Ancient Mexico, edited by Elizabeth P. Benson and Beatriz de la Fuente, pp. 186–187. Washington, D.C.: National Gallery of Art.

1996c   Catalogue Entry 25: Acrobat Effigy Vessel. In Olmec Art of Ancient Mexico, edited by Elizabeth P. Benson and Beatriz de la Fuente, p. 189. Washington, D.C.: National Gallery of Art.

O'Neale, Lila M.

1932   Yurok-Karok Basket Weavers. University of California Publications in American Archaeology and Ethnology, vol. 32, no. 1. Berkeley, Calif.

1945   Textiles of Highland Guatemala. Carnegie Institution of Washington Publication 567. Washington, D.C.

Ortiz, Alfonso

1969   The Tewa World: Space, Time, Being, and Becoming in a Pueblo Society. Chicago: University of Chicago Press.

Ortner, Sherry

1974   Is Female to Male as Nature Is to Culture? In Woman, Culture, and Society, edited by Michelle Rosaldo and Louise Lamphere, pp. 67–88. Stanford: Stanford University Press.

Ortner, Sherry, and Harriet Whitehead

1981   Introduction. In Sexual Meanings: The Cultural Construction of Gender and Sexuality, edited by Sherry Ortner and Harriet Whitehead, pp. 1–28. Cambridge: Cambridge University Press.

Paine, Richard, and AnnCorrine Freter

1996   Environmental Degradation and the Classic Maya Collapse at Copan, Honduras (A.D. 600–1250): Evidence from Studies of Household Survival. Ancient Mesoamerica 7(1):37–47.

Paine, Richard, AnnCorrine Freter, and David Webster

1996   Mathematical Projection of Population Growth in the Copan Valley, Honduras, A.D. 400–800. Latin American Antiquity 7(1):51–60.

Parmentier, Richard

1987   The Sacred Remains: Myth, History, and Polity in Belau. Chicago: University of Chicago Press.

Parry, Jonathan, and Maurice Bloch, eds.

1989   Money and the Morality of Exchange. Cambridge: Cambridge University Press.

Parsons, Jeffrey R., Elizabeth Brumfiel, and Mary Hodge
1996   Developmental Implications of Earlier Dates for Early Aztec in the Basin of
        Mexico. *Ancient Mesoamerica* 7(2):217–230.

Pasztory, Esther
1988   A Reinterpretation of Teotihuacan and Its Mural Tradition. In *Feath-
        ered Serpents and Flowering Trees: Reconstructing the Murals of Teotihua-
        can*, edited by Kathleen Berrin, pp. 45–77. San Francisco: The Fine Arts
        Museums of San Francisco.
1992   Abstraction and the Rise of a Utopian State at Teotihuacan. In *Art, Ideology,
        and the City of Teotihuacan*, edited by Janet Catherine Berlo, pp. 281–320.
        Washington, D.C.: Dumbarton Oaks.

Pendergast, David
1986   Stability through Change: Lamanai, Belize, from the Ninth to the Seven-
        teenth Century. In *Late Lowland Maya Civilization: Classic to Postclassic*,
        edited by Jeremy A. Sabloff and E. Wyllys Andrews V, pp. 223–249. Albu-
        querque: University of New Mexico Press.

Piña Chan, Román
1958   *Tlatilco* 2 vols. Serie de Investigaciones, no. 1. Mexico City: Instituto Nacio-
        nal de Antropología e Historia.

Pires-Ferreira, Jane Wheeler
1976   Obsidian Exchange in Formative Mesoamerica. In *The Early Mesoameri-
        can Village*, edited by Kent V. Flannery, pp. 292–306. New York: Aca-
        demic Press.

Pohl, Mary
1981   Ritual Continuity and Transformation in Mesoamerica: Reconstructing the
        Ancient Maya *cuch* Ritual. *American Antiquity* 46(3):513–529.
1983   Maya Ritual Faunas: Vertebrate Remains from Burials, Caches, Caves, and
        Cenotes in the Maya Lowlands. In *Civilization in the Ancient Americas*,
        edited by Richard M. Leventhal and Alan L. Kolata, pp. 55–103. Albu-
        querque: University of New Mexico Press.
1985   Privileges of Maya Elites: Prehistoric Vertebrate Fauna from Seibal. In *Exca-
        vations at Seibal*, edited by Gordon R. Willey, pp. 133–145. Peabody Museum
        of Archaeology and Ethnology Papers, vol. 77. Harvard University, Cam-
        bridge, Mass.
1991   Women, Animal Rearing, and Social Status: The Case of the Formative
        Period Maya of Central America. In *The Archaeology of Gender*, edited by
        Dale Walde and Noreen D. Willows, pp. 391–399. Proceedings of the 22d
        Annual Chacmool Conference. Calgary: Archaeological Association, Uni-
        versity of Calgary.

Pohl, Mary, and Lawrence Feldman
1982   The Traditional Role of Women and Animals in Lowland Maya Economy.
        In *Maya Subsistence*, edited by Kent V. Flannery, pp. 295–311. New York:
        Academic Press.

Pohl, Mary, and John Pohl
1994   Cycles of Conflict: Political Factionalism in the Maya Lowlands. In *Fac-
        tional Competition and Political Development in the New World*, edited by

Elizabeth M. Brumfiel and John W. Fox, pp. 138–157. Cambridge: Cambridge University Press.

Pohorilenko, Anatole
1996   Portable Carvings in the Olmec Style. In *Olmec Art of Ancient Mexico,* edited by Elizabeth P. Benson and Beatriz de la Fuente, pp. 119–132. Washington, D.C.: National Gallery of Art.

Pope, Kevin
1985   Palaeoecology of the Ulua Valley, Honduras: An Archaeological Perspective. Ph.D. diss., Stanford University. Ann Arbor: University Microfilms International.

Popenoe, Dorothy
1930   Two Expeditions in Search of Painted Pottery. Field report, March 1930. Peabody Museum of Archaeology and Ethnology, Accession File 30–46. Harvard University, Cambridge, Mass.

1934   Some Excavations at Playa de los Muertos, Ulua River, Honduras. *Maya Research* 1:62–86.

Porter, James
1989   Olmec Colossal Heads as Recarved Thrones: "Mutilation," Revolution, and Recarving. *Res: Anthropology and Aesthetics* 17-18:23-29.

Porter, Muriel
1953   *Tlatilco and the Pre-Classic Cultures of the New World.* Publications in Anthropology, no. 18. New York: Viking Fund.

Prindiville, Mary, and David C. Grove
1987   The Settlement and Its Architecture. In *Ancient Chalcatzingo,* edited by David C. Grove, pp. 63–81. Austin: University of Texas Press.

Proskouriakoff, Tatiana
1944   An Inscription on a Jade Probably Carved at Piedras Negras. In *Notes on Middle American Archaeology and Ethnology* 2:142–147. Cambridge, Mass.: Carnegie Institution of Washington, Division of Historical Research.

1960   Historical Implications of a Pattern of Dates at Piedras Negras, Guatemala. *American Antiquity* 25:454–475.

1961   Portraits of Women in Maya Art. In *Essays in Pre-Columbian Art and Archaeology,* edited by Samuel K. Lothrop, pp. 81–99. Cambridge, Mass.: Harvard University Press.

1963   Historical Data in the Inscriptions of Yaxchilan. Part 1. *Estudios de Cultura Maya* 3:149–167.

1964   Historical Data in the Inscriptions of Yaxchilan. Part 2. *Estudios de Cultura Maya* 4:177–201.

1970   On Two Inscriptions at Chichen Itza. In *Monographs and Papers in Maya Archaeology,* edited by William R. Bullard, Jr., pp. 459–467. Peabody Museum of Archaeology and Ethnology Papers, vol. 61. Harvard University, Cambridge, Mass.

1974   *Jades from the Cenote of Sacrifice, Chichen Itza, Yucatan.* Peabody Museum of Archaeology and Ethnology Memoirs 10(1). Harvard University, Cambridge, Mass.

1993   *Maya History.* Austin: University of Texas Press.

Pyburn, K. Anne
1990   Settlement Patterns at Nohmul: Preliminary Results of Four Excavation Seasons. In *Precolumbian Population History in the Maya Lowlands,* edited by T. Patrick Culbert and Don Rice, pp. 183–197. Albuquerque: University of New Mexico Press.

Pyne, Nannette
1976   The Fire-Serpent and Were-Jaguar in Formative Oaxaca: A Contingency Table Analysis. In *The Early Mesoamerican,* edited by Kent V. Flannery, pp. 272–282. New York: Academic Press.

Rands, Robert
1973   The Classic Collapse in the Southern Maya Lowlands: Chronology. In *The Classic Maya Collapse,* edited by T. Patrick Culbert, pp. 43–62. Albuquerque: University of New Mexico Press.

Rands, Robert, and Barbara Rands
1965   Pottery Figurines of the Maya Lowlands. In *Handbook of Middle American Indians* 2:535–560. Edited by Robert Wauchope and Gordon Willey. Austin: University of Texas Press.

Reents, Doris
1985   The Late Classic Maya Holmul-Style Polychrome Pottery. Ph.D. diss., University of Texas at Austin. Ann Arbor: University Microfilms.

Reents-Budet, Dorie
1991   The "Holmul Dancer" Theme in Maya Art. In *Sixth Palenque Round Table, 1986,* edited by Virginia M. Fields, pp. 217–222. Norman: University of Oklahoma Press.
1994   *Painting the Maya Universe: Royal Ceramics of the Classic Period.* Durham: Duke University Press.

Rice, Don
1986   The Peten Postclassic: A Settlement Perspective. In *Late Lowland Maya Civilization: Classic to Postclassic,* edited by Jeremy A. Sabloff and E. Wyllys Andrews V, pp. 301–344. Albuquerque: University of New Mexico Press.

Rice, Don, and Prudence Rice
1990   Population Size and Population Change in the Central Peten Lakes Region, Guatemala. In *Precolumbian Population History in the Maya Lowlands,* edited by T. Patrick Culbert and Don Rice, pp. 123–148. Albuquerque: University of New Mexico Press.

Rice, Prudence
1986   The Peten Postclassic: Perspectives from the Central Peten Lakes. In *Late Lowland Maya Civilization: Classic to Postclassic,* edited by Jeremy A. Sabloff and E. Wyllys Andrews V, pp. 251–299. Albuquerque: University of New Mexico Press.

Ringle, William M.
1990   Who Was Who in Ninth-Century Chichen Itza. *Ancient Mesoamerica* 1(2): 233–243.
1999   Preclassic Cityscapes: Ritual Politics among the Early Lowland Maya. In *Social Patterns in Pre-Classic Mesoamerica,* edited by David C. Grove and Rosemary A. Joyce, pp. 183–223. Washington, D.C.: Dumbarton Oaks.

Robertson, Merle Greene

1974　The Quadripartite Badge—A Badge of Rulership. In *Primera Mesa Redonda de Palenque, Part 1*, edited by Merle Greene Robertson, pp. 77–83. Pebble Beach, Calif.: The Robert Louis Stevenson School.

1991　*The Sculpture of Palenque*. Vol. 4, *The Cross Group, the North Group, the Olvidado, and Other Pieces*. Princeton: Princeton University Press.

Rojas, José Luis de

1986　*México Tenochtitlan: Economía y sociedad en el siglo XVI*. Mexico City: Fondo de Cultura Económica.

Rosaldo, Michelle Zimbalist, and Louise Lamphere, eds.

1974　*Woman, Culture, and Society*. Stanford: Stanford University Press.

Rue, David J., AnnCorrine Freter, and Diane A. Ballinger

1989　The Caverns of Copan Revisited: Preclassic Sites in the Sesesmil River Valley, Copan, Honduras. *Journal of Field Archaeology* 16(4):395–404.

Ruppert, Karl

1931　Temple of the Wall Panels, Chichen Itza. In *Contributions to American Archaeology* 1(3):117–140. Carnegie Institution of Washington Publication 403. Washington, D.C.

1935　*The Caracol at Chichen Itza, Yucatan, Mexico*. Carnegie Institution of Washington Publication 454. Washington, D.C.

1943　The Mercado, Chichen Itza, Yucatan. In *Contributions to American Anthropology and History* 8(43):223–260. Carnegie Institution of Washington Publication 546. Washington, D.C.

1950　Gallery-Patio Type Structures at Chichen Itza. In *For the Dean: Essays in Anthropology in Honor of Byron Cummings on his Eighty-ninth Birthday, September 20, 1950*, edited by Erik Reed and Dale King, pp. 249–258. Tucson and Santa Fe: Hohokam Museums Association and the Southwestern Monuments Association.

1952　*Chichen Itza, Architectural Notes and Plans*. Carnegie Institution of Washington Publication 595. Washington, D.C.

Ruppert, Karl, and A. Ledyard Smith

1955　Two New Gallery-Patio Type Structures at Chichen Itza. In *Notes on Middle American Archaeology and Ethnology* 5(122):59–62. Cambridge, Mass.: Carnegie Institution of Washington, Division of Historical Research.

Ruppert, Karl, J. Eric S. Thompson, and Tatiana Proskouriakoff

1955　*Bonampak, Chiapas, Mexico*. Carnegie Institution of Washington Publication 602. Washington, D.C.

Ruscheinsky, Lynn

1995　The Construction and Reproduction of Gender Hierarchy. In *Debating Complexity*, edited by David A. Meyer, Peter C. Dawson, and Donald T. Hanna, pp. 629–634. Proceedings of the 26th Annual Chacmool Conference. Calgary: Archaeological Association, University of Calgary.

Rust, William F., III

1992　New Ceremonial and Settlement Evidence at La Venta, and Its Relation to Preclassic Maya Cultures. In *New Theories on the Ancient Maya*, edited by Elin Danien and Robert J. Sharer, pp. 123–129. University Museum Monograph 77. Philadelphia: University Museum of Archaeology and Anthropology, University of Pennsylvania.

Sabloff, Jeremy

1973   Continuity and Disruption during Terminal Late Classic Times at Seibal: Ceramic and Other Evidence. In *The Classic Maya Collapse*, edited by T. Patrick Culbert, pp. 107-131. Albuquerque: University of New Mexico Press.

Sabloff, Jeremy, and Gordon Willey

1967   The Collapse of Maya Civilization in the Southern Lowlands: A Consideration of History and Process. *Southwestern Journal of Anthropology* 23(4): 311-336.

Sabloff, Jeremy A., and John S. Henderson, eds.

1993   *Lowland Maya Civilization in the Eighth Century A.D.* Washington, D.C.: Dumbarton Oaks.

Sahagún, Bernardino de

1951   *Florentine Codex: General History of the Things of New Spain, Book 2 — The Ceremonies.* Translated by Arthur J. O. Anderson and Charles E. Dibble. Monographs of the School of American Research, number 14, Part 3. Santa Fe: School of American Research and the University of Utah Press.

1953a   *Florentine Codex: General History of the Things of New Spain, Book 3 — The Origins of the Gods.* Translated by Arthur J. O. Anderson and Charles E. Dibble. Monographs of the School of American Research, number 14, Part 4. Santa Fe: School of American Research and the University of Utah Press.

1953b   *Florentine Codex: General History of the Things of New Spain, Book 7 — The Sun, Moon, and Stars, and the Binding of the Years.* Translated by Arthur J. O. Anderson and Charles E. Dibble. Monographs of the School of American Research, number 14, Part 8. Santa Fe: School of American Research and the University of Utah Press.

1954   *Florentine Codex: General History of the Things of New Spain, Book 8 — Kings and Lords.* Translated by Arthur J. O. Anderson and Charles E. Dibble. Monographs of the School of American Research, number 14, Part 9. Santa Fe: School of American Research and the University of Utah Press.

1957   *Florentine Codex: General History of the Things of New Spain, Book 4 — The Soothsayers.* Translated by Arthur J. O. Anderson and Charles E. Dibble. Monographs of the School of American Research, number 14, Part 5. Santa Fe: School of American Research and the University of Utah Press.

1959   *Florentine Codex: General History of the Things of New Spain, Book 9 — The Merchants.* Translated by Arthur J. O. Anderson and Charles E. Dibble. Monographs of the School of American Research, number 14, Part 10. Santa Fe: School of American Research and the University of Utah Press.

1961   *Florentine Codex: General History of the Things of New Spain, Book 10 — The People.* Translated by Arthur J. O. Anderson and Charles E. Dibble. Monographs of the School of American Research and the Museum of New Mexico, number 14, Part 11. Santa Fe: School of American Research and the University of Utah Press.

1969   *Florentine Codex: General History of the Things of New Spain, Book 6 —*

Rhetoric and Moral Philosophy. Translated by Arthur J. O. Anderson and Charles E. Dibble. Monographs of the School of American Research, number 14, Part 7. Santa Fe: School of American Research and the University of Utah Press.

1970 *Florentine Codex: General History of the Things of New Spain, Book 1 — The Gods.* Rev. ed. Translated by Arthur J. O. Anderson and Charles E. Dibble. Monographs of the School of American Research, number 14, Part 2. Santa Fe: School of American Research and the University of Utah Press.

Sallnow, Michael

1989 Precious Metals in the Andean Moral Economy. In *Money and the Morality of Exchange,* edited by Jonathan Parry and Maurice Bloch, pp. 209–231. Cambridge: Cambridge University Press.

Sanday, Peggy Reeves, and Ruth Gallagher Goodenough, eds.

1990 *Beyond the Second Sex: New Directions in the Anthropology of Gender.* Philadelphia: University of Pennsylvania Press.

Sanders, William T., and David Webster

1988 The Mesoamerican Urban Tradition. *American Anthropologist* 90(3):521–546.

Sandstrom, Alan

2000 Toponymic Groups and House Organization: The Nahuas of Northern Veracruz, Mexico. In *Beyond Kinship: Social and Material Reproduction in House Societies,* edited by Rosemary A. Joyce and Susan D. Gillespie, pp. 53–72. Philadelphia: University of Pennsylvania Press.

Saul, Frank

1973 Disease in the Maya Area: The Pre-Columbian Evidence. In *The Classic Maya Collapse,* edited by T. Patrick Culbert, pp. 301–324. Albuquerque: University of New Mexico Press.

Schele, Linda

1976 Accession Iconography of Chan-Bahlum in the Group of the Cross at Palenque. In *Art, Iconography, and Dynastic History of Palenque, Part 3: Proceedings of the Segunda Mesa Redonda de Palenque, Palenque, Chiapas, Mexico, December 14–21, 1974,* edited by Merle Greene Robertson, pp. 9–34. Pebble Beach, Calif.: Robert Louis Stevenson School, Pre-Columbian Art Research.

1979 Genealogical Documentation on the Tri-Figure Panels at Palenque. In *Tercera Mesa Redonda de Palenque, Volume 4,* edited by Merle Greene Robertson and Donnan Call Jeffers, pp. 41–70. Palenque: Pre-Columbian Art Research Center.

1982 *Maya Glyphs, The Verbs.* Austin: University of Texas Press.

1990 House Names and Dedication Rituals at Palenque. In *Vision and Revision in Maya Studies,* edited by Flora S. Clancy and Peter D. Harrison, pp. 143–157. Albuquerque: University of New Mexico Press.

1991a An Epigraphic History of the Western Maya Region. In *Classic Maya Political History: Hieroglyphic and Archaeological Evidence,* edited by T. Patrick Culbert, pp. 72–101. Cambridge: Cambridge University Press.

1991b The Demotion of Chac-Zutz': Lineage Compounds and Subsidiary Lords at

Palenque. In *Sixth Palenque Round Table, 1986,* edited by Virginia M. Fields, pp. 6-11. Norman: University of Oklahoma Press.

Schele, Linda, and David Freidel

1990   *A Forest of Kings: The Untold Story of the Ancient Maya.* New York: William Morrow.

1991   The Courts of Creation: Ballcourts, Ballgames, and Portals to the Maya Otherworld. In *The Mesoamerican Ballgame,* edited by Vernon L. Scarborough and David R. Wilcox, pp. 289-315. Tucson: University of Arizona Press.

Schele, Linda, and Peter Mathews

1991   Royal Visits and Other Intersite Relationships among the Classic Maya. In *Classic Maya Political History: Hieroglyphic and Archaeological Evidence,* edited by T. Patrick Culbert, pp. 226-252. Cambridge: Cambridge University Press.

Schele, Linda, and Mary Ellen Miller

1986   *The Blood of Kings: Dynasty and Ritual in Maya Art.* Fort Worth: Kimball Art Museum.

Schele, Linda, and Khristaan D. Villela

1996   Creation, Cosmos, and the Imagery of Palenque and Copan. In *Eighth Palenque Round Table, 1993,* edited by Martha J. Macri and Jan McHargue, pp. 15-30. San Francisco: Pre-Columbian Art Research Institute.

Schneider, David

1984   *A Critique of the Study of Kinship.* Ann Arbor: University of Michigan Press.

Sedat, David W.

1992   Preclassic Notation and the Development of Maya Writing. In *New Theories on the Ancient Maya,* edited by Elin Danien and Robert J. Sharer, pp. 81-90. University Museum Monograph 77. Philadelphia: University Museum of Archaeology and Anthropology, University of Pennsylvania.

Seler, Eduard

1923   Die Ruinen von Chich'en Itzá in Yucatan. In *Gesammelte Abhandlungen zur amerikanischen Sprach- und Alterthumskunde, 5,* pp. 197-388. Berlin: A. Asher.

Serra, Mari Carmen, and Yoko Sugiura

1987   Funerary Rites at Two Historical Moments in Mesoamerica: Middle and Late Formative. In *Studies in the Neolithic and Urban Revolutions: The V. Gordon Childe Colloquium, Mexico, 1986,* edited by Linda Manzanilla, pp. 345-351. BAR International Series 349. Oxford.

Sharer, Robert J.

1978   Excavations in the El Trapiche Group. In *The Prehistory of Chalchuapa, El Salvador,* Vol. 1, *Introduction, Surface Surveys, Excavations, Monuments, and Special Deposits,* edited by Robert J. Sharer, pp. 61-87. Philadelphia: University of Pennsylvania Press.

1985   Terminal Events in the Southeastern Lowlands: A View from Quirigua. In *The Lowland Maya Postclassic,* edited by Arlen F. Chase and Prudence Rice, pp. 245-253. Austin: University of Texas Press.

1992   The Preclassic Origin of Lowland Maya States. In *New Theories on the An-*

cient Maya, edited by Elin Danien and Robert J. Sharer, pp. 131–136. University Museum Monograph 77. Philadelphia: University Museum of Archaeology and Anthropology, University of Pennsylvania.

1993   Social Organization of the Late Classic Maya: Problems of Definition and Approaches. In *Lowland Maya Civilization in the Eighth Century A.D.*, edited by Jeremy Sabloff and John S. Henderson, pp. 91–109. Washington, D.C.: Dumbarton Oaks.

Sharer, Robert J., and David W. Sedat

1973   Monument 1, El Portón, Guatemala, and the Development of Maya Calendrical and Writing Systems. In *Studies in Ancient Mesoamerica*, edited by John Graham, pp. 177–194. University of California Archaeological Research Facility Contributions no. 18. Berkeley, Calif.

Sheets, Payson

1978   Artifacts. In *The Prehistory of Chalchuapa, El Salvador*, Vol. 2, *Artifacts and Figurines*, edited by Robert J. Sharer, pp. 2–131. Philadelphia: University of Pennsylvania Press.

Sherzer, Joel

1983   *Kuna Ways of Speaking: An Ethnographic Perspective.* Austin: University of Texas Press.

Shimkin, Demitri

1973   Models for the Downfall: Some Ecological and Culture-Historical Considerations. In *The Classic Maya Collapse*, edited by T. Patrick Culbert, pp. 269–299. Albuquerque: University of New Mexico Press.

Silverblatt, Irene

1987   *Moon, Sun, and Witches: Gender Ideologies and Class in Inca and Colonial Peru.* Princeton: Princeton University Press.

1988   Women in States. *Annual Reviews in Anthropology* 17:427–460.

Smith, Michael E.

1979   The Aztec Marketing System and Settlement Pattern in the Valley of Mexico: A Central Place Analysis. *American Antiquity* 44(1):110–125.

1980   The Role of the Marketing System in Aztec Society and Economy: Reply to Evans. *American Antiquity* 45(4):876–883.

1990   Long-Distance Trade under the Aztec Empire: The Archaeological Evidence. *Ancient Mesoamerica* 1(2):153–169.

Smith, Michael E., and Frances F. Berdan

1992   Archaeology and the Aztec Empire. *World Archaeology* 23(3):353–367.

Smith, Michael E., and Kenneth G. Hirth

1988   Development of Prehispanic Cotton-Spinning Technology in Western Morelos, Mexico. *Journal of Field Archaeology* 15(3):349–358.

Sperber, Dan

1992   Culture and Matter. In *Representations in Archaeology*, edited by Jean Gardin and Christopher Peebles, pp. 56–65. Bloomington: Indiana University Press.

Stark, Barbara

1981   The Rise of Sedentary Life. In *Handbook of Middle American Indians, Supplement* 1:345–372. Edited by Victoria Bricker and Jeremy Sabloff. Austin: University of Texas Press.

Stone, Andrea
1988   Sacrifice and Sexuality: Some Structural Relationships in Classic Maya Art. In *The Role of Gender in Precolumbian Art and Architecture,* edited by Virginia Miller, pp. 75–103. Lanham, Md.: University Press of America.
1991   Aspects of Impersonation in Classic Maya Art. In *Sixth Palenque Round Table, 1986,* edited by Virginia Fields, pp. 194–202. Norman: University of Oklahoma Press.
1995   *Images from the Underworld: Naj Tunich and the Tradition of Maya Cave Painting.* Austin: University of Texas Press.
1999   Architectural Innovation in the Temple of the Warriors at Chichen Itza. In *Mesoamerican Architecture as a Cultural Symbol,* edited by Jeff Karl Kowalski, pp. 298–319. New York: Oxford University Press.
Stone, Doris
1941   *Archaeology of the North Coast of Honduras.* Peabody Museum of Archaeology and Ethnology Memoirs 9(1). Harvard University, Cambridge, Mass.
Storey, Rebecca
1992   Children of Copan: Issues in Paleopathology and Paleodemography. *Ancient Mesoamerica* 3(1):161–167.
Strathern, Marilyn, ed.
1987   *Dealing with Inequality: Analysing Gender Relations in Melanesia and Beyond.* Cambridge: Cambridge University Press.
Stromsvik, Gustav
1937   Notes on Metates from Calakmul, Campeche, and from the Mercado, Chichen Itza, Yucatan. In *Contributions to American Archaeology* 3(16):121–127. Carnegie Institution of Washington Publication 456. Washington, D.C.
Strong, William Duncan, A. V. Kidder II, and A. J. Drexel Paul
1938   *Preliminary Report of the Smithsonian Institution–Harvard University Archaeological Expedition to Northwestern Honduras, 1936.* Miscellaneous Collections 97. Washington, D.C.: Smithsonian Institution.
Stuart, David
1984   Royal Auto-Sacrifice among the Maya. *Res: Anthropology and Aesthetics* 7-8:6–20.
1985   The Inscriptions on Four Shell Plaques from Piedras Negras. In *Fourth Palenque Round Table, 1980,* edited by Elizabeth P. Benson, pp. 175–183. San Francisco: Pre-Columbian Art Research Institute.
1988a   Blood Symbolism in Maya Iconography. In *Maya Iconography,* edited by Elizabeth P. Benson and Gillett G. Griffin, pp. 175–221. Princeton: Princeton University Press.
1988b   The Río Azul Cacao Pot: Epigraphic Observations on the Function of a Maya Ceramic Vessel. *Antiquity* 62(234):153–157.
1997   Kinship Terms in Maya Inscriptions. In *The Language of Maya Hieroglyphs,* edited by Martha Macri and Anabel Ford, pp. 1–12. San Francisco: Pre-Columbian Art Research Institute.
Sullivan, Thelma
1980   O Precious Necklace, O Quetzal Feather! Aztec Pregnancy and Childbirth Orations. *Alcheringa: Ethnopoetics* (Boston), n.s., 4(2):38–52.

1982   Tlazolteotl-Ixcuina: The Great Spinner and Weaver. In *The Art and Iconography of Late Post-Classic Central Mexico,* edited by Elizabeth Boone, pp. 7-35. Washington, D.C.: Dumbarton Oaks.

Taggart, James
1983   *Nahuat Myth and Social Structure.* Austin: University of Texas Press.

Tate, Carolyn
1985   Summer Solstice Ceremonies Performed by Bird Jaguar III of Yaxchilan, Chiapas, Mexico. *Estudios de Cultura Maya* 16:85-112.

1991   The Period-Ending Stelae of Yaxchilan. In *Sixth Palenque Round Table, 1986,* edited by Virginia Fields, pp. 102-109. Norman: University of Oklahoma Press.

1992   *Yaxchilan: The Design of a Maya Ceremonial City.* Austin: University of Texas Press.

Taube, Karl
1983   The Teotihuacan Spider Woman. *Journal of Latin American Lore* 9(2):107-189.

1985   The Classic Maya Maize God: A Reappraisal. In *Fifth Palenque Round Table, 1983,* edited by Virginia Fields, pp. 171-181. San Francisco: Pre-Columbian Art Research Institute.

Tedlock, Barbara
1986   On a Mountain Road in the Dark: Encounters with the Quiché Maya Culture Hero. In *Symbol and Meaning beyond the Closed Community: Essays in Mesoamerican Ideas,* edited by Gary Gossen, pp. 125-138. Albany: Institute for Mesoamerican Studies, State University of New York at Albany.

Tedlock, Dennis
1985   *Popol Vuh.* New York: Simon and Schuster.

Thomson, Charlotte
1987   Chalcatzingo Jade and Fine Stone Objects. In *Ancient Chalcatzingo,* edited by David C. Grove, pp. 295-304. Austin: University of Texas Press.

Thompson, Edward H.
1938   *The High Priest's Grave, Chichen Itza, Yucatan, Mexico, A Manuscript, by Edward H. Thompson.* Prepared for publication, with notes and introduction, by J. Eric S. Thompson. Field Museum of Natural History Publication 412. Chicago: Fieldiana: Anthropology vol. 27, no. 1.

Thompson, J. Eric S.
1961   A Blood-Drawing Ceremony Painted on a Maya Vase. *Estudios de Cultura Maya* 1:13-20.

1962   *A Catalogue of Maya Hieroglyphs.* Norman: University of Oklahoma Press.

1970   The Bacabs: Their Portraits and Their Glyphs. In *Monographs and Papers in Maya Archaeology,* edited by William R. Bullard, Jr., pp. 469-485. Peabody Museum of Archaeology and Ethnology Papers, vol. 61. Harvard University, Cambridge, Mass.

Thompson, Philip C.
1982   Dynastic Marriage and Succession at Tikal. *Estudios de Cultura Maya* 14: 261-287.

Tolstoy, Paul
1989   Coapexco and Tlatilco: Sites with Olmec Materials in the Basin of Mexico.

In *Regional Perspectives on the Olmec,* edited by Robert J. Sharer and David C. Grove, pp. 85–121. Cambridge: Cambridge University Press.

Toren, Christina
1989   Drinking Cash: The Purification of Money through Ceremonial Exchange in Fiji. In *Money and the Morality of Exchange,* edited by Jonathan Parry and Maurice Bloch, pp. 142–164. Cambridge: Cambridge University Press.

Tourtellot, Gair
1983   Assessment of Classic Maya Household Composition. In *Prehistoric Settlement Patterns: Essays in Honor of Gordon R. Willey,* edited by Evon Z. Vogt and Richard Leventhal, pp. 35–54. Albuquerque: University of New Mexico Press.

Tozzer, Alfred M.
1957   *Chichen Itza and Its Cenote of Sacrifice: A Comparative Study of Contemporaneous Maya and Toltec.* Peabody Museum of American Archaeology and Ethnology Memoirs 11 and 12. Harvard University, Cambridge, Mass.

Turner, Terence
1980   The Social Skin. In *Not Work Alone: A Cross-Cultural View of Activities Superfluous to Survival,* edited by Jeremy Cherfas and Roger Lewin, pp. 112–140. Beverly Hills, Calif.: Sage Publications.

Vaillant, George
1930   *Excavations at Zacatenco.* American Museum of Natural History Anthropological Papers 32(1). New York.

Valdés, Juan Antonio
1992   Beginnings of Preclassic Maya Art and Architecture. In *Ancient Americas: Art from Sacred Landscapes,* edited by Richard Townsend, pp. 146–157. Chicago and Munich: Art Institute of Chicago.
1997   Tamarindito: Archaeology and Regional Politics in the Petexbatun Region. *Ancient Mesoamerica* 8(2):321–352.

van de Guchte, Maarten
1992   *Masquerades and Demons: Tukuna Bark-Cloth Painting.* Champaign, Ill.: Board of Trustees of the University of Illinois.

van Zantwijk, Rudolf
1985   *The Aztec Arrangement: The Social History of Pre-Hispanic Mexico.* Norman: University of Oklahoma Press.

Viel, René, and Charles Cheek
1983   Sepulturas. In *Introducción a la arqueología de Copán, Honduras,* vol. 1, edited by Claude Baudez, pp. 551–609. Tegucigalpa: SECTUR.

Visweswaran, Kamala
1997   Histories of Feminist Ethnography. *Annual Reviews in Anthropology* 26: 591–621.

Waterson, Roxana
1990   *The Living House: An Anthropology of Architecture in South-East Asia.* Singapore and New York: Oxford University Press.
1995   Houses and Hierarchies in Island Southeast Asia. In *About the House: Lévi-Strauss and Beyond,* edited by Janet Carsten and Stephen Hugh-Jones, pp. 47–68. Cambridge: Cambridge University Press.

Webster, David
1993   The Study of Maya Warfare: What It Tells Us about the Maya and What
        It Tells Us about Maya Archaeology. In *Lowland Maya Civilization in the
        Eighth Century A.D.*, edited by Jeremy Sabloff and John S. Henderson, pp.
        415–444. Washington, D.C.: Dumbarton Oaks.

Webster, David, and AnnCorrine Freter
1990   The Demography of Late Classic Copan. In *Precolumbian Population His-
        tory in the Maya Lowlands*, edited by T. Patrick Culbert and Don Rice, pp.
        37–61. Albuquerque: University of New Mexico Press.

Webster, David, and Nancy Gonlin
1988   Household Remains of the Humblest Maya. *Journal of Field Archaeology*
        15(2):169–190.

Webster, David, David Rue, and AnnCorrine Freter
1993   Obsidian Hydration Dating Project at Copan: A Regional Approach and
        Why It Works. *Latin American Antiquity* 4(4):303–324.

Weiner, Annette B.
1976   *Women of Value, Men of Renown: New Perspectives in Trobriand Exchange.*
        Austin: University of Texas Press.

1989   Why Cloth? Wealth, Gender, and Power in Oceania. In *Cloth and Human
        Experience*, edited by Annette Weiner and Jane Schneider, pp. 33–72. Wash-
        ington, D.C.: Smithsonian Institution Press.

1992   *Inalienable Possessions: The Paradox of Keeping-while-Giving.* Berkeley: Uni-
        versity of California Press.

Whitehead, Harriet
1981   The Bow and the Burden Strap: A New Look at Institutionalized Homo-
        sexuality in Native North America. In *Sexual Meanings: The Cultural Con-
        struction of Gender and Sexuality*, edited by Sherry Ortner and Harriet
        Whitehead, pp. 80–115. Cambridge: Cambridge University Press.

Whitten, Norman
1985   *Sicuanga Runa: The Other Side of Development in Amazonian Ecuador.*
        Urbana: University of Illinois Press.

Wilk, Richard R., and Harold L. Wilhite, Jr.
1991   The Community of Cuello: Patterns of Household and Settlement Change.
        In *Cuello: An Early Maya Community in Belize*, edited by Norman Ham-
        mond, pp. 118–133. Cambridge: Cambridge University Press.

Willey, Gordon R.
1972   *The Artifacts of Altar de Sacrificios.* Peabody Museum of Archaeology and
        Ethnology Papers, vol. 64(1). Harvard University, Cambridge, Mass.

1973   Certain Aspects of the Late Classic to Postclassic Periods in the Belize Val-
        ley. In *The Classic Maya Collapse*, edited by T. Patrick Culbert, pp. 93–106.
        Albuquerque: University of New Mexico Press.

1978   *Excavations at Seibal, Department of Peten, Guatemala: Artifacts.* Peabody
        Museum of Archaeology and Ethnology Memoirs 14(1). Harvard Univer-
        sity, Cambridge, Mass.

1981   Maya Lowland Settlement Patterns: A Summary Review. In *Lowland Maya
        Settlement Patterns*, edited by Wendy Ashmore, pp. 385–415. Albuquerque:
        University of New Mexico Press.

Winter, Marcus C.
1976 The Archeological Household Cluster in the Valley of Oaxaca. In *The Early Mesoamerican Village,* edited by Kent V. Flannery, pp. 25–31. New York: Academic Press.

Wonderley, Anthony W.
1981 *Late Postclassic Excavations at Naco, Honduras.* Dissertation Series no. 86. Ithaca, N.Y.: Latin American Studies Program, Cornell University.
1985 Land of Ulua: Postclassic Research in the Naco and Sula Valleys, Honduras. In *The Lowland Maya Postclassic,* edited by Arlen F. Chase and Prudence Rice, pp. 254–269. Austin: University of Texas Press.

Wren, Linnea H.
1991 The Great Ball Court Stone from Chichen Itza. In *Sixth Palenque Round Table, 1986,* edited by Virginia M. Fields, pp. 51–58. Norman: University of Oklahoma Press.
1994 Ceremonialism in the Reliefs of the North Temple, Chichen Itza. In *Seventh Palenque Round Table, 1989,* edited by Virginia M. Fields, pp. 25–31. San Francisco: Pre-Columbian Art Research Institute.

Wren, Linnea H., and Peter Schmidt
1991 Elite Interaction during the Terminal Classic Period: New Evidence from Chichen Itza. In *Classic Maya Political History: Hieroglyphic and Archaeological Evidence,* edited by T. Patrick Culbert, pp. 199–225. Cambridge: Cambridge University Press.

Wren, Linnea H., Peter Schmidt, and Ruth Krochock
1989 The Great Ball Court Stone of Chichen Itza. *Research Reports on Ancient Maya Writing,* no. 25. Washington, D.C.: Center for Maya Research.

Wright, Lori E.
1997 Biological Perspectives on the Collapse of the Pasión Maya. *Ancient Mesoamerica* 8(2):267–274.

Wright, Lori E., and Christine D. White
1996 Human Biology in the Classic Maya Collapse: Evidence from Paleopathology and Paleodiet. *Journal of World Prehistory* 10(2):147–198.

Wright, Rita
1991 Women's Labor and Pottery Production in Prehistory. In *Engendering Archaeology: Women and Prehistory,* edited by Joan Gero and Margaret Conkey, pp. 194–223. Oxford and Cambridge, Mass.: Basil Blackwell.

Yanagisako, Sylvia, and Jane Fishburne Collier, eds.
1987 *Gender and Kinship: Essays toward a Unified Analysis.* Stanford: Stanford University Press.

Zavella, Patricia
1991 *Mujeres* in Factories: Race and Class Perspectives on Women, Work, and Family. In *Gender at the Crossroads of Knowledge: Feminist Anthropology in the Postmodern Era,* edited by Micaela di Leonardo, pp. 312–336. Berkeley: University of California Press.

Index

Bonampak, 57, 79, 95, 110, 123, 124, 180
Boon, James A., 22
Bourdieu, Pierre, 187
breast, 43, 49, 65, 79, 80, 103, 105, 106, 109, 116
Bruhns, Karen, 76
Brumfiel, Elizabeth M., 136, 146, 164, 165
burials, 5, 8, 28, 70, 91, 132, 180, 189; at Chalcatzingo, 42, 48; at Chiapa de Corzo, 183; at Copan, 93; at La Venta, 43-47, 50; at Los Naranjos, 39; at Playa de los Muertos, 39; at Tikal, 59, 91; at Tlatilco, 29, 30-34, 48. See also mortuary rituals
Butler, Judith, 7, 9, 177, 187-191, 197

cacao, 140, 143
caches, 70, 82, 91
Calakmul, 13, 57, 74, 75, 77, 82, 103, 193
calendars, 10, 193; Aztec, 140, 143, 147, 151, 152, 158, 166-168; Maya, 56, 57, 81, 118, 119-120, 121
calli, 136, 139
calmecac, 148-149
Calnek, Edward E., 135, 136
calpulli, 136-139, 143, 152, 167, 170
canals, 135
Cancuen, 74
capture, 68, 72, 96, 115, 123, 146, 155, 156, 163, 171-172
Caracol (Belize), 23, 57, 96, 115
Caracol (Chichen Itza), 101
Carlson, John B., 47
Casa Colorada (Chichen Itza), 100-101, 102
Cashinahua, 11, 12
Castillo (Chichen Itza), 101
causeways. See walkways
caves, 59-60, 79, 196-197
Cenote (Chichen Itza), 14, 15, 101, 113, 114
ceramics. See pottery
Cerro Palenque, 93
Chalcatzingo, 23, 28, 39, 41-43, 44,

46, 48-49, 180, 183; Monument 10, 43; Monument 14, 43; Monument 28, 43; Relief 1, 43
Chance, John, 138
Chase, Arlen F., 23
Chase, Diane Z., 23
Chiapa de Corzo, 28, 39, 183
Chichen Itza, 14, 15, 90, 92, 93, 94, 97-117, 121, 136, 143, 173
childbirth: and adult status, 155; as capture, 163, 170-172; and curing, 119, 186; in life cycle, 81, 120, 145, 146, 156; in representation, 41; in text, 124, 128, 144
childhood, 37-38, 120-132, 140, 145-162
chinampas, 135
Cholan, 55
cihuacoatl, 173, 192
cinnabar, 44
Cipactonal, 173-174, 191
cities, 135, 178; regal-ritual, 57, 65
Clancy, Flora S., 64
clans, 136
Clark, John E., 25, 26, 50-51, 183, 185
class, 4, 28, 48, 135, 186-187
Clendinnen, Inga, 151, 152
Closs, Michael P., 64
cloth. See textiles
Coba, 74
Codex Mendoza, 148, 149, 150, 152, 153, 154, 155
Coggins, Clemency C., 113
collapse, Maya, 91-96
Comalcalco, 55
commoners, 58, 68, 94, 95, 97, 135, 136, 140, 143, 159-160
Conides, Cynthia, 70
Conkey, Margaret, 4
Connerton, Paul, 9, 10, 188, 189
consumption, 49, 57, 58, 97, 122
control, 9, 17, 135, 150, 157, 158, 161, 162-165, 177, 179-182, 197
Copan, 27, 68, 75, 77, 79, 80, 81, 93, 96, 101, 115, 186
copper, 93, 97
Cortés, Hernán, 134, 140